RIDING THE WAVES OF CULTURE

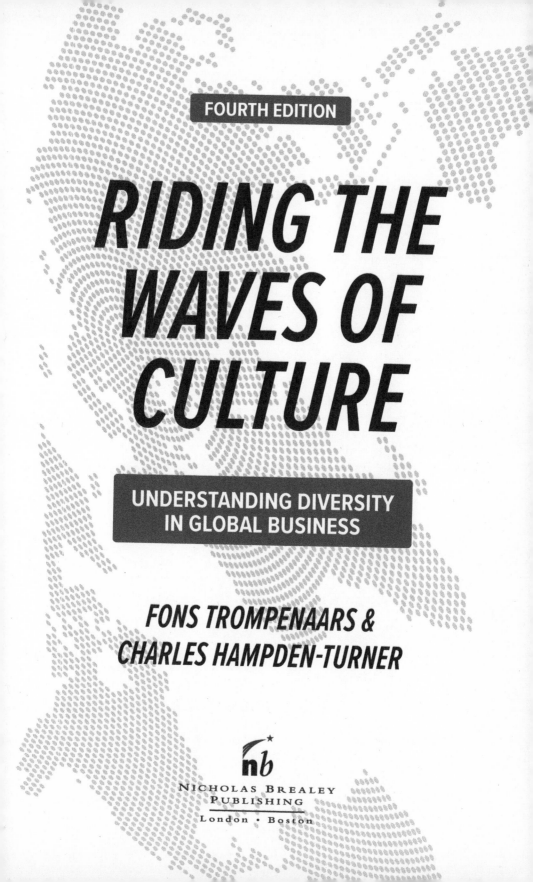

FOURTH EDITION

RIDING THE WAVES OF CULTURE

UNDERSTANDING DIVERSITY IN GLOBAL BUSINESS

FONS TROMPENAARS & CHARLES HAMPDEN-TURNER

nb
NICHOLAS BREALEY
PUBLISHING
London · Boston

To Cens for her continued support

First published by McGraw-Hill Education in 2020.

First published in Great Britain by Nicholas Brealey Publishing in 2020
An imprint of John Murray Press
A division of Hodder & Stoughton Ltd,
An Hachette UK company

2

The acknowledgments on pp. xi constitute
an extension of this copyright page.

A CIP catalogue record for this title is available from the British Library

Trade Paperback ISBN 9781529346183
eBook ISBN 9781904838401

Typeset in Palatino LT Std

Printed and bound in Great Britain by Clays Ltd, Elcograf S.p.A.

John Murray Press policy is to use papers that are natural, renewable
and recyclable products and made from wood grown in sustainable
forests. The logging and manufacturing processes are expected to
conform to the environmental regulations of the country of origin.

John Murray Press
Carmelite House
50 Victoria Embankment
London EC4Y 0DZ

Nicholas Brealey Publishing
Hachette Book Group
Market Place, Center 53, State Street
Boston, MA 02109, USA

www.nicholasbrealey.com

Contents

Foreword

SINCE THE first edition of this book in 1993, the central premise has remained—namely, that to be effective in leading and doing business with both an international and diverse environment, leaders and managers will have to recognize and respect cultural differences.

In the second edition we extended support of the core constructs by providing a number of country-specific examples, paying particular attention to the statistical significance and reliability of the underlying cultural database. In addition, we presented a new framework to reconcile the dilemmas that arise from cultural diversity. In a three-step structure, we gave an exhaustive treatment to the three Rs of Recognition, Respect, and Reconciliation.

The context for the third edition (2012) was that the world of business continued to move ever rapidly to the global village, accelerated by changing political, social, and economic forces enabled by air travel and communications technology. While cultural factors had long been recognized as critical, the earlier more anthropological ideas that emphasized differences needed to be supplemented and extended by a new body of knowledge that is more relevant to today's world. The focus and need was shifting from simply understanding cultural differences and how to prevent embarrassments and resolve communication issues to how to leverage difference for competitive advantage, in a world where even local business may involve leading a diverse workforce.

In the third edition we added the fourth step to build on the first three given in earlier editions. We introduced the fourth R, for Realization, in this edition, so that culture is ever more explicitly linked to the bottom line.

Studies of cultures are now further clouded by the consequences of migrations, immigration and acculturation, and cultural differences across generations, along with new players such as India and South America as well as China in the center stage.

This new fourth edition goes further as we seek to respond to the rapidly accelerating "new ways of working" that owe their origin to ever greater diversity, advances in Internet technologies and online meetings, sociopolitical dynamics (equality through "me too" and BLN), global warming, autonomous vehicles, and at a time when the coronavirus epidemic is changing the world.

To serve these changes and to make the knowledge and associated wisdom more accessible to a wider audience, we have captured both the earlier and more recent constructs in digital formats. Along with conventional printed copies of this book and electronic delivery of e-books, this fourth edition serves as a central portal from which readers can follow their interest and go deeper by exploring the many web links provided. These will enable readers to test themselves online with interactive cases and explore the increasing portfolio of apps developed by the authors and their research and support team that focus on the many aspects of culture presented in the text.

New content on realizing the business benefits of international and transnational operations is considered in some depth. Added to that, special treatment is given to cultural differences in alliances, mergers, and acquisitions. We illustrate the power of these ideas by showing how they can be applied in the cultural integration of organizations to significant advantage over conventional (financial) due diligence. The interactive apps bring these ideas to life as readers can explore for themselves.

The cultural databases that underpin this book have been extended to include not only more cases and more country data from more respondents but also a whole wealth of cultural measurements of competences, dilemmas and their reconciliations, servant leadership across cultures, innovation paradigms across cultures, and multicultural and remote team effectiveness.

None of the value of the earlier editions has been lost, and this new edition provides an evidence-driven framework essential for all business leaders and managers, whether they serve as CEO of a major global corporation or play an important middle-management role in a section of their smaller local company. The latter more than ever need to interact with a diverse workforce, as well as with a diverse customer and supplier base, and therefore require a certain level of cultural competence.

The book will also be of value to students of business and management to help prepare them for the new world of business, which is so different from only a few years ago.

Professor Peter Woolliams, PhD
Emeritus Professor, Anglia Ruskin University, UK

Acknowledgments

SINCE THE first edition of this book in 1993, many people have contributed to its further development. We wish to thank all the colleagues of our consulting firm Trompenaars Hampden-Turner Consultancy B.V. They all have contributed in many ways to the fine-tuning of the data and development of the conceptual models.

It all started with my masters studies at the Free University of Amsterdam (VU) in which Professor Frits Haselhoff helped me use systems thinking as a foundation for looking at the world and its diversity. After being selected for a European PhD grant by Geert Hofstede, André Laurent, and Gunnar Hedlund, I was admitted to a PhD program at Wharton, Social Systems Sciences. In this mind-blowing program Russ Ackoff, Giorgio Inzerilli, and Hasan Ozbekhan helped me translate cross-cultural models into actionable processes. I am also thankful to the Royal Dutch Shell organization that allowed me to do empirical research on top of its financial support.

After completing my PhD in 1982, I started a job in HR at Shell in Rotterdam. I vividly remember Jaap Leemhuis, VP of Group Planning Netherlands, advising me to contact Charles Hampden-Turner as he was responsible at Shell for framing the dilemmas between the different scenarios that Group Planning in London designed on a regular basis. Charles helped me find a way through the dilemmas created by cultural diversity. Together we could make a difference. But this would all have been impossible without the intellectual and professional support of Peter Woolliams. He supported all our models and processes with digital means, which we are still using and developing as is well documented in this fourth edition. Thank you all.

We have always subscribed to Lewin's maxim "there is nothing so practical as a good theory" but also recognize the corollary that "there is nothing like good professional practice to develop good theory." So we also thank the myriad of participants in our presentations and workshops from our client organizations who took the time to complete our online diagnostic questionnaires and interactive tools and apps. Their input has been of enormous value and has helped in both the development of the new constructs and their validation.

Professor Fons Trompenaars, PhD
CEO, THT Consulting and professor of the Vrije Universiteit of Amsterdam

1

An Introduction to Culture

Fons Trompenaars and Charles Hampden-Turner

THIS BOOK is about cultural differences and how they affect the process of doing business and managing. It is not about how to understand the people of different nationalities. It is our belief that you can never understand other cultures. Those who are married know that it is impossible ever completely to understand even people of your own culture. The Dutch author (Fons Trompenaars) became interested in this subject before it grew popular because his father is Dutch and his mother is French. It gave him an understanding of the fact that if something works in one culture, there is little chance that it will work in another. No Dutch "management" technique his father tried to use ever worked very effectively in his French family.

This is the context in which we started wondering if any of the American management techniques and philosophies with which we were brainwashed in many years of the best business education money could buy would apply in the Netherlands or the UK, where we came from, or indeed in the rest of the world.

Both authors have been studying the effect of culture on management for many years. This book describes much of what we have discovered. The different cultural orientations described result from 25 years of academic and field research. Many of the anecdotes and cases used in the text have come up in the course of more than 1,000 cross-cultural training programs we have given in over 25 countries. The names of the companies used in most of the cases are disguised.

Apart from the training program material, a diverse range of companies, including most of the global corporates and other major players with departments spanning over 60 different countries, have contributed to the research. In order to gather comparable samples, a minimum of 100 people with similar backgrounds and occupations were originally taken in each of the countries in which the companies operated to provide basic reference cultural norms. Approximately 75 percent of these participants belong to management (managers in operations, marketing, sales, and so on), while the remaining 25 percent were general administrative staff (typists, personal assistants, etc.). Our original cultural database comprised some 80,000 of these respondents and has been extended in several ways. We have added more responses from managers and business leaders across the world, which has resulted in much more than just an increase in sample sizes. This database now extends to some 140,000 participants. Another 20,000 have completed partial responses to this basic cultural diagnostic in combination with other surveys.

With the continuing growth and pervasion of the Internet, we have continued to add many other cultural measurement instruments and have developed associated ancillary databases and apps to disclose them. These include another 20,000 responses to our deductive assessments of intercultural competence and transcultural leadership, corporate effectiveness and sustainability, cultural aspects of personality and team development, and innovation. In a separate text-oriented database, we have collected and coded data comprising nearly 50,000 dilemmas and associated reconciliations.

In response to demand, we increasingly make adapted versions of our online tools available to other responses such as students of business and management and spouse of expatriates. These are flagged appropriately as different respondents.

With much more data to draw on, we are able to reaffirm the constructs presented in earlier editions but also to extend debate to issues of longitudinal studies of cultural shifts. We can also drill down to age and generation differences as well as functional areas and discuss issues of cultural convergence and acculturation.

The empirical results are, however, just an illustration of what we are trying to say.

This book attempts to do three things: dispel the notion that there is "one best way" of managing and organizing; give readers a better understanding of their own culture and cultural differences in general, by learning how to recognize and cope with these in a business context; and provide some cultural insights into the "global" versus "local" dilemma facing international organizations. Possibly the most important aspect of the book is the second. We believe understanding our own culture and our own assumptions and expectations about how people "should" think and act is the basis for success.

The Impact of Culture on Business

Take a look at the new breed of international managers, educated according to the most modern management philosophies. They all know that in the SBU, TQM should reign, with products delivered JIT, where CFTs distribute products while subject to MBO, AI, and tested through MVPs. If this is not done appropriately, we need to BPR. (SBU = strategic business unit; TQM = total quality management; JIT = just-in-time; CFT = customer first team; MBO = management by objectives; AI = artificial intelligence; MVP=Minimum Viable Product; BPR = business process reengineering.)

But just how universal are these management solutions? Are these "truths" about what effective management really is: truths that can be applied anywhere, under any circumstances?

Even with experienced international companies, many well-intended "universal" applications of management theory have turned out badly. For example, pay-for-performance has in many instances been a failure on the African continent because there are particular, though unspoken, rules about the sequence and timing of rewards and promotions. Similarly, management-by-objectives schemes have generally failed within subsidiaries of multinationals in southern Europe, because managers have not wanted to conform to the abstract nature of preconceived policy guidelines.

Even the notion of human-resource management is difficult to translate to other cultures, coming as it does from a typically Anglo-Saxon doctrine. It borrows from economics the idea that human beings are "resources" like physical and monetary resources. It tends to assume almost unlimited capacities for individual development. In countries without these beliefs, this concept is hard to grasp and unpopular once it is understood.

International managers have it tough. They must operate on a number of different premises at any one time. These premises arise from their culture of origin, the culture in which they are working, and the culture of the organization that employs them.

In every culture in the world such phenomena as authority, bureaucracy, creativity, good fellowship, verification, and accountability are experienced in different ways. That we use the same words to describe them tends to make us unaware that our cultural biases and our accustomed conduct may not be appropriate or shared.

There is a presumption that internationalization will create, or at least lead to, a common culture worldwide. This would make the life of international managers much simpler. People point to McDonald's or Coca-Cola as examples of tastes, markets, and hence cultures becoming similar everywhere. Indeed, many products and services are becoming common to world markets. What is important to consider, however, is not what they are and where they are found physically, but *what they mean to the people in each culture*. As we will describe later, the essence of culture is not what is visible on the surface. It is the shared ways groups of people understand and interpret the world. So the fact that we can all communicate with iPhones, listen to iTunes and Spotify, and eat hamburgers tells us that there are some novel products that can be sold on a universal message, but it does not tell us what eating hamburgers or listening to iTunes and Spotify means in different cultures. Dining at McDonald's was at one time a show of status in Moscow, whereas it is a fast meal for a fast buck in New York. If businesspeople want to gain understanding of and allegiance to their corporate goals, policies, products, or services wherever they are doing business, they must understand what those and other aspects of management mean in different cultures.

In addition to exploring why universal applications of Western management theory may not work, we will also try to deal with the growing dilemma facing international managers known as "glocalization."

As markets globalize, the need for standardization in organizational design, systems, and procedures increases. Yet managers are also under pressure to adapt their organization to the local characteristics of the market, the legislation, the fiscal regime, the sociopolitical system, and the cultural system. This balance between consistency and adaptation is essential for corporate success.

Paralysis Through Analysis: The Elixir of the Management Profession

Peters and Waterman in *In Search of Excellence* hit the nail on the head with their critique of "the rational model" and "paralysis through analysis." Western analytical thinking (taking a phenomenon to pieces) and rationality (reckoning the consequences before you act) have led to many international successes in fields of technology. Indeed, technologies do work by the same universal rules everywhere, even on the moon. Yet the very success of the universalistic philosophy now threatens to become a handicap when applied to interactions between human beings from different cultures.

The human being is a special piece of technology, and the results of our studies, extensively discussed in this book, indicate that the social world of the international organization has many more dimensions to deal with.

Some managers, especially in Japan, recognize the multidimensional character of their company. They seem able to use a logic appropriate to machines (analytic-rational) *and* a logic more appropriate to social relations (synthetic-intuitive), switching between these as needed.

In the process of internationalization the Japanese increasingly take the functioning of local society seriously. They were not the first to observe *"Si fueris Romae, Romano vivito more"* ("When in Rome, do as the Romans do"), but they seem to act on this more than Westerners do. The Japanese have, moreover, added another dimension: "When in Rome, understand the behavior of the Romans, and thus become an even more complete Japanese."

In opposition we have our Western approach, based on American business education, which treats management as a profession and regards emotionally detached rationality as "scientifically" necessary. This numerical, cerebral approach dominates not only American business schools, but also other economic and business faculties. Such schools educate their students by giving them the right answers to the wrong questions. Statistical analysis, forecasting techniques, and operational studies are not "wrong." These are important technical skills. The mistake is to assume that technical rationality should characterize the human element in the organization. No one is denying the existence of universally applicable scientific laws with objective consequences. These are, indeed, culture-free. However, the belief that human cultures in the workplace should resemble the laws of physics and engineering is a *cultural*, not a scientific, belief. It is a universal assumption that does not win universal agreement, or even come close to doing so.

The internationalization of business life requires more knowledge of cultural patterns. Pay-for-performance, for example, can work out well in the cultures where we have had most of our training: the USA, the Netherlands, and the UK. In more communitarian cultures like France, Germany, and large parts of Asia it may not be so successful, at least not the Anglo-Saxon version of pay-for-performance. Employees may not accept that individual members of the group should excel in a way that reveals the shortcomings of other members. Their definition of an "outstanding individual" is one who benefits those closest to him or her. Customers in more communitarian cultures also take offense at the "quick buck" mentality of the best salespeople; they prefer to build up relationships carefully and maintain them.

How Proven Formulas Can Lead to Wrong Result

Why is it that many management processes lose effectiveness when cultural borders are crossed?

Many multinational companies apply formulas in overseas areas that are derived from, and are successful in, their own culture. International management consulting firms of Anglo-Saxon origin are still using similar methods to the neglect of cultural differences.

An Italian computer company received advice from a prominent international management consulting firm to restructure to a matrix organization. It did so and failed; the task-oriented approach of the matrix structure challenged loyalty to the functional boss. In Italy bosses are like fathers, and you cannot have two fathers.

Culture is like gravity: you do not experience it until you jump six feet into the air. Local managers may not openly criticize a centrally developed appraisal system or reject the matrix organization, especially if confrontation or defiance is not culturally acceptable to them. In practice, though, beneath the surface, the silent forces of culture operate a destructive process, biting at the roots of centrally developed methods that do not "fit" locally.

The flat hierarchy, SBUS, MBO, matrix organizations, assessment centers, TQM, BPR, AI, MVP, and pay-for-performance are subjects of discussion in nearly every bestseller about management, and not only in the Western world. Reading these books (for which managers happily do not have much time anymore) creates a feeling of euphoria. "If I follow these Ten Commandments, I'll be the *modern leader*, the *change master*, the *champion*." A participant from Korea told us in quite a cynical tone that he admired the USA for solving one of the last major problems in business—how to get rid of people in the process of reengineering. The idea of the "one best way" is a management fallacy that is dying a slow death.

Although the organizational theory developed in the 1970s introduced the environment as an important consideration, it was unable to kill the dream of the one best way of organizing. It did not measure the effects of national culture, but systematically pointed to the importance of the market, the technology, and the product for determining the most effective methods of management and organization.

If you study similar organizations in different cultural environments, they often turn out to be remarkably uniform by major criteria: number of functions, levels of hierarchy, degree of specialization, and so on. Instead of proving anything, this may mean little more than that uniformity has been imposed on global operations, or that leading company practices have been carefully imitated, or even that technologies have their own imperatives. Research of this kind has often claimed that this "proves" that the organization is culture-free. But the wrong questions have been asked. The issue is not whether a hierarchy in the Netherlands has six levels, as does a similar company in Singapore, but what the hierarchy and those levels mean to the Dutch and Singaporeans. Where the meaning is totally different—for example, a "chain of command" versus "a family"—then human-resource policies developed to implement the first will seriously miscommunicate in the latter context.

In this book we examine the visible and invisible ways in which culture impacts on organizations. The more fundamental differences in culture and their effects may not be directly measurable by objective criteria, but they will certainly play a very important role in the success of an international organization.

Culture Is the Way in Which People Solve Problems

A useful way of thinking about where culture comes from is the following: *culture is the way in which a group of people solves problems and reconciles dilemmas.*[1] The particular problems and dilemmas each culture must resolve will be discussed below. If we focus first on what culture is, perhaps it is easiest to start with this example.

Imagine you are on a flight to South Africa and the pilot says, "We have some problems with the engine, so we will land temporarily in Burundi" (for those who do not know Burundi, it is next to Rwanda). What is your first impression of Burundi culture once you enter the airport building? It is not "what a nice set of values these people have," or even "don't they have an interesting shared system of meaning." It is the concrete, observable things like language, food, or dress. Culture comes in layers, like an onion. To understand it you have to unpeel it layer by layer.

On the outer layer are the products of culture, like the soaring skyscrapers of Manhattan, pillars of private power, with congested public streets between them. These are expressions of deeper values and norms in a society that are not directly visible (values such as upward mobility, "the more, the better," status, material success). The layers of values and norms are deeper within the "onion" and are more difficult to identify.

But why do values and norms sink down into semi-awareness and unexamined beliefs? Why are they so different in different parts of the world?

A problem that is regularly solved disappears from consciousness and becomes a basic assumption, an underlying premise. It is not until you are trying to get rid of the hiccups and hold your breath for as long as you possibly can that you think about your need for oxygen. These basic assumptions define the meaning that a group shares. They are implicit.

Take the following discussion between a medical doctor and a patient. The patient asks the doctor: "What's the matter with me?" The doctor answers: "Pneumonia." "What causes pneumonia?" "It is caused by a virus." "Interesting," says the patient, "what causes a virus?" The doctor shows signs of severe irritation and the discussion dies. Very often that is a sign that the questioner has hit a basic assumption, or in the words of Collingwood, an absolute presupposition about life.[2] What is taken for granted, unquestioned reality: this is the core of the onion.

National, Corporate, and Professional Culture

Culture also presents itself on different levels. At the highest level is the culture of a *national* or regional society, the French or west European versus the Singaporean or Asian. The way in which attitudes are expressed within a specific organization is described as a *corporate* or organizational culture. Finally, we can even talk about the culture of particular functions within organizations: marketing, research and development, personnel. People within certain functions will tend to share certain *professional* and ethical orientations. This book will focus on the first level, the differences in culture at a national level.

Cultural differences do not only exist with regard to faraway, exotic countries. In the course of our research it has become increasingly clear that there are at several levels as many differences between the cultures of West Coast and East Coast America as there are between different nations (although for the purposes of this book most American references are averaged). All the examples show that there is a clear-cut cultural border between the northwest European (analysis, logic, systems, and rationality) and the Euro-Latin (more person-related, more use of intuition and sensitivity). There are even significant differences between the neighboring Dutch and Belgians.

The average Belgian manager has a family idea of the organization. He or she experiences the organization as paternalistic and hierarchical, and, as in many Latin cultures, father decides how it should be done. The Belgian sees the Dutch manager as overly democratic: what nonsense that everybody consults everybody. The Dutch manager thinks in a way more consistent with the Protestant ethic than the Belgian, who thinks and acts in a more Catholic way. Most Dutch managers distrust authority, while Belgian managers tend to respect it.

Nearly all discussions about the unification of Europe deal with techno-legal matters. But when these problems are solved, the real problem emerges. Nowhere do cultures differ so much as inside Europe. If you are going to do business with the French, you will first have to learn how to lunch extensively. The founder of the European Community, Jean Monnet, once declared: "If I were again facing the challenge to integrate Europe, I would probably start with culture."[3] Culture is the context in which things happen; out of context, even legal matters lack significance.

On this last point we need to consider that it has therefore become very popular to say that culture eats strategy for breakfast. True. But please also consider the truth of the fact that strategy eats culture for lunch. We strongly believe that culture and strategy should have dinner together.

The Basis of Cultural Differences

Every culture distinguishes itself from others by the specific solutions it chooses to certain problems that reveal themselves as dilemmas. It is convenient to look at these problems under three headings: those that arise from our relationships with other people; those that come from the passage of time; and that which relate to the environment. Our research, to be described in the following chapters, examines culture within these three categories. From the solutions different cultures have chosen to these universal problems, we can further identify seven fundamental dimensions of culture. Five of these come from the first category.

Relationships with People

There are five orientations covering the ways in which human beings deal with each other. We have taken Parsons's five relational orientations as a starting point.[4]

Universalism versus particularism. The universalist approach is roughly: "What is good and right can be defined and always applies." In particularist cultures far greater attention is given to the obligations of relationships and unique circumstances. For example, instead of assuming that the one good way must always be followed, the particularist reasoning is that friendship has special obligations and hence may come first. Less attention is given to abstract societal codes.

Individualism versus communitarianism. Do people regard themselves primarily as individuals or primarily as part of a group? Furthermore, is it more important to focus on individuals so that they can contribute to the community as and if they wish, or is it more important to consider the community first since that is shared by many individuals?

Neutral versus emotional. Should the nature of our interactions be objective and detached, or is expressing emotion acceptable? In North America and northwest Europe business relationships are typically instrumental and all about achieving objectives. The brain checks emotions because these are believed to confuse the issues. The assumption is that we should resemble our machines in order to operate them more efficiently. But further south and in many other cultures, business is a human affair and the whole gamut of emotions is deemed appropriate. Loud laughter, banging your fist on the table, or leaving a conference room in anger during a negotiation is all part of business.

Specific versus diffuse. When the whole person is involved in a business relationship there is a real and personal contact, instead of the specific relationship prescribed by a contract. In many countries a diffuse relationship is not only preferred but necessary before business can proceed.

In the case of one American company trying to win a contract with a South American customer (see Chapter 7), disregard for the importance of the relationship lost the deal. The American company made a slick, well-thought-out presentation that it thought clearly demonstrated its superior product and lower price. Its Swedish competitor took a week to get to know the customer. For five days the Swedes spoke about everything except the product. On the last day the product was introduced. Though somewhat less attractive and slightly higher priced, the diffuse involvement of the Swedish company got the order. The Swedish company had learned that to do business in particular countries involves more than overwhelming the customer with technical details and fancy slides.

Achievement versus ascription. Achievement means that you are judged on what you have recently accomplished and on your record. Ascription means that status is attributed to you by birth, kinship, gender, or age, but also by your connections (who you know) and your educational record (a graduate of Tokyo University or Haute Ecole Polytechnique).

In an achievement culture, the first question is likely to be "*What* did you study?" while in a more ascriptive culture the question will more likely be "*Where* did you study?" Only if it is a lousy university or one they do not recognize will ascriptive people ask what you studied; and that will be to enable you to save face.

Attitudes with Regard to Time

The way in which societies look at *time* also differs. In some societies what somebody has achieved in the past is not that important. It is more important to know what plan the person has developed for the future. In other societies you can make more of an impression with your past accomplishments than those of today. These are cultural differences that greatly influence corporate activities.

With respect to time, the American Dream is the French Nightmare. Americans generally start from zero, and what matters is their present performance and their plan to "make it" in the future. This is *nouveau riche* for the French, who prefer the *ancien pauvre*; they have an enormous sense of the past and relatively less focus on the present and future than Americans.

In certain cultures like the American, Swedish, and Dutch, time is perceived as passing in a straight line, a sequence of disparate events. Other cultures think of time more as moving in a circle, the past and present together with future possibilities. This distinction makes for considerable differences to planning, strategy, investment, and views on home-growing your talent, as opposed to buying it in.

Attitudes with Regard to the Environment

An important cultural difference can also be found in the attitude to the *environment*. Some cultures see the major focus affecting their lives and the origins of vice and virtue as residing within the person. Here, motivations and values are derived from within. Other cultures see the world as more powerful than individuals. They see nature as something to be feared or emulated.

The then chairman of Sony, Mr. Morita, explained how he came to conceive of the Walkman. A lover of classical music, he wanted to have a way of listening to recordings on his way to work without bothering any fellow commuters. The device was a way of not imposing on the outside world, but of being in harmony with it. Contrast that to the way most Westerners think about such technology: "I can listen to music without being disturbed by other people."

Another obvious example is the use of face masks that are worn over the nose and mouth during the Corona crisis. In Tokyo you see many people wearing them in great numbers. When you inquire why, you are told by the majority that when people have a virus, they wear them so they will not likely infect other people by breathing on them. In London or New York masks are worn by the majority of people who do not want to be infected by others.

Structure of the Book

This book will describe why there is no "one best way of managing," and how some of the difficult dilemmas of international management can be mediated. Throughout, it will attempt to give readers more insight into their own culture and how it differs from others.

For this fourth edition we have structured the book in five main sections:

Section I: National Culture and Personal Values (Chapters 2–12)

Section II: Corporate Cultures and Change Management (Chapters 13–15)

Section III: Reconciling Cultural Dilemmas (Chapters 16–17)

Section IV: Culture in Practice (Chapters 18–20)

And finally Appendices A and B for an extensive overview of the tools: apps, questionnaires and other supporting digital means. This is followed by the technical aspects of our databases.

Section I. National Culture and Personal Values

Chapters 2 through 8 will initiate the reader into the world of cultural diversity in relations with other people. How do cultures differ in this respect? In what ways do these differences impact on organizations and the conduct of international business? How are the relationships between employees affected? In what different ways do they learn and solve conflicts?

Chapters 9 and 10 discuss variations in cultural attitudes to time and the environment, which have very similar consequences for organizations.

Chapter 11 discusses a new approach to measuring intercultural competence that overcomes many of the limitations of other methods—including the researchers' own earlier frameworks. The reader is introduced to four aspects of Intercultural Competence:

1. **Recognition:** How competent is a person to recognize cultural differences around him or her?
2. **Respect:** How respectful is a person about those differences?
3. **Reconciliation:** How competent is a person to reconcile cultural differences?
4. **Realization:** How competent is a person to realize the necessary actions to implement the reconciliation of cultural differences?

Chapter 12 considers how managers can prepare the organization for the process of internationalization through some specific points of intervention. This chapter is intended to deal in a creative way with the dilemmas of internationalization, as well as to repeat the message that an international future depends on achieving a balance between any two extremes.

What will emerge is that the whole centralization versus decentralization debate is really a false dichotomy. What is needed is the skill, sensitivity, and experience to draw upon all the decentralized capacities of the international organization.

Section II. Corporate Cultures and Change Management

Chapter 13 discusses how general cultural assumptions about mankind, time, and the environment affect the culture of organizations. It identifies the four broad types of organization that have resulted with their hierarchies, relationships, goals, and structures.

Chapter 14 offers a new way of looking at managing cultural change. The main message is focused around how to enrich the existing organizational culture by its opposite. For example, if the preference is short-term results, how can one contextualize that within the context of a long-term vision? And if you push your products and services, how can you do it in a way that involves the customer?

Chapter 15 reflects on some of the ways one can sustain an organizational culture such as introducing programs to embed yin and yang values and Values to Behavior programs.

Section III: Reconciling Cultural Dilemmas

Chapter 16 analyses the different steps that are needed to reconcile cultural dilemmas. This is explored through a case study that elicits the various problems that occur when professional people from different cultures meet.

Chapter 17 discusses the challenges of managing cultural integration in mergers, acquisitions, and strategic alliances. These are increasingly pursued, not only to implement globalization strategies, but as a consequence of political, monetary, and regulatory convergence. Realizing the business benefits and creating wealth in an integration process is not easy since it demands joining values that are not easily joined; two out of three deals still do not achieve anywhere near the benefits that were originally anticipated. It is assumed too often that delivering benefits simply requires the alignment of technical, operational, and financial systems and market approaches. An alternative is given in how to reconcile the cultural diversity of the organizations involved.

Section IV: Culture in Practice

In this last section we introduce a series of frequently occurring dilemmas in areas ranging from recruitment to digitalization. All of these areas are supported by our portfolio of apps that help users to diagnose the dilemmas they are facing ranging from personal and organizational values to risk avoidance and risk taking and to serving and leading.

Much has been written previously about the recruitment, selection, and retention of creative talent and separately about product and process innovation. Even more has been written about corporate culture and mechanistic and structural approaches to innovation in organizations. What is severely lacking is an overall framework that integrates these components and informs the HR professional to help the organization create a culture of innovation. Chapter 18 discusses the way HR can contribute to the sustainability of creative cultures.

Although much has been written and hypothesized about leadership competencies and styles, the advent of leadership in the digital age has further complicated the issue. In Chapter 19, we propose a model of reconciliation based on seven golden "dilemmas" that digital leaders face. The approaches to these dilemmas are culturally defined. The premise is that, by thinking and acting to reconcile these issues, leaders are better able to work digitally *and* cross-culturally.

Chapter 20 shows how different cultures might define integrity and ethical behavior differently. Some definitions might work in a single culture, but can be done when cultures meet in multicultural environments? People in all cultures, organizations, and institutions agree that great leaders can be respected across cultures and institutions. Indeed, they have integrity. In this article it is suggested that integrity is creating wholeness through the integration of opposites. This is something that is not taught at educational institutions.

What this book attempts to make possible is the genuinely transnational organization, in which each national culture contributes its own particular insights and strengths to the solution of worldwide issues and the company is able to draw on whatever it is that nations do best.

CULTURAL DATA

Throughout the book, we give examples of "stereotypical" responses to our basic cultural instruments from updated representative samples from major countries to illustrate the concepts being discussed based on our earlier cultural data. These serve to illustrate what we might describe as the underlying cultural norms of that country relevant to the development of business and management styles prior to the boom in globalization over the last 30 years. They are intended to help the reader reflect on the origins of cultural differences relevant to business rather than for modern day tourists.

The effects of globalization, immigration, and other socioeconomic shifts (e.g., European convergence) based on our more recent cultural data are given special consideration in Section IV. It is now too simplistic to try to describe the (single) culture of a country without taking into consideration the effects of immigration, the development of multicultural societies, age and generation differences, and corporate culture.

For this fourth edition, we have provided access links to more information and our online tools in a dedicated website. This includes the country culture scores for research purposes.

For a much more in-depth picture we also refer to very specific online tools such as the comprehensive detailed tips on doing business in 144 countries given in our Culture for Business app.

See: www.ridingthewavesofculture.com.

National Culture and Personal Values

2

The One Best Way of Organizing Does Not Exist

Fons Trompenaars and Charles Hampden-Turner

HOWEVER OBJECTIVE and uniform we try to make organizations, they will not have the same meaning for individuals from different cultures. The meanings perceived depend on certain cultural preferences, which we shall describe. Likewise, the meaning that people give to the organization, their concept of its structure, practices, and policies, is culturally defined.

Culture is a shared system of meanings. It dictates what we pay attention to, how we act, and what we value. Culture organizes such values into what Geert Hofstede calls "mental programs."[1] The behavior of people within organizations is an enactment of such programs.

Each of us carries within us the ways we have learned about organizing our experience to mean something. This approach is described as phenomenological, meaning that the way people perceive phenomena around them is coherent, orderly, and makes sense.

A fellow employee from a different culture makes one interpretation of the meaning of an organization while we make our own. Why? What can we learn from this alternative way of seeing things? Can we let that employee contribute in his or her own way?

This approach to understanding an international organization is in strong contrast to the traditional approach, in which managers or researchers decide unilaterally how the organization should be defined. Traditional studies have been based on the physical, verifiable characteristics of organizations, which are assumed to have a common definition for all people, everywhere, at all times. Instead of this approach, which looks for laws and common properties among "things" observed, we shall look for consistent ways in which cultures structure the perceptions of what they experience.

Our more recent research confirms that different cultures share similar business problems but how they (initially) approach these is culturally determined. The significance of these different points of view has important implications for doing business and managing in today's world, and we will discuss how these can be accommodated through reconciliation.

What the Gurus Tell Us

Management gurus like Frederick Taylor, Henri Fayol, Peter Drucker, Tom Peters, Jim Collins, and Jerry Porras have one thing in common: they all gave the impression, consciously or unconsciously, that there was one best way to lead, to manage, and to organize. We shall be showing how very American and, in the case of Fayol, how French these assumptions were. Not much has changed in this respect since they wrote their seminal books. Is it not desirable to be able to give management a box of tools that will reduce the complexities of managing? Of course it is. We see the manager reach for the tools to limit complexity, but unfortunately the approach tends to limit innovation and intercultural success as well.

Yet studies in the 1970s already showed that the effectiveness of certain methods depends on the environment in which we operate.

Since then, most so-called contingency studies have asked how the major structures of the organization vary in accordance with major variables in the environment. They have tended to show that if the environment is essentially simple and stable, then steep hierarchies survive, but if it is complex and turbulent, flatter hierarchies engage it more profitably. Such studies have mainly been confined to one country, usually the UK and USA. Both structure and environment are measured, and the results explain that X amount of environmental turbulence evokes Y amount of hierarchical levels, leading to Z amount of performance. The fact that Japanese corporations engaged in very turbulent environments with much steeper hierarchies has not as a rule been addressed.

We should note that these contingency studies are still searching for one best way in specified circumstances. They still believe their universalism is scientific, when in fact it is a cultural preference. "One best way" is a yearning, not a fact. Michel Crozier, the French sociologist, working in 1964, could find no studies that related organizations to their sociocultural environments.[2] Of course those who search for sameness will usually find it, and if you stick to examining common objects and processes, like refining oil according to chemical science, then pipes will be found to have the same function the world over. If the principles of chemical engineering are the same, why not all principles? It seems a plausible equation.

Talcott Parsons, an American sociologist, has suggested that organizations have to adapt not simply to the environment but also to the views of participating employees.[3] It has been only in recent years that this consideration of employee perceptions, and differing cultures, has surfaced in management literature.

Neglect of Culture in Action

Take the following meeting of a management team trying to internationalize a company's activities. This case is a summary of an interview with a North American human-resource manager, a case history that will be referred to throughout the book. Although the case is real, the names of the company and the participants are fictitious.

THE MISSOURI COMPUTATIONAL COMPANY (MCC)

MCC, founded in 1952, is a very successful American company. It develops, produces, and sells midsize and large computers. The company currently operates as a multinational in North and South America, Europe, Southeast Asia, Australia, and the Middle East. Sales activities are regionally structured. The factories are in St. Louis and Newark (New Jersey); the most important research activities take place in St. Louis.

Production, R&D, personnel, and finance are coordinated at the American head office. Business units handle the regional sales responsibilities. This decentralized structure does have to observe certain centralized limitations regarding logos, letter types, types of products, and financial criteria. Standardization of labor conditions, function classification, and personnel planning is coordinated centrally, whereas hiring is done by the regional branches. Each regional branch has its own personnel and finance departments. The management meets every two weeks, and this week is focusing on global-ization issues.

Internationalization. Mr. Johnson paid extra attention in the management meeting. As vice president of human resources worldwide, he could be fac-ing serious problems. Management recognizes that the spirit of globalization is becoming more active every day. Not only do the clients have more inter-national demands, but production facilities need to be set up in more and more countries.

This morning a new logo was introduced to symbolize the worldwide image of the company. The next item on the agenda was a worldwide mar-keting plan.

Mr. Smith, the CEO, saw a chance to bring forward what his MBA taught him to be universally applicable management tools. In addition to global images and marketing, he saw global production, finance, and human-resources management as supporting the international breakthrough.

Johnson's hair started to rise as he listened to his colleague's presentation. "The organization worldwide should be flatter. An excellent technique for this would be to follow the project approach that has been so successful in the USA." Johnson's question about the acceptance of this approach in southern Europe and South America was brushed aside with a short reply regarding the extra time that would be allotted to introduce it in these cultures. The generous allocation of six months would be provided to make even the most unwilling cul-ture understand and appreciate the beauty of shorter lines of communication.

Finally, all of this would be supported by a strong pay-for-performance system so that, in addition to more effective structures, the employees would also be directed toward the right goals.

Johnson's last try to introduce a more "human" side to the discussion concerning the implementation of the techniques and policy instruments was useless. The finance manager, Mr. Finley, expressed the opinion of the entire management team: "We all know that cultural differences are decreasing with the increasing reach of the media. We should be world leaders and create a future environment that is a microcosm of Missouri."

Mr. Johnson frowned at the prospect of next week's international meeting in Europe.

Mr. Johnson knew from experience there would be trouble in com-municating this stance to European human-resource managers. He could empathize with the Europeans, while knowing that central management did not really intend to be arrogant in extending a central policy worldwide. What could he do to get the best outcome from his next meeting? We shall follow this through in Chapter 4.

Culture as a Side Dish?

Culture still seems like a luxury item to most managers, a dish on the side. In fact, culture pervades and radiates meanings into every aspect of the enterprise. Culture patterns the whole field of business relationships. The Dutch author remembers a conversation he had with a Dutch expatriate in Singapore. This expatriate was very surprised when questioned about the ways in which he accommodated to the local culture when implementing management and organization techniques. Before answering, he tried to find out why he had been asked such a stupid question. "Do you work for personnel, by any chance?" Then he took me on a tour through the impressive refinery. "Do you really think the products we have and the technology we use allow us to take local culture into consideration?"

Indeed, it would be difficult for a continuous-process company to accommodate to the wishes of most Singaporeans to be home at night. In other words, reality seems to show us that variables such as product, technology, and markets are much more of a determinant than culture is. In one sense this conclusion is correct. Integrated technologies have a logic of their own that operates regardless of where the plant is located. Cultures do not compete with or repeal these laws. They simply supply the social context in which the technology operates. A refinery is indeed a refinery, but the culture in which it is located may see it as an imperialist plot, a precious lifeline, the last chance for an economic takeoff, a prop for a medieval potentate, or a weapon against the West. It all depends on the cultural context.

It is quite possible that organizations can be the same in such objective dimensions as physical plant, layout, or product, yet totally different in the meanings the surrounding human cultures read into them. We once interviewed a Venezuelan process operator, showing him the company organizational chart and asking him to indicate how many layers he had above and below him. To our surprise he indicated more levels than there were on the chart. We asked him how he could see these. "This person next to me," he explained, "is above me, because he is older."

One of the exercises we conduct in our workshops is to ask participants to choose between the following two extreme ways to conceive of a company, asking them which they think is usually true, and which most people in their country would opt for.

A. One way is to see a company as a system designed to perform functions and tasks in an efficient way. People are hired to perform these functions with the help of machines and other equipment. They are paid for the tasks they perform.

B. A second way is to see a company as a group of people working together. They have social relations with other people and with the organization. The functioning is dependent on these relations.

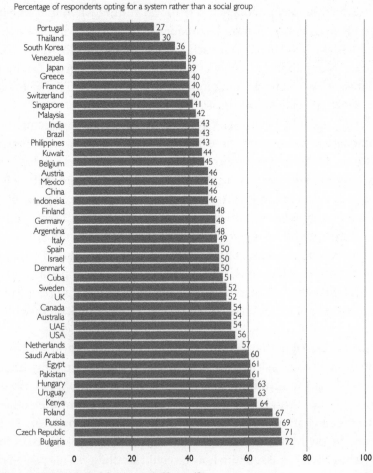

Percentage of respondents opting for a system rather than a social group

Portugal	27
Thailand	30
South Korea	36
Venezuela	39
Japan	39
Greece	40
France	40
Switzerland	40
Singapore	41
Malaysia	42
India	43
Brazil	43
Philippines	43
Kuwait	44
Belgium	45
Austria	46
Mexico	46
China	46
Indonesia	46
Finland	48
Germany	48
Argentina	48
Italy	49
Spain	50
Israel	50
Denmark	50
Cuba	51
Sweden	52
UK	52
Canada	54
Australia	54
UAE	54
USA	56
Netherlands	57
Saudi Arabia	60
Egypt	61
Pakistan	61
Hungary	63
Uruguay	63
Kenya	64
Poland	67
Russia	69
Czech Republic	71
Bulgaria	72

FIGURE 2.1. Which Kind of Company Is Normal?

Figure 2.1 shows the wide range of national responses. Only a little over a third of French, Korean, or Japanese managers see a company as a system rather than a social group, whereas the British and Americans are fairly evenly divided, and there is a large majority in favor of the system in Russia and several countries of eastern Europe.

These differing interpretations are important influences on the interactions between individuals and groups. Formal structures and management techniques may appear uniform. Indeed they imitate hard technologies in order to achieve this, but just as plant and equipment have different cultural meanings, so do social technologies.

An Alternative Approach

All organizational instruments and techniques are based on *paradigms* (sets of assumptions). An assumption often taken for granted is that social reality is "out there," separated from the manager or researcher in the same way as the matter of a physics experiment is "out there." The physics researchers can give the physical elements in their experiments any name they want. Dead things do not talk back and do not define themselves.

The human world, however, is quite different. As Alfred Schutz pointed out, when we encounter other social systems they have already given names to themselves, decided how they want to live and how the world is to be interpreted.[4] We may label them if we wish, but we cannot expect them to understand or accept our definitions unless these correspond to their own. We cannot strip people of their commonsense constructs or routine ways of seeing. They come to us as whole systems of patterned meanings and understandings. We can only try to understand, and to do so means starting with the way they think and building from there.

Hence organizations do not simply react to their environment as a ship might to waves. They actively select, interpret, choose, and create their environments.

Summary

In spite of globalization and many merger failures, it is surprising that individuals and organizations act as they do without considering the *meanings* they attribute to their environment. "A complex market" is not an objective description so much as a cultural perception. Complex to whom? To an Ethiopian or to an American? Feedback sessions where people explore their mistakes can be "useful feedback" according to American management culture and "enforced admissions of failure" in a German management culture. One culture may be inspired by the very thing that depresses another.

The organization and its structures are thus more than objective reality; they comprise fulfillments or frustrations of the mental models held by real people.

Rather than there being "one best way of organizing" there are several ways, some very much more culturally appropriate and effective than others, but all of them giving international managers additional strings to their bow if they are willing and able to clarify the reactions of foreign cultures.

3

The Meaning of Culture

Fons Trompenaars and Charles Hampden-Turner

A FISH DISCOVERS its need for water only when it is no longer in it. Our own culture is like water to a fish. It sustains us. We live and breathe through it. And we are not very conscious of it. What one culture may regard as essential, a certain level of material wealth for example, may not be so vital to other cultures.

The Concept of Culture

Social interaction, or meaningful communication, presupposes common ways of processing information among the people interacting. These have consequences for doing business as well as managing across cultural boundaries. Even "at home," managers are faced with an increasingly diverse and multicultural workforce. The mutual dependence of the actors is because together they constitute a connected system of meanings: a shared definition of a situation by a group.

How do these shared beliefs come about, and what is their influence on the interactions between members of an organization? An absolute condition for meaningful interaction in business and management is the existence of mutual expectations.

On a cold winter night in Amsterdam the Dutch author sees someone enter a cigar shop. His Burberry coat and horn spectacles reveal him to be well off. He buys a pack of cigarettes and takes a box of matches. He then visits the newspaper stand, purchases a Dutch newspaper, and quickly walks to a wind-free corner near the shopping gallery. I approach him and ask if I can smoke a cigarette with him and whether he would mind if I read the second section of his paper. He looks at me unbelievingly and says, "I need this corner to light my paper." He throws me the pack of cigarettes because he does not smoke. When I stand back, I see that he lights the newspaper and holds his hands above the flames. He turns out to be homeless, searching for warmth and too shy to purchase a single box of matches without the cigarettes.

In this situation my expectations are not met by the individual observed. My expectations about the behavior of the man say more about myself than about him. What I expect depends on where I come from and the meanings I give to what I experience. Expectations occur on many different levels, from concrete, explicit levels to implicit and subconscious ones. I am misled not only by the "meaning" of the man's clothing and appearance, but also on the simple level of the newspaper and cigarettes. When we observe such symbols they trigger certain expectations. When the expectations of who we are communicating with meet our own, there is mutuality of meaning.

The existence of mutual beliefs is not the first thing that comes to mind when you think about culture. In cultural training workshops we often start by asking participants: "What does the concept of culture mean to you? Can you differentiate a number of components?" In 25 years we have seldom encountered two or more groups or individuals with identical suggestions regarding the concept of culture. This shows the inclusiveness of the concept. The more difficult question is perhaps: "Can you name anything that is *not* encompassed by the concept of culture?"

The Layers of Culture

Figure 3.1 shows a model of culture that has three layers, which we will explore in this section.

The Outer Layer: Explicit Products

Go back to the temporary flight detour to Burundi from Chapter 1. What are the first things you encounter on a cultural level? Most likely it is not the strange combination of norms and values. Nor is it the sharing of meanings and value orientations. An individual's first experience of a new culture is the less esoteric, more concrete factors. This level consists of *explicit* culture.

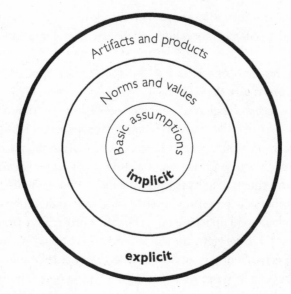

FIGURE 3.1. A Model of Culture

Explicit culture is the observable reality of the language, food, buildings, houses, monuments, agriculture, shrines, markets, fashions, and art. They are the symbols of a deeper level of culture. Prejudices mostly start on this symbolic and observable level. We should never forget that, as in the Burberry coat example, each opinion we voice regarding explicit culture usually says more about where *we* come from than about the community we are judging.

If we see a group of Japanese managers bowing, we are obviously observing explicit culture as the sheer act of bending. However, if we ask the Japanese "Why do you bow?"—a question they may not welcome—we penetrate the next layer of culture.

The Middle Layer: Norms and Values

Explicit culture reflects deeper layers of culture, the norms and values of an individual group. *Norms* are the mutual sense a group has of what is "right" and "wrong." Norms can develop on a formal level as written laws, and on an informal level as social control. *Values*, on the other hand, determine the definition of "good and bad," and are therefore closely related to the ideals shared by a group.

A culture is relatively stable when the norms reflect the values of the group. When this is not the case, there will most likely be a destabilizing tension. In Eastern Europe we have seen for years how the norms of Communism failed to match the values of society. Disintegration is a logical result.

While the norms, consciously or subconsciously, give us a feeling of "this is how I normally *should* behave," values give us a feeling of "this is how I *aspire* or *desire* to behave." A value serves as a criterion to determine a choice from existing alternatives. It is the concept an individual or group has regarding the desirable. For instance, in one culture people might agree with the value "Hard work is essential to a prosperous society." Yet the behavioral norm sanctioned by the group may be "Do not work harder than the other members of the group because then we would all be expected to do more and would end up worse off." Here the norm differs from the value. If you attend a job interview, do you wear a smart business suit (because that is the expected "norm"), or do you select your dress code on the basis of what you believe in (your own "value(s)")? If the decision outcomes are the same, then there is no tension, but if you prefer to dress casually but you are expected to dress more formally, then there is a conflict.

Some Japanese might say that they bow because they like to greet people: that is a value. Others might say they don't know why except that they do it because the others do it. Then we are talking about a norm.

It takes stable and salient shared meanings of norms and values for a group's cultural tradition to be developed and elaborated.

Why have different groups of people, consciously or subconsciously, chosen different definitions of good or bad, right or wrong?

The Core: Assumptions About Existence

To answer questions about basic differences in values between cultures, it is necessary to go back to the core of human existence. The most basic value people strive for is survival. Historically, and presently, we have witnessed civilizations fighting daily with nature: the Dutch with rising water; the Swiss with mountains and avalanches; the Central Americans and Africans with droughts; and the Siberians with bitter cold.

Each culture has organized itself to find the ways to deal most effectively with its environment, given its available resources. Such continuous problems are eventually solved automatically. "Culture" comes from the same root as the verb "to cultivate," meaning to till the soil: the way people act upon nature. The problems of daily life are solved in such obvious ways that the solutions disappear from our consciousness. If they did not, we would go crazy. Imagine having to concentrate on your need for oxygen every 30 seconds. The solutions disappear from our awareness and become part of our system of absolute assumptions.

The best way to test if something is a basic assumption is when the question provokes confusion or irritation. You might, for example, observe that some Japanese bow deeper than others. Again, if you ask why they do it the answer might be that they don't know but that the other person does it too (norm) or that they want to show respect for authority (value). A typical Dutch question that might follow is: "Why do you respect authority?" The most likely Japanese reaction would be either puzzlement or a smile (which might be hiding their irritation). When you question basic assumptions, you are asking questions that have never been asked before. It might lead to deeper insights, but it also might provoke annoyance. Try in the USA or the Netherlands to raise the question of why people are equal and you will see what we mean.

Groups of people organize themselves in such a way that they increase the effectiveness of their problem-solving processes. Because different groups of people have developed in different geographic regions, they have also formed different sets of logical assumptions.

We see that a specific organizational culture or functional culture is nothing more than the way in which groups have organized themselves over the years to solve the problems and challenges presented to them. Changes in a culture happen because people realize that certain old ways of doing things do not work anymore. It is not difficult to change culture when people are aware that the survival of the community is at stake, where survival is considered desirable.

From this fundamental relationship with the (natural) environment humankind, and after humankind the community, takes the core meaning of life. This deepest meaning has escaped from conscious questioning and has become self-evident, because it is a result of routine responses to the environment. In this sense culture is anything but nature.

Culture Directs Our Actions

Culture is beneath awareness in the sense that no one bothers to verbalize it, yet it forms the roots of action. This made one anthropologist liken it to an iceberg, with its largest implicit part beneath the water.

Culture is man-made, confirmed by others, conventionalized, and passed on for younger people or newcomers to learn. It provides people with a meaningful context in which to meet, to think about themselves and face the outer world.

In the language of Clifford Geertz, culture is the means by which people "communicate, perpetuate, and develop their knowledge about attitudes towards life. Culture is the fabric of meaning in terms of which human beings interpret their experience and guide their action."[1]

Over time, the habitual interactions within communities take on familiar forms and structures, which we will call the *organization of meaning*. These structures are imposed upon the situations that people confront and are not determined by the situation itself. For example, the wink of an eye: Is it a physical reflex from dust in the eye or an invitation to a prospective date? Or could it be someone making fun of you to others? Perhaps a nervous tic? The wink itself is real, but its meaning is attributed to it by observers. The attributed meaning may or may not coincide with the intended meaning of the wink. Effective social interaction, though, depends on the attributed meaning and intended meaning coinciding.

Cultures can be distinguished from each other by the differences in shared meanings they expect and attribute to their environment. Culture is not a "thing," a substance with a physical reality of its own. Rather, it is made by people interacting, and at the same time determining further interaction.

Culture as a "Normal Distribution"

People within a culture do not all have identical sets of artifacts, norms, values, and assumptions. Within each culture there is a wide spread of these. This spread does have a pattern around an average. So, in a sense, the variation around the norm can be seen as a normal distribution. Distinguishing one culture from another depends on the limits we want to make on each side of the distribution.

In principle, each culture shows the total variation of its human components. So while the USA and France have great variations, there are also many similarities. The "average" or "most predictable" behavior, as depicted by Figure 3.2, will be different for these two countries.

Cultures whose norms differ significantly tend to speak about each other in terms of extremes (Figure 3.3). Americans might describe the French as having the behavioral characteristics listed on the left in the figure, or the tail of the normal distribution. The French will use a similar caricature for

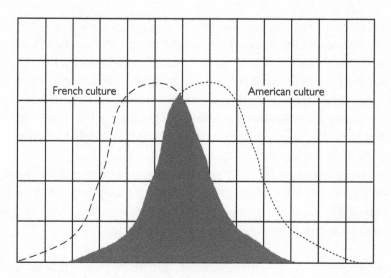

Norms and values

FIGURE 3.2. Culture as Normal Distribution

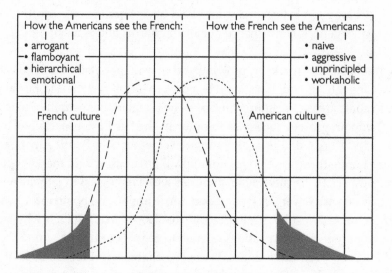

How the Americans see the French: How the French see the Americans:

- arrogant
- flamboyant
- hierarchical
- emotional

- naive
- aggressive
- unprincipled
- workaholic

French culture   American culture

Norms and values

FIGURE 3.3. Culture and Stereotyping

the Americans, as listed on the right. This is because we tend to notice differences rather than sameness.

Using extreme, exaggerated descriptions of behavior is *stereotyping*. It is, quite understandably, the result of registering what surprises us, rather than what is familiar. But there are dangers in doing this. First, a stereotype is a very limited view of the average behavior in a certain environment. It exaggerates and caricatures the culture observed and, unintentionally, the observer.

Second, people often equate something different with something wrong, thinking, "Their way is clearly different from ours, so it cannot be right." Finally, stereotyping ignores the fact that individuals in the same culture do not necessarily behave according to the cultural norm. Individual personality mediates in each cultural system.

Of course, business leaders have always been concerned with changing demographics in order to profile customers and subgroups of customers. Business leaders are discovering how rapidly they need to rethink and reassess such groupings. We have to be concerned with:

- Structural changes (in population, age distributions, fecundity/ birth rates of different cultures)
- Migrations—net of immigration and emigration (acculturation, ethnicity, diversity, the development of multicultural societies)
- Changes in beliefs and values held by different people (shifts, divergences, convergence of cultural norms and values)

The total potential market is growing as the world population expands at an increasing rate, although it should be noted that this growth is not uniform, and in some areas—including Europe—the population is actually declining.

The main growth continues to occur in the Far East, especially China, India, and Korea, and in accelerating developments in South America. Of course population growth does not imply a direct growth in market opportunity, especially because those countries with larger growth rates also tend to be those with lower GNP per capita. More important, population growth in these regions results in a larger low-cost labor force, which is why many US and European organizations operate in these countries.

However, even more dramatic are the changes in the structure of the population due to birth rates and life expectancy. These result because of differences in fecundity (fertility, health of mothers, and survival rates) and other changes in society (women in more developed societies restricting pregnancies and/or choosing to delay the onset of childbearing) combined with longer life expectancy. In some countries, such as Bangladesh, Pakistan, and India, life expectancy will double over the course of less than a century.

Whilst migration has very little effect on overall population levels, it does contribute to changes in the population structure. Immigrants usually come from different cultural backgrounds and offer and create different opportunities as well as challenges for business. Entirely new markets have been identified and satisfied (such as one for adhesive bandages in darker skin colors) for these immigrants as new customers. In addition immigrants often become a new source of suppliers as they offer new, culturally led products and services to the host community—such as ethnic food shops and restaurants.

So we have to be careful when describing what we mean by the "typical" French person, for example, given demographic changes in the population. Do we mean today or 20 years ago, or even before the French revolution? Throughout this book and in explaining the fundamentals ideas of culture, we will use the notion of "traditional" stereotypes to assist the reader in understanding the more important constructs. Later, we will consider what real population changes mean and where and how we will need to consider acculturation and issues of cultural convergence and changes arising from aging populations and generation differences.

Cultures Vary in Solutions to Common Problems and Dilemmas

To explain variations in the meaning organizations have for people working in them, we need to consider variations in meanings for different cultures. If we can identify and compare categories of culture that affect organizations, this will help us understand the cultural differences that must be managed in international business.

In every culture a limited number of general, universally shared human problems need to be solved. One culture can be distinguished from another by the specific solution it chooses for those problems. The anthropologists F. Kluckhohn and F.L. Strodtbeck identify five categories of problems, arguing that all societies are aware of all possible kinds of solution but prefer them in different orders.[2] Hence in any culture there is a set of "dominant," or preferred, value orientations. The five basic problems mankind faces, according to this scheme, are as follows:

1. What is the relationship of the individual to others? (relational orientation)
2. What is the temporal focus of human life? (time orientation)
3. What is the modality of human activity? (activity orientation)

4. What is a human being's relation to nature? (man-nature orientation)
5. What is the character of innate human nature? (human nature orientation)

In short, Kluckhohn and Strodtbeck argue that mankind is confronted with universally shared problems emerging from relationships with fellow beings, time, activities, and (human) nature. One culture can be distinguished from another by the arrangement of the specific solutions it selects for each set of problem situations. The solutions depend on the meaning given by people to life in general, and to their fellows, time, and nature in particular.

In our research we have distinguished seven dimensions of culture (see Chapter 1), also based on societies' differing solutions to relationships with other people, time, and nature. The following chapters will explain these dimensions and how they affect the process of managing across cultures.

Instead of running the risk of getting stuck by perceiving cultures as static points on a dual axis map, we believe that cultures *dance* from one preferred end to the opposite and back. In that way we do not risk one cultural category excluding its opposite, as has happened in so many similar studies, of which Hofstede's five mutually exclusive categories are the best known. Rather, we believe that one cultural category seeks to "manage" its opposite and that value dimensions self-organize in systems to generate new meanings. Cultures are circles with preferred arcs joined together. In this revised edition we have therefore introduced new questions that measure the extent to which managers seek to *integrate and reconcile* values. And we are testing the hypothesis that cultures that have a natural tendency to reconcile seemingly opposing values have a better chance of being successful economically than cultures that lack that inclination. All cultures are similar in the dilemmas they confront, yet different in the solutions they find, which creatively transcend the opposites.

Summary

This chapter described how common meanings arise and how they are reflected through explicit symbols. We saw that culture presents itself to us in layers. The outer layers are the products and artifacts that symbolize the deeper, more basic values and assumptions about life. The different layers are not independent from one another, but are complementary.

The shared meanings that are the core of culture are man-made, are incorporated into people within a culture, yet transcend the people in the culture. In other words, the shared meanings of a group are within them and cause them to interpret things in particular ways, but are also open to be changed if more effective solutions to problems of survival are desired by the group.

The solutions to three universal problems faced by humankind distinguish one culture from another. The problems—people's relationship to time, nature, and other human beings—are shared by humankind; their solutions are not. The latter depend on the cultural background of the group concerned. The categories of culture that emerge from the solutions cultures choose will be the subject of the next seven chapters. Their significance to work-related relationships, management instruments, and organizational structures will also be explored.

4

Rules and Exceptions

Fons Trompenaars and Charles Hampden-Turner

PEOPLE EVERYWHERE are confronted with three sources of challenge. They have exceptional relationships with other people, such as friends, employees, customers, and bosses. They must manage time and aging. And they must somehow come to terms with the external nature of the world, be it benign or threatening.

We have already identified the five dimensions of human relationships. It is easiest to summarize these in abstract terms, which may seem rather abstruse. We list them again with some translations in parentheses.

1. Universalism versus particularism (rules versus exceptions)
2. Communitarianism versus individualism (the group versus the individual)
3. Neutral versus emotional (the degree to which feelings are expressed)
4. Diffuse versus specific (the degree of involvement)
5. Achievement versus ascription (how status is accorded)

These five value orientations greatly influence our ways of doing business and managing as well as our responses in the face of moral dilemmas. Our relative position along these dimensions guides our beliefs and actions through life. For example, we all confront situations in which the established rules do not quite fit a particular circumstance. Do we do what is deemed "right," or do we adapt to the circumstances of the situation? If we are in a difficult meeting, do we show how strongly we feel and risk the consequences, or do we show "admirable restraint"? When we encounter a difficult problem, do we break it apart into pieces to understand it, or do we see everything as related to everything else? On what grounds do we show respect for someone's status and power: because that person has achieved it or because other circumstances (like age, education, or lineage) define it? These are all dilemmas to which cultures have differing answers. Part of the purpose of culture is to provide answers and guide behavior in otherwise vexatious situations.

Before discussing the first dimension—universal versus particular forms of relating to other people—let us rejoin the perplexed Mr. Johnson of the Missouri Computational Company (MCC) from Chapter 2. He is due to preside over an international human resources meeting in which 15 national representatives are expected to agree on the uniform implementation of a pay-for-performance system. Here is some background on MCC and a summary of its main policy directives.

Since the late 1970s MCC has been operating in more than 20 countries. As its foreign sales have grown, top management has become increasingly concerned about international coordination. Overseas growth, while robust, has been unpredictable. The company has therefore decided to coordinate the processes of measuring and rewarding achievement worldwide. Greater consistency in managing country operations is also on the agenda. There is not a complete disregard for national differences; the general manager worked in Germany for five years, and the marketing manager spent seven years in the Singapore operation.

It has been agreed to introduce a number of policy principles that will permeate MCC plants worldwide. They envisage a shareable definition of "How we do things in MCC" to let everyone in MCC, wherever they are in the world, know what the company stands for. Within this, there will be centrally coordinated policies for human resources, sales, and marketing.

This would benefit customers since they, too, are internationalizing in many cases. They need to know that MCC could provide high levels of service and effectiveness to their businesses, which increasingly cross borders. MCC needs to achieve consistent, recognizable standards regardless of the country in which it is operating. There is already a history of standardizing policies.

The reward system. Two years ago, confronted with heavy competition, the company decided to use a more differentiated reward system for the personnel who sold and serviced midsize computers. One of the reasons was to see whether the motivation of the American sales force could be increased. In addition, the company became aware that the best salespeople often left the firm for better-paying competitors. They decided on a two-year trial with the 15 active salespeople in the St. Louis area.

Experiment with pay-by-performance. The experiment consisted of the following elements:

- A bonus was introduced that depended on the turnover figures each quarter for each salesperson: 100 percent over salary for the top salesperson; 60 percent for the second best; 30 percent for numbers three and four; and no bonus for the remainder.
- The basic salary of all salespeople of midsize computers was decreased by 10 percent.

During the first year of the trial period there were continuous discussions among the affected employees. Five salespeople left the company because they were convinced the system treated them unjustly. Total sales did not increase. Despite this disaster, management continued the experiment because leaders believed that this kind of change was necessary and would take time to be accepted.

The Universal Versus the Particular

MCC in the USA is of course operating in a universalist culture. But even here a universalist solution has run into particularist problems. This first dimension defines how we judge other people's behavior. There are two "pure" yet alternative types of judgment. At one extreme we encounter an obligation to adhere to standards that are universally agreed to by the culture in which we live: "Do not lie. Do not steal. Do unto others as you would have them do unto you" (the Golden Rule), and so on. At the other extreme we encounter particular obligations to people we know: "X is my dear friend, so obviously I would not lie to him or steal from him. It would hurt us both to show less than kindness to one another."

Universalist, or rule-based, behavior tends to be abstract. Try crossing the street when the light is red in a very rule-based society like Switzerland or Germany. Even if there is no traffic, you will still be frowned at. It also tends to imply equality in the sense that all persons falling under the rule should be treated the same. But situations are ordered by categories. For example, if "others" to whom you "do unto" are not categorized as human, the rules may not apply. Finally, rule-based conduct has a tendency to resist exceptions that might weaken that rule. There is a fear that once you start to make exceptions for illegal conduct the system will collapse.

Particularist judgments focus on the exceptional nature of present circumstances. This person is not "a citizen" but my friend, brother, husband, child, or person of unique importance to me, with special claims on my love or my hatred. I must therefore sustain, protect, or discount this person *no matter what the rules say.*

Businesspeople from both societies will tend to think each other corrupt. A universalist will say of particularists, "They cannot be trusted because they will always help their friends," and a particularist, conversely, will say of universalists, "You cannot trust them; they would not even help a friend."

In practice we use both kinds of judgment, and in most situations we encounter they reinforce each other. If an employee is harassed in the workplace we would disapprove of this because "harassment is immoral and against company rules" and/or because "it was a terrible experience for Jennifer and really upset her." The universalist's chief objection, though, will be the breach of rules: "Employees should not have to deal with harassment in the workplace; it is wrong." The particularist is likely to be more disapproving of the fact that it caused distress to poor Jennifer.

Problems are not always so easily agreed upon as this one. Sometimes rules of supposed universal application do not cover a case of particular concern very well. There are circumstances much more complex than the rules appear to have envisaged. Consider the further adventures of the Missouri Computational Company, with its head office in St. Louis intent on imposing general policy guidelines on employees of many nations.

MCC has recently acquired a small but successful Swedish software company. Its head founded it three years ago with his son Carl, and was joined by his newly graduated daughter Clara and his youngest son, Peter, 12 months ago. Since the acquisition MCC has injected considerable capital and also given the company its own computer distribution and servicing in Sweden. This has given a real boost to the business.

MCC is now convinced that rewards for salespeople must reflect the increasing competition in the market. It has decreed that at least 30 percent of remuneration must depend on individual performance. At the beginning of this year Carl married a very rich wife. The marriage is happy, and this has had an effect on his sales record. He will easily earn the 30 percent bonus, though this will be small in relation to his total income, supplemented by his wife's wealth and by his share of the acquisition payment.

Peter has a less happy marriage and much less money. His only average sales figures mean that his income will be reduced when he can ill afford it. Clara, who married while still in school, has two children and this year lost her husband in an air crash. This tragic event caused her to have a weak sales year.

At the international sales conference national MCC managers present their salary and bonus ranges. The head of the Swedish company believes that performance should be rewarded and that favoritism should be avoided; he has many nonfamily members in his company. Yet he knows that unusual circumstances in the lives of his children have made this contest anything but fair. The rewards withheld will hurt more deeply than the rewards bestowed will motivate. He tries to explain the situation to the American HR chief and the British representative, who both look skeptical and talk about excuses. He accedes to their demands.

His colleagues from France, Italy, Spain, and the Middle East, who all know the situation, stare in disbelief. They would have backed him on the issue. His family members later says they feel let down. This was not what they joined the company for.

This episode from our ongoing MCC case shows that universalist and particularist points of view are not always easy to reconcile. The culture you come from and your personality, religion, and bonds with those concerned lead you to favor one approach more than another.

Universalist Versus Particularist Orientations in Different Countries

Much of the early research into this cultural dimension has come from the USA, and is influenced by American cultural preferences. The emerging consensus among these researchers, though, is that universalism is a feature of modernization per se, of more complex and developed societies. Particularism, they argue, is a feature of smaller, largely rural communities in which everyone knows everyone personally. The implication is that universalism and sophisticated business practice go together and all nations might be better off for more nearly resembling the USA.

We do not accept this conclusion. Instead, we believe that cultural dilemmas need to be reconciled in a process of understanding the advantages of each cultural preference. The creation of wealth and the development of industry should be an evolving process of discovering more and better universals covering and sustaining more particular cases and circumstances.

The story below, created by Americans Stouffer and Toby,[1] is another exercise used in our workshops. It takes the form of a dilemma that measures universal and particularist responses.

You are riding in a car driven by a close friend. He hits a pedestrian. You know he was going at least 35 miles per hour in an area of the city where the maximum allowed speed is 20 miles per hour. There are no witnesses. His lawyer says that if you testify under oath that he was only driving 20 miles per hour it may save him from serious consequences.

What right has your friend to expect you to protect him?

　A. My friend has a definite right as a friend to expect me to testify to the lower figure.
　B. He has some right as a friend to expect me to testify to the lower figure.
　C. He has no right as a friend to expect me to testify to the lower figure.

What do you think you would do in view of the obligations of a sworn witness and the obligation to your friend?

　D. Testify that he was going 20 miles an hour.
　E. Not testify that he was going 20 miles an hour.

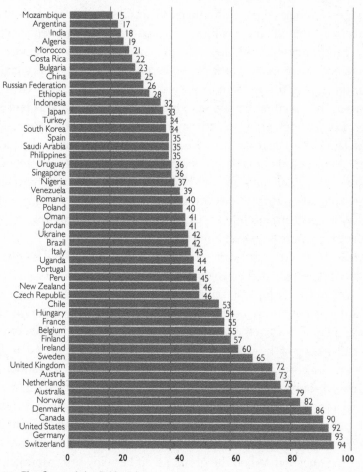

FIGURE 4.1. The Car and the Pedestrian

Figure 4.1 shows the result of putting these questions to a variety of nationalities.* The percentage shown represents those who answered that the friend had no right or some right and would then not testify (C or B + E). North Americans and most north Europeans emerge as almost totally

---

* As explained in Chapter 1, these charts are illustrative from representative samples from major countries to our basic cultural instruments to illustrate the concepts being discussed based on our earlier cultural data. These serve to illustrate what we might describe as the underlying cultural norms of that country relevant to the development of business and management styles prior to the boom in globalization over the last 20 years. It is the rank order rather than absolute scores that are relevant at this stage of discussion. For details of more recent data, cultural changes, and all other countries see www.ridingthewavesofculture.com.

universalist in their approach to the problem. The proportion falls to under 50 percent for the Italians, Spanish, and Japanese, while in Venezuela two-thirds of respondents would lie to the police to protect their friend.

Time and again in our workshops, the universalists' response is that, as the seriousness of the accident increases, the obligation to help their friend decreases. They seem to be saying to themselves, "The law was broken and the serious condition of the pedestrian underlines the importance of uphold-ing the law." This suggests that universalism is rarely used to the exclusion of particularism, rather that it forms the first principle in the process of moral reasoning. Particular consequences remind us of the need for universal laws.

Particularist cultures, however, are rather more likely to support their friend as the pedestrian's injuries increase. They seem to reason, "My friend needs my help more than ever now that he is in serious trouble with the law." Universalists would regard such an attitude as corrupt. What if we all started to lie on behalf of those close to us? Society would fall apart. There is indeed something to this argument. But particularism, which is based on a logic of the heart and human friendship, may also be the chief reason that citizens would not break laws in the first place. Do you love your children or present them with a copy of the civil code? And what if the law becomes a weapon in the hands of a corrupt elite? You can choose what you call corruption.

In a workshop we were giving some time ago we presented this dilemma. There was one British woman, Fiona, among the group of French participants. Fiona started the discussion of the dilemma by asking about the condition of the pedestrian. Without that information, she said, it would be impossible to answer the question. When the group asked her why this information was so indispensable, Dominique, an employee of a French airline, interjected: "Naturally it is because if the pedestrian is very seriously injured or even dead, then my friend has the absolute right to expect my support. Other-wise, I would not be so sure." Fiona, slightly irritated but still laughing, said: "That's amazing. For me it is absolutely the other way around."

This illustration shows that we "anchor" our response in one of the two principles. All nations might agree that universals and particulars should ideally be resolved—that is, that all exceptional cases be judged by more humane rules. What differs is their starting points.

As Figure 4.1 shows, universalists are more common in Protestant cul-tures, where the congregation relates to God by obedience to his written laws. There are no human intermediaries between God and his adherents, no one with the discretion to hear particular confessions, forgive sins, or make special allowances. Predominantly Catholic cultures retained these features of religion, which are more relational and particularist. People can break commandments and still find compassion for their unique circumstances. God for the Catholics is like them, moreover; he will probably understand that you were lying for your friend, particularly one who had the bad luck to have the stupid pedestrian crossing in front of his or her car.

Countries with strongly universalist cultures try to use the courts to mediate conflicts. An American book on automobile insurance is called *Hit Me—I Need the Money.* Indeed, the USA, credited with being the most litigious society on earth, has considerably more lawyers per capita than relatively particularist Japan. The more universal the country, the greater the need for an institution to protect the truth. (Incidentally, there is a strong correlation between universalism and expenditure per capita on pet food. This is not the same as pet ownership; particularist France has more dogs than universalist Germany, but French dogs are integrated into the family and eat leftovers.)

However, countries may be more or less universalist depending on what the rules are *about*. French and Italian managers, who were particularist on the traffic accident, believe that when writing on a subject as important as food you have a universal obligation to truth. Consider the following scenario, described by Stouffer and Toby.

You are a newspaper journalist who writes a weekly review of new restaurants. A close friend of yours has sunk all her savings in a new restaurant. You have eaten there, and you really think the restaurant is no good.

What right does your friend have to expect you to go easy on her restaurant in your review?

   A. She has a definite right as a friend to expect me to go easy on her restaurant in my review.
   B. She has some right as a friend to expect me to do this for her.
   C. She has no right as a friend to expect me to do this for her.

Would you go easy on her restaurant in your review given your obligations to your readers and your obligation to your friend?

   D. Yes.
   E. No.

In this second example, a universalist's view is that as a journalist you are writing for everyone, the universe of readers, not for your friend. Your obligation is to be "truthful and unbiased." In some cultures, then, it seems more important to universalize good taste than legal procedure. For them it is easier to leave the pedestrian in trouble than to judge the quality of food wrongly. (See Figure 4.2.)

A third dilemma we use to explore this dimension has to do with the rule of confidentiality concerning the secret deliberations of a business.

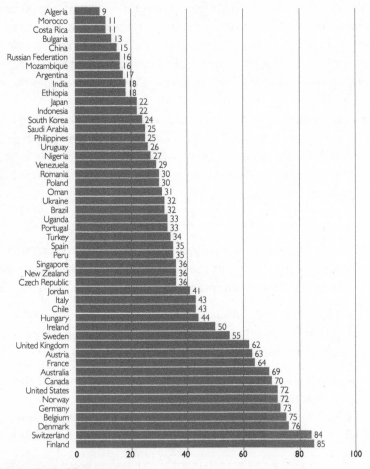

FIGURE 4.2. The Bad Restaurant

You are a doctor for an insurance company. You examine a close friend who needs more insurance. You find he is in pretty good shape, but you are doubtful on one or two minor points that are difficult to diagnose.

What right does your friend have to expect you to tone down your doubts in his favor?

A. My friend has a definite right as a friend to expect me to tone down my doubts in his favor.
B. He has some right as a friend to expect me tone down my doubts in his favor.
C. He has no right as a friend to expect me to tone down my doubts in his favor.

Would you help your friend in view of the obligations you feel toward your insurance company and your friend?

D. Yes.
E. No.

There are some interesting differences here between the scores on this dilemma and the previous two. (See Figure 4.3, next page.) The Japanese and Indonesians, especially, jump from the situational ethics they showed previously to a strongly universalistic stance on corporate confidentiality. Quite possibly this occurs because the situation is broader than a particular friend; at stake here is loyalty to a group or corporation versus loyalty to an individual outside that group.

This dilemma thus may also be presenting issues of communitarianism versus individualism, to be considered in Chapter 5. As these dimensions are related as well as relational, we must be careful in interpreting the meaning different national groups give them.

Universalism Versus Particularism in International Business

When companies go global, there is an almost inevitable move toward universalist ways of thinking. After all, products and services are being offered

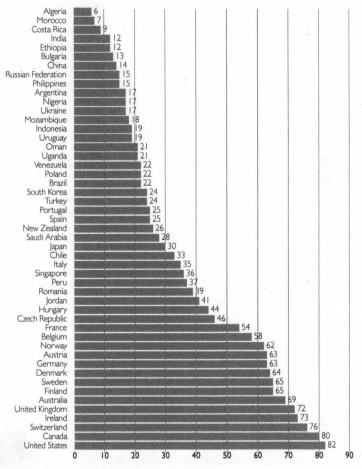

FIGURE 4.3. The Doctor and the Insurance Company

to a wider and wider universe of people. Their willingness to buy is "proof" of a universal appeal. It follows that the ways of producing the product, managing those who make it, and distributing it to customers should also be universalized. Let us consider the following examples of some of the areas where the universalist versus particularist dilemma shows up:

- The contract
- Timing a business trip
- Building a relationship with the client
- The role of the head office
- Job evaluations and rewards

The Contract

Weighty contracts are a way of life in universalist cultures. A contract serves to record an agreement on principle and codifies what the respective parties have promised to do. It also implies consent to the agreement and provides recourse if the parties do not keep to their side of the deal. Introducing lawyers into the process of negotiation puts the parties on notice that any breach could be costly and that promises made initially must be kept, even if these prove inconvenient.

How might a legal contract be perceived by a more particularist business partner? There is another reason why people tend to keep their promises. They have a personal relationship with their customer, whom they hold in particular regard. If you introduce contracts with strict requirements and penalty clauses, the implied message is that one party would cheat the other if not legally restrained from doing so. Those who feel they are not trusted may accordingly behave in untrustworthy ways. Alternatively they may terminate their relationship with a universalist business partner because that partner's precautions offend them and the contract terms are too rigid to allow a good working relationship to evolve.

One serious pitfall for universalist cultures in doing business with more particularist ones is that the importance of the relationship is often ignored. The contract will be seen as definitive by the universalist, but only as a rough guideline or approximation by the particularist. The latter will want to make the contract as vague as possible and may object to clauses that tie them down. This is not necessarily a sign of impending subterfuge, but a preference for mutual accommodation. Given the rise of Chinese, Japanese, and Indian economic power, the automatic superiority of the universalist position can no longer be assumed. Good customer relationships and good employee relationships may involve doing *more* than the contract requires. Moreover, relationships have a flexibility and durability that contracts often lack. Asian, Arab, and Latin businesspeople may expect contracts to be qualified where circumstances have changed.

In a 10-year contract between a Canadian ball bearing producer and an Arabic machine manufacturer, a minimum annual quantity of ball bearings was agreed upon. After about six years the orders from the Middle East stopped coming in. The Canadians' first reaction: "This is illegal."

A visit to the customer only increased their confusion. The contract had apparently been cancelled unilaterally by the Arabs because the Canadian contract-signer had left the company. The so-called universally applicable law was not considered relevant anymore in the eyes of the Arabs. What could the Canadians say against this logic, especially when they discovered that the ball bearings were never even used? It turned out that the product was purchased solely out of the particular loyalty to the Canadian contract-signer, not because of a felt legal obligation.

Timing a Business Trip

A universalist businessperson—a North American, British, Dutch, German, or Scandinavian—is wise to take much longer than usual when visiting a particularist culture. Particularists get suspicious when hurried. At least twice the time normally necessary to establish a contractual agreement is necessary to forge what has to be a closer relationship. It is important to create a sound relational and trustworthy basis that equates the quality of the product with the quality of the personal relationship. Rolls-Royce gave Toyota a deadline to make an acquisition offer, and Toyota promptly withdrew. Something similar happened in negotiations between Samsung and Fokker, when after a Dutch deadline Samsung pulled out. This process takes a considerable amount of time, but for particularists, the time taken to grow close to your partner is saved in the avoidance of trouble in the future. If you are not willing to take time now, the relationship is unlikely to survive vicissitudes.

The Role of the Head Office

In those Western countries that are high in universalism, the head office tends to hold the keys to global marketing, global production, and global human-resource management. Our own experience, though, is that, within more particularist national cultures, the writ of the head office fails to shape local ways of operating. Different groups develop their own local standards that become the basis of their solidarity and resistance to centralized edicts. Stratified boundaries are created by the national subsidiary between itself and the head office, and differentiation is deliberately sought.

Particularist groups seek gratification through relationships, especially relationships to the leader. Generally, the more particularist, the greater the commitment between employer and employee. The employer in these cultures strives to provide a broad array of satisfactions to employees: security, money, social standing, goodwill, and socioemotional support. Relationships are typically close and long-lasting. Job turnover is low, and commitments to the labor force are long-term. The local chief wishes all this to redound to his or her own credit, not that of the foreign owner. Research done in an American bank with branches in Mexico found Mexican staff to be far more particularist, with a tendency to distance themselves as far as possible from the head office in the USA in order to minimize universalist pressures.[2]

What frequently occurs is that foreign-based subsidiaries will *pretend* to comply with head office directives, which leads to a kind of ritualistic "corporate rain dance." They will go through the motions so long as they are under scrutiny, but they do not believe that rain will result. As soon as the attention of the head office is diverted to other matters, normal life proceeds.

Job Evaluations and Rewards

Head office policies in the human-resource area often lay down systems that all expatriate managers are required to apply locally. The logic of this universal system—that all jobs should be described, all candidates should have their qualifications compared with these descriptions, and all job occupants should have their performance evaluated against what their contracts specified they would do—is surely "beyond culture." It seems a demonstrably fair and universal way of managing. This general system sprang up in the postwar years when companies, especially American multinationals, saw very rapid growth. Thousands of employees within the USA needed fair methods of appraisal and promotion, and before long this spread to the rest of the developed world. Labor unions often gave their support to these methods, seeing them as protection from arbitrary discipline or anti-union activity. A worker could be fired only for demonstrable failure to do a defined piece of work. In such regulations there was, indeed, protection for many employees. Managers had to behave consistently. They could not take harsh steps in one instance and be lenient in another.

A system designed by Colonel Hay of the American army, called the Hay job evaluation system, is now widely used in businesses to evaluate what base salaries should be for the performance of various functions. Each function and job within it is scored with the help of the employee, his or her direct superior, and a panel that includes people doing similar jobs elsewhere. This helps to maintain internal consistency and facilitates transfers between different subsidiaries throughout a company's network without changes in salary or training. Minor concessions are usually made to local conditions by way of a cost-of-living allowance, but otherwise uniformity is maintained. All this sounds highly plausible. All such procedures may appear to be working with the paperwork duly completed. But what in fact happens in more particularist societies?

The following incident occurred in a multinational oil company. During a presentation to a group of Venezuelan managers, representatives from the head office were explaining new developments in the Hay function assessment system for R&D functions. They explained that the function would be less clearly separated from the function-holder, and that there would now be "benchmarks" determining the level of the function. The Venezuelans showed the pro forma response by concluding the presentation with a loud round of applause.

After a good lunch and a third glass of wine, a few of the Venezuelan managers became quite talkative. They asked whether the visiting group would be interested in hearing about the Venezuelan way of assessing functions in the laboratory. "Would you like to hear what we say we do or what we really do?" they asked. Already aware of what their "party line" was, the head office representatives asked for what really went on.

Reality turned out to be much simpler than the complex system. Each year, they explained, the six-person management team got together after the assessment round. In the meeting this group decided on the most appropriate candidates for promotion. The employees selected were then rushed to the HR department in order to set up the function description required by the head office. HR had already been informed of what the score was to be for the particular functions.

This is an interesting example of reverse causality. Instead of the job description and evaluation "choosing" the person that best filled it, the person was first informally and intuitively chosen and then wrote his or her own description and evaluation.

This begs the question of whether a process in which universals guide particulars is necessarily better than a process in which particular people guide and choose their universals. As the local Venezuelan boss put it: "Who decides on the promotion of *my* subordinates, Colonel Hay or me?" The same kind of question and circularity will arise when we consider performance and achievement in Chapter 8.

Reconciling Universalism and Particularism

In all the seven cultural dichotomies we have identified, of which universalism versus particularism is the first, the two extremes can always in a sense be found in the same person. The two horns of the dilemma are very close to each other, as it is easy to realize if, as a universalist, you substitute

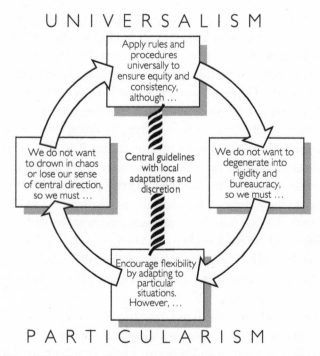

FIGURE 4.4. Reconciling Universalism and Particularism

your father or daughter for the friend who is driving the car. In fruitful cross-cultural encounters both sides avoid pathological excesses. Figure 4.4, whose methodology is explained in Chapter 16, illustrates this.

This figure shows the beginnings of a *vicious* circle. If you follow the logic of the flow, you see that the universalist approach at best helps us to avoid the pathologies of particularism taken too far; the particularist position needs to be taken to avoid the pathologies of universalism taken too far. In fact, the universalist position is encouraging opposition from the particularist position.

When the two are working effectively together, we talk about a *virtuous* circle. Here cross-cultural encounters can synergize and come out on a level much higher than any of the cultures could achieve on their own.

In one case the resolution brought a company to a higher level. A group of European microprocessor salespeople were complaining that they lost a large part of their potential market because the American headquarters could not produce the adaptations that different European clients were requesting. The Americans at the HQ in California said that they couldn't understand why their European colleagues could not grasp the loss of economies of scale and the gross undercapacity that their chips facilities experienced. It is obviously not enough simply to map the problematic nature of a dilemma as two horns, one opposing the other, as in Figure 4.5.

When approaching this dilemma between the two extremes, we may seek a compromise. However, a compromise is frequently worse than just choosing between one of the two horns. It could mean, for example, going for two chips instead of one universal chip. By doing this you would lose both economies of scale and most of your clients. The best approach is to frame the dilemmas as two axes, X and Y, and then try to find a 10/10 solution. This means that the drive for the universal chip needs to be connected in some way to the process of fulfilling the particular need in Europe.

In our workshop the Americans proposed to invite the R&D people from some of their clients to co-develop the next (universal) chip. The Europeans, in turn, thought it would be preferable to get American R&D people over to work with local R&D people in Europe. The principle was the same, but the starting point was different. The Americans preferred to start from a universal position and have some input from the particular needs of the client. The Europeans felt more at home with first testing the value of their particular need by some universal Californian rules. But both were aiming for the creation of a unique, particular, customized microprocessor that might lead to a renewed spate of "universal sales."

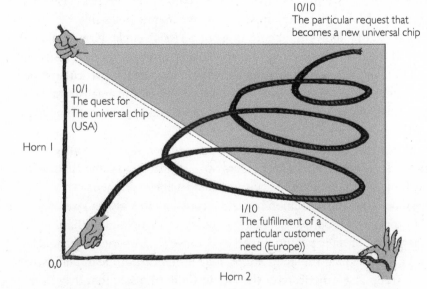

FIGURE 4.5. A Virtuous Circle

THE CASE OF THE PHARMACEUTICAL JOINT VENTURE

Mr. Geddy Teok, an American-Chinese (second generation) employee of a large New Jersey pharmaceutical firm, was based in Tokyo, Japan. His main aim was to get a major joint venture going with one of the largest Japanese pharmaceutical manufacturers. After four years of negotiating, the supreme moment had come for signing contracts. Obviously, the lawyers from HQ in New Jersey were well prepared and sent the contract to Geddy one week before the "ceremony."

After four years of Japanese experience, Geddy was shocked when he received the document from the USA. He told us: "I could not even count the number of pages. There were just too many. But I remember the number of inches it measured when laying it on the table. I would guess that with every inch one of the Japanese would leave the room in despair. I hope they will come with a group of 10. Then at least I will keep one person to talk to. The Japanese will sign contracts, but you should not take it too far."

Geddy Teok decided to call HQ and ask for some help. The legal department said that the relationship was so complex that the contract needed to cover many possible instances. Moreover, a consultancy firm that advised them regularly said that Asians in general and Japanese in particular had a reputation of being quite loose in defining what was developed by them and what came from the USA: "We better have some pain now and be clear in the terms of our relationship, than to run into problems later because of miscommunication. If they sign it at least they show they are serious."

Geddy was in despair, but he only had a day to decide what to do. The meeting was tomorrow. Should he perhaps call the Japanese CEO, with whom he had built up quite a relationship? Or should he just go for it? Geddy framed his dilemma quite clearly to us: "Whatever I would do, it would hurt my career. If I insist on the Japanese partners signing the contract they will see it as proof of how little trust has been developed over the years of negotiation. This might mean a postponement of the discussions and in the worst case the end of the deal. If I reduce the contract to a couple of pages and present it as a "letter of intent," HQ in general and even worse the whole legal department will jump on me, jeopardizing my career."

If you were Geddy, what would you do?

Being aware of the cultural dynamics does not really help you (although if you were not aware of the cultural differences between the Japanese and the Americans your situation would be even worse). It is not enough to say that the Americans tend to be universalist so they believe the Japanese should sign the contract. Nor does it suffice to say that the Japanese tend to be particularist in their approach. Transcultural effectiveness is not measured only by the degree to which you are able to grasp the opposite value. It is measured by your competence in reconciling the dilemmas—the degree to which you are able to make both values work together—as in the microprocessor case.

It might be advisable for Geddy to ask what the logic of the typical universalist would be in order to have the contract signed. In fact, the Americans' position is: "Our trust in the other party is not sufficient so we need the backing of a binding contract." For the Japanese, who do frequently sign contracts, the logic would be: "I'll sign the contract only if I have trust in the other party and they see this as a sign of respect for our relationship. Where the relationship is good enough we can easily change the details of the contract later if the particular circumstances have changed."

We would advise Geddy to do the following. First, make culture a point of discussion and tell the Japanese counterpart what kind of problem you are facing: "Our American headquarters have sent me a 1,100-page contract. Obviously, this is normal practice in the USA, but it was not meant to insult you." By doing this you are sharing the dilemma. Try to establish and respect the Japanese logic by asking "What would you do in my case?"

The actual Japanese response was another question: "How long would you stay here, Mr. Teok?" Geddy's answer was honest and brilliant at the same time: "Until the job is done, Mr. Samamoto." "In that case I'll sign the contract," replied the Japanese.

Test Yourself

In order to measure the degree to which individuals and cultures tend to reconcile, we have developed a series of questions that measure not only the degree to which you identify with one of the opposing values, but also your tendency to reconcile. We are currently testing the hypothesis that the creation of wealth is highly correlated with people's capacity to reconcile. In the first dimension the questions would be the following:

Six months after the ABC mining company had signed a long-term contract with a foreign buyer to buy bauxite in 10 annual installments, the world price of bauxite collapsed. Instead of paying $4 a ton below world market price, the buyer now faced the prospect of paying $3 above.

The buyer faxed ABC to say it wished to renegotiate the contract. The final words of the fax read: "You cannot expect us as your new partner to carry alone the now ruinous expense of these contract terms."

ABC negotiators had a heated discussion about this situation. Several views were offered:

1. A contract is a contract. It means precisely what its terms say. If the world price had risen we would not be crying, nor should they. What partnership are they talking about? We had a deal. We bargained. We won. End of story.
2. A contract symbolizes the underlying relationship. It is an honest statement of original intent. Where circumstances transform the mutual spirit of that contract, then terms must be renegotiated to preserve the relationship.
3. A contract symbolizes the underlying relationship. It is an honest statement of original intent. But such rigid terms are too brittle to withstand turbulent environments. Only tacit forms of mutuality have the flexibility to survive.
4. A contract is a contract. It means precisely what the terms say. If the world price had risen we would not be crying, nor should they. We would, however, consider a second contract whose terms would help offset their losses.

Allocate "1" to the approach you prefer and "2" to your second choice. Similarly, indicate what you believe would be favored by your closest colleagues at work.

The problem that this simple case study illustrates is common to all cultures. All cultures recognize the tension from this and similar scenarios that we have expressed as a dilemma. But where cultures differ is how they interpret (give meaning to) this problem and the direction from which they would approach a reconciled solution. Universalists will view the problem from option 1 if they reject the opportunity to connect their viewpoint with the particularist. Particularists will view the problem from option 2 if they reject the opportunity to connect their viewpoint with the universalist.

But if universalists opt for 4, they start to view the problem from their own perspective of a universalist but seek to accommodate the opposite viewpoint of the particularist, leading to a reconciliation between the cultural differences. And similarly for the particularists who approach a reconciliation from their own perspective from option 3.

Our research has generated evidence (through triangulation) that leaders and managers who choose 3 and 4 sustain improved bottom-line business performance (see Appendix 1).

Finally, we should return to Mr. Johnson of MCC.

- What do you think will happen when he tries to introduce pay-for-performance worldwide, especially in particularistic cultures?
- Do you believe that bonuses of 30 percent, 60 percent, and 100 percent over salary, taken from the salaries of other employees, will be deemed fair?
- Will high performers be encouraged or discouraged in their work by those whose salaries have been cut in order to pay them?
- Will local management cooperate wholeheartedly in this change or find ways of getting around it?
- Does local management have it in its power to organize sales territories so that it can choose who performs well for particular areas?

The following tables highlight differences between universalist and particularist approaches and give some tips for achieving reconciliation between the two views.

Recognizing the Differences

UNIVERSALIST	PARTICULARIST
• Focus is more on rules than on relationships.	• Focus is more on relationships than on rules.
• Legal contracts are readily drawn up.	• Legal contracts are readily modified.
• A trustworthy person is the one who honors his or her word or contract.	• A trustworthy person is the one who honors changing mutualities.
• There is only one truth or reality, that which has been agreed to.	• There are several perspectives on reality relative to each participant.
• A deal is a deal.	• Relationships evolve.

Tips for Reconciliation

PARTICULARISTS DOING BUSINESS WITH UNIVERSALISTS	UNIVERSALISTS DOING BUSINESS WITH PARTICULARISTS
• Be prepared for "rational," "professional" arguments and presentations that push for your acquiescence.	• Be prepared for personal "meandering" or "irrelevancies" that do not seem to be going anywhere.
• Do not take impersonal, "get down to business" attitudes as rude.	• Do not take personal, "get to know you" attitudes as small talk.
• Carefully prepare the legal ground with a lawyer if in doubt.	• Carefully consider the personal implications of your legal "safeguards."

Differences in Managing and Being Managed

UNIVERSALISTS	PARTICULARISTS
• Strive for consistency and uniform procedures.	• Build informal networks and create private understandings.
• Institute formal ways of changing the way business is conducted.	• Try to alter informally accustomed patterns of activity.
• Modify the system so that the system will modify you.	• Modify relations with you, so that you will modify the system.
• Signal changes publicly.	• Pull levers privately.

5

The Individual and the Group

Fons Trompenaars and Charles Hampden-Turner

THE CONFLICT between what each of us wants as an individual and the interests of the group we belong to is the second of our five dimensions covering how people relate to other people. Do we relate to others by discovering what each one of us individually wants and then trying to negotiate the differences, or do we place ahead of this some shared concept of the public and collective good?

Individualism has been described (Parsons and Shils[1]) as "a prime orientation to the self," and communitarianism as "a prime orientation to common goals and objectives." Just as for our first dimension, cultures do typically vary in putting one or the other of these approaches first in their thinking processes, although both may be included in their reasoning. The 140,000 managers who have answered the following question show this, although the division here is not quite so sharp* as for the universal versus the particular example.

---

* However, combining these responses with other questions based on similar constructs that differentiate orientation to individuals or groups does provide a reliable and statistically significant index along this cultural dimension.

Two people were discussing ways in which individuals could improve the quality of life.

A. One said: "It is obvious that if individuals have as much freedom as possible and the maximum opportunity to develop themselves, the quality of their life will improve as a result."

B. The other said: "If individuals are continuously taking care of their fellow human beings, the quality of life will improve for everyone, even if it obstructs individual freedom and individual development."

Which of the two ways of reasoning do you think is usually best, A or B?

As Figure 5.1 shows, the highest scoring individualists are the Norwegians, Russians, and Americans, closely followed by the Finns, Israelis, and Swiss, all over 75 percent in favor of A. Some of the lowest scoring Europeans are the French at 25 percent. This may come as a surprise. But remember that the French all take vacations in August, on the same date. They join the Club Méditerranée in order to be together. For the French, the community is France and the family. They become individualists in other social encounters. Remember that many of the French words expressing subtle relationships in a group are popular even in English-speaking environments: *ensemble, esprit de corps, entente, ménage a trois, clique,* etc. That the Japanese are more group oriented in their answers to this question than the French is expected; also expected is that the Chinese score as more individualist than the Indians, though only slightly.

Concepts of Individualism and Communitarianism

Individualism is often regarded as the characteristic of a modernizing society, while communitarianism reminds us of both more traditional societies and the failure of the Communist experiment. We shall see, though, that the success of growth in Asia (especially Japan, Hong Kong, Singapore, South Korea, and Taiwan) raises serious questions about both the success and the inevitability of individualism.

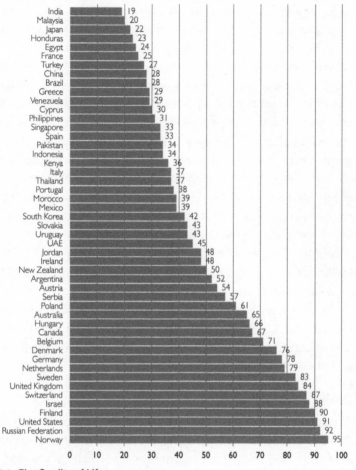

FIGURE 5.1. The Quality of Life

As in the case of universalism and particularism, it is probably truer to say that these dimensions are complementary, not opposing, preferences. They can be effectively reconciled by an integrative process, a universalism that learns its limitations from particular instances, for example, and by the individual voluntarily addressing the needs of the larger group.

International management is seriously affected by individualist or communitarian preferences within various countries. Negotiations, decision-making, and motivation are the most crucial areas. Practices such as promotion for recognized achievements and pay-for-performance, for example, assume that individuals seek to be distinguished within the group and that their colleagues approve of this happening. They also rest on the assumption that the contribution of any one member to a common task is easily distinguishable and that no problems arise from singling him or her out for praise. None of this may, in fact, be true in more communitarian cultures.

Most of our received wisdom on this subject derives from the individualistic West, especially from theorists writing in English. The capital letter "I" is one of the most used capitals in the English language. So the idea that rising individualism is part of the rise of civilization itself needs to be treated as a cultural belief rather than a fact beyond dispute. Clearly, however, it took many centuries for the individual to emerge from the surrounding community. It is generally believed that the essence of the relationship between the individual and society, at least in the West, has changed considerably since the Renaissance. In earlier societies individuals were defined primarily in terms of their surrounding community: the family, the clan, the tribe, the city-state, or the feudal group.

Individualism was very much in the fore during the periods of intense innovation such as the Renaissance, the Age of Exploration, the Netherlands' Golden Age, the French Enlightenment, and the industrial revolutions of Britain and the USA. A whole range of causes and effects have been offered to explain this. And access to the Internet offers both individual control as well as communities through social networking.

Individualism and Religion

There is considerable evidence that individualism and communitarianism follow the Protestant–Catholic religious divide. Calvinists had contracts or covenants with God and with one another for which they were personally responsible. Each Puritan worshipper approached God as a separate being, seeking justification through works. Roman Catholics have always approached God as a community of the faithful. Research has found that Catholics score higher on group choices and Protestants significantly lower. Geert Hofstede's research[2] confirms this, as do our own findings that Latin Catholic cultures, along with Asian cultures of the Pacific Rim, score lower on individualism than the Protestant West: for instance, the UK, Scandinavia (as a rule), the Netherlands, Germany, the USA, and Canada.

Individualism and Politics

Individualism has been adopted or opposed by different political factions in the history of countries, and the strength of that ethic today depends greatly on the fortune of its advocates. It triumphed in the USA but is still strongly opposed by the French Catholic tradition. Eighteenth-century

France, though, was exposed to the pleasures of individualism by Voltaire and Rousseau. Later, in the nineteenth century, the French socialists pointed to the positive effects of individualism, while outlining a new independence from traditional structures and rejecting the authority of religious, economic, and intellectual hierarchies. French business may have been affected forever by the fact that the pro-business French liberal party was in power when France fell suddenly to the Nazis in 1940. The fortunes of British individualism, at least in commerce, have been affected by Prime Minister Thatcher and her revolution.

Does Modernization Imply Individualism?

That individualism, or self-orientation, is a crucial element of modern society has been argued by Ferdinand Tönnies.[3] He suggested that in modernizing we emerge from *Gemeinschaft*, a family-based intimate social context in which the person is not sharply differentiated, into *Gesellschaft*, a workplace of individual tasks and separated responsibilities. Adam Smith, too, saw the division of labor as individualizing.[4] Max Weber saw many meanings in individualism: dignity, autonomy (meaning "self-rule"), privacy, and the opportunity for the person to develop.[5]

We take it for granted in many Western countries that individual geniuses create businesses, invent new products, deserve high salaries, and shape our futures. But do they? How much credit is due to them, and how much due to the patterns of organized employees? Why are Nobel prizes for science awarded to single individuals becoming the exception? If a creative genius combines ideas, where did such ideas come from if not the community? Are we really self-made, or did our parents, teachers, families, and friends have a hand in it?

The following dilemma, which explores this dimension, shows that people from different cultures make different choices about appropriate ways of working.

Which kind of job is found more frequently in your organization?

A. Everybody works together and you do not get individual credit.

B. Everybody is allowed to work individually and individual credit can be received.

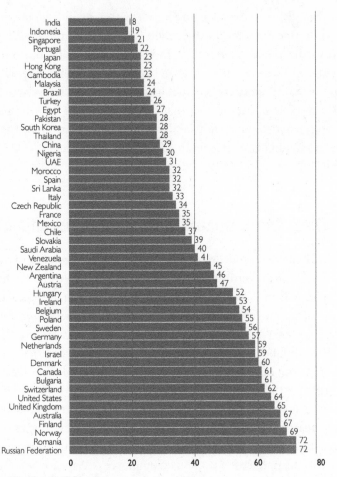

FIGURE 5.2. Working Individually

Figure 5.2 shows the results of these answers. It differs from the previous illustrations of responses to dilemmas in that nationals are much more divided in their approach. However, the range between countries remains very great. Only 23 percent of the Japanese believe that a job is where one is allowed to work individually, whereas at the other extreme this is the experience of approximately 72 percent of Russians and around 60 percent of Americans, Fins, Norwegians, and Israelis. Again, we would emphasize the rank order of country samples rather than absolute percentages.

Which Community?

Individuals are either self- or community-oriented, though we must be careful in generalizing about which "community" a particular culture identifies with. The high internal variation of scores in our research, we believe, has to do with the numerous communities with which different cultures choose to identify. Take, for example, the following question.

There is a defect in an installation. It was caused by negligence of one of the members of a team. Responsibility for this mistake can be carried in various ways.

  A. The person causing the defect by negligence is the one responsible.

  B. Because he or she happens to work in a team, the responsibility should be carried by the group.

Which one of these two ways of taking responsibility do you think is usually the case in your society, A or B?

This question triggers a number of scores that are consistent with the previous question, but we can also identify a number of shifts. This has to do with the heterogeneity of the concept of "community" or "group." For each single society, it is necessary to determine the group with which individuals have the closest identification. They could be keen to identify with their trade union, their family, their corporation, their religion, their profession, their nation, or the state apparatus. The French tend to identify with *la France, la famille, le cadre*; the Japanese with the corporation; the former eastern bloc with the Communist Party; and Ireland with the Roman Catholic Church. Communitarian goals may be good or bad for industry depending on the community concerned, its attitude, and the relevance to business development.

As Figure 5.3 illustrates a slightly different set of country samples than Figure 5.2, we can clearly see here that the impact of Communist organization on Russian and east European managers has been extremely limited. They score highest on the individual responsibility assumption. Americans are significantly above the middle of the range at 64 percent and below some European countries. Japan scores at 23 percent individualist, while India and Indonesia take the communitarian crown with 18 percent and 19 percent.

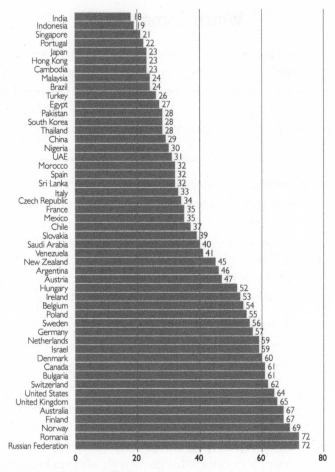

FIGURE 5.3. Individual Responsibility

The approach to the situation will of course differ in relation to third parties; if Americans are criticized there is a good chance that Bill will put an elbow into the stomach of Pete, while asking whose rotten idea it was, while the Italians will walk out as having suffered a group insult, regardless of the fact that it was Giorgio who did it.

Is Individualism a Corporate Requirement?

While the French experience individualism more negatively, the more optimistic philosophy of Germany sees, in the words of Simmel, "an organic unity of individual and society."[6] The USA, with its vast acreage available to migrating individuals, is often seen as the world's major exponent of individualism and indeed scores highest, or nearly so, on most of our research instruments. De Tocqueville, the nineteenth-century French aristocrat, described Americans as exhibiting "a strong confidence in self, or reliance upon one's own exertion and resources." The "Commission of National Goals" reporting to President Eisenhower claimed that the possibility of individual self-realization was the central goal of American civilization.

Yet there were and are dissenting voices on the usefulness of individualism even in the USA. The Harvard sociologist Daniel Bell accused consumerist-type individualism, what he terms modernism, of weakening America's industrial infrastructure.[7] As the information society develops, those with a communitarian ethos disseminate information faster. Information is shareable in a way physical products are not. Bell and Nelson saw a shift from "tribal brotherhood," which excludes individuality, to "universal otherhood," which includes it while still focusing upon superordinate group goals.[8]

A visionary call for the integration of individualism and communitarianism came from Emile Durkheim, the nineteenth-century French sociologist. He saw communitarianism taking both primitive and more modern forms. In its primitive form, the society has a communitarian conscience from which none dare deviate. The individual is dominated by the community. Durkheim called this mechanical solidarity, which he saw as losing ground because industry requires a division of labor, which mechanical solidarity is slow to accommodate. This would help explain the early economic success of individualist (and Protestant) nations.

But Durkheim also saw a later, more sophisticated form of voluntary integration among sovereign beings, which he called organic solidarity. The extension of the division of labor would cause the individual to share fewer and fewer characteristics with other individuals in the same society and would call for a new form of social integration. This involved biological-type integration as found in developing organisms, which are both differentiated and integrated. In 1965 Paul Lawrence and Jay Lorsch found that highly creative plastics companies, prospering in turbulent environments, were both more highly differentiated and more highly integrated.[9] It was a vindication of the model of organic growth, and pointed to an increasingly necessary synthesis of individualism and communitarianism in increasingly complex, differentiated, and interdependent societies. We see the issue as essentially

I N D I V I D U A L I S M

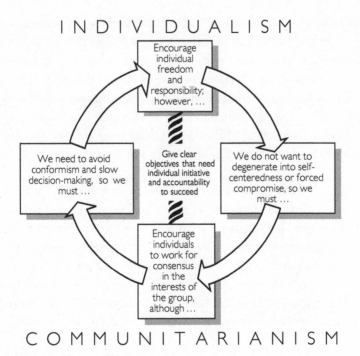

FIGURE 5.4. Reconciling Individualism and Communitarianism

circular, with two "starting points" (see Figure 5.4)[10] as a complex of events that reinforces itself through a feedback loop. A virtuous circle has favorable results, and a vicious circle has detrimental results. A virtuous circle can transform into a vicious circle if eventual negative feedback is ignored.

We all go through these cycles, but start from different points and conceive of them as means or ends. The individualist culture sees the individual as "the end" and improvements to communal arrangements as the means to achieve it. The communitarian culture sees the group as its end and improvements to individual capacities as a means to that end. Yet if the relationship is truly circular, the decision to label one element as an end and another as a means is arbitrary. By definition circles never end. Every "end" is also the means to another goal.

This is closer to our own conviction that individualism finds its fulfillment in service to the group, while group goals are of demonstrable value to individuals only if those individuals are consulted and participate in the process of developing them. The reconciliation is not easy, but possible.

Every parent knows this intuitively. Are you raising your child to become independent at the age of 18, or do you try to develop the child to become a good family member? We all know the answer to both is yes. Parents around the world try to develop a child into a self-supporting person who will choose to become a good family member. Here again we find the essence of reconciliation. One value increases the quality of the seemingly opposing one.

Individualism Versus Communitarianism in International Business

What are the practical issues raised by differences in degrees of individualism or communitarianism? Consider our ongoing case of MCC and the luckless Mr. Johnson.

During a meeting in Milan, Mr. Johnson presented ideas for the payment scheme to motivate the sales force. He became annoyed at the way these meetings were always run and decided to introduce guidelines on how all future meetings should be conducted. He did not like the Singaporean and African representatives always turning up in groups. They should, he said, confine themselves to one representative only, please. And could Mr. Sin from Singapore make sure that his boss was always represented by the same person and not different people on each occasion?

These suggestions were not very popular among some of the managers. Mr. Sin, Mr. Nuere from Nigeria, and Mr. Calamier from France wanted to know the reasons for these comments. Mr. Sin asked why, since different issues were on the agenda, they should not have different representatives knowledgeable on the various items. The discussion was going nowhere, and, after an hour had passed, Mr. Johnson suggested it be put to a vote, confident that most of his European managers would back him.

But this, too, proved controversial. Mr. Calamier threw up his hands and said he was "shocked that on such a sensitive and important issue you seek to impose this decision upon a minority." He said there really should be a consensus on this even if it took another hour. Mr. Sin agreed that "voting should be saved for trivial questions." Johnson looked to the German and Scandinavian representatives for support, but to his surprise they agreed that consensus should be given more of a chance. He was too frustrated to respond to the Dutch manager's suggestion that they should vote on whether to vote. Finally, the Nigerians recommended that at the very least a discussion and/or voting should be postponed until the next meeting. How else were those present supposed to solicit the views of their colleagues in their home offices? Wearily, Mr. Johnson agreed. Further discussions about the reward system would have to wait too.

Representation

It should be evident from the passage above that communitarian cultures prefer plural representation. The Singaporeans, Nigerians, and French seek negotiating groups, which are microcosms of the interests of their entire national subsidiaries. In the face of unexpected demands, communitarians will wish to confer with those back home. Rarely does a single Japanese go to an important negotiation. Yet to Anglo-Saxons a single representative voting his or her private conscience on behalf of constituents is the foundation stone of parliamentary democracy. To more communitarian cultures, those at the meeting are delegates, bound by the wishes of those who sent them.

Status

Unaccompanied people in communitarian cultures are assumed to lack status. If there is no one to take notes for you or help you carry bags, you cannot be very important. If you arrive unaccompanied in Thailand, for example, they may seriously underestimate your status and power at home.

Translators

In Anglo-Saxon negotiations the translator is supposed to be neutral, like a black box through which words in one language enter and words in another language exit. The translator in more communitarian cultures will usually serve the national group, engaging them in lengthy asides and attempting to mediate misunderstandings arising from culture as well as language. Very often he or she may be the top negotiator in the group and is an interpreter rather than a translator.

Decision-Making

Communitarian decision-making typically takes much longer, and there are sustained efforts to win over everyone to achieve consensus. Voting down the dissenters, as often happens in English-speaking Western democracies, is not acceptable. There will usually be detailed consultations with all those concerned and, because of pressures to agree on collective goals, consensus will usually be achieved. If the group or home office is not consulted first, an initial yes can easily become a no later. The many minor objections raised are typically practical rather than personal or principled, and the consensus may be modified in many respects. Since, however, those consulted will usually have to implement the consensus, this latter phase of implementation typically proceeds smoothly and easily. The time "wasted" (from an individualist's perspective) is saved when the new procedures operate as envisioned. The Japanese *ringi* process, where proposals circulate and are initialed by agreeing participants, is the most famous example of communitarian decision-making, but it can lead to very lengthy delays.

A Japanese company had a factory built in the south of the Netherlands. As usual, this was carried out with acute attention to detail. In the designing phase, though, the company discovered that it had not considered one restriction. The legal minimum height for workshops was four centimeters higher than the design. A new design, which needed extensive consultation with many people at the head office in Tokyo, took one full month per centimeter for approval.

But it is far too easy for North Americans and northwest Europeans, used to individualism, to jeer at such delays. Our own procedures can err in the opposite direction. The decision-making process in individualistic cultures is usually very short, with a "lonely individualist" making decisions in a few fateful seconds. While this may make for quicker deliberations, "one-minute managers," and so on, it will often be discovered months later that the organization has conspired to defeat decisions the other managers never liked or agreed to. Saving time in decision-making is often followed by significant delays due to implementation problems.

The individualist society, with its respect for individual opinions, will frequently ask for a vote to get all noses pointing in the same direction. The drawback to this is that within a short time participants are likely to have reverted to their original orientation. The communitarian society will intuitively refrain from voting because this will not show respect to the individuals who are against the majority decision. It prefers to deliberate until consensus is reached. The final result takes longer to achieve but will be much more stable. In individualistic societies there is frequently disparity between decision and implementation.

Individualism, Communitarianism, and Motivation

The relationship between individual and group also plays an important role in what motivates people. Mr. Johnson believed that he and MCC knew what motivated people: extra salary rewards paid to high-performing individuals. It had seemed so obvious in the meetings back in Missouri, but now he was having doubts. After the earlier discussion, could he be sure of anything?

Mr. Johnson finally managed to compromise on the representation issue by allowing each national office to send up to three people, if they wished, but no more. This decision had not been voted on. Everyone had agreed. Now he could start to tackle the introduction of pay-by-performance, bonuses, and merit pay for next year.

He started, as usual, with an overview of the situation in the USA. It had been three years since the system was first introduced. In general, he explained, they could detect a link between the use of this system and computer sales, although it had to be mentioned that a similar system had failed miserably in the manufacturing department. A different type of achievement-based reward system was currently being tested. No problems were anticipated with this revised system. "In summary," Johnson said, "we are strongly convinced that we need to introduce this system worldwide."

The northwest European representatives voiced their carefully considered, but positive comments. Then the Italian representative, Mr. Gialli, began describing his experience with the system. In his country, the pay-for-performance experiment did much better than he had expected during the first three months. But the following three months were disastrous. Sales were dramatically lower for the salesperson who had performed the best during the previous period. "After many discussions," he continued, "I finally discovered what was happening. The salesperson who received the bonus for the previous period felt guilty in front of the others and tried extremely hard the next quarter not to earn a bonus."

The Italian manager concluded that for the next year of this experiment, the Italian market should be divided into nine regions. All sales representatives within one region should be allowed to allocate the bonus earned in their region either to individual performers or to share it equally. The blunt Dutch manager's reaction: "I have never heard such a crazy idea."

This incident shows that there are at least two sources of motivation. People work for extrinsic money rewards or for the positive regard and support of their colleagues. In more communitarian cultures, this second source of motivation may be so strong that high performers prefer to share the fruits of their efforts with colleagues than to take extra money for themselves as individuals.

Western theories of motivation have individuals growing out of early, and hence primitive, social needs into an individually resplendent self-actualization at the summit of the hierarchy. Needless to say, this does not achieve resonance the world over, however good a theory it may be for the USA and northwest Europe. The Japanese notion of the highest good is harmonious relationships within and with the patterns of nature; the primary orientation is to other people and to the natural world.

Differences in Organizational Structure

In individualistic cultures organizations (from the Greek *organon*) are essentially instruments. They have been deliberately assembled and contrived in order to serve individual owners, employees, and customers. Members of organizations enter relationships because it is in their individual interests to do so. Their ties are abstract, legal ones, regulated by contract. The organization is a means to what its actors want for themselves. Insofar as they cooperate, it is because they have particular interests at stake. Each performs a differentiated and specialized function and receives an extrinsic reward for doing so. Authority originates in an individual's skill at performing tasks, and an individual's knowledge is used to make the organizational instrument work effectively.

In communitarian cultures the organization is not the creation or instrument of its founders so much as a social context all members share that gives them meaning and purpose. Organizations are often likened to a large family, community, or clan that develops and nurtures its members and may live longer than they do. The growth and prosperity of organizations are not considered bonanzas for individual shareholders or gravy trains for top managers, but are valuable ends in themselves. These considerations will be discussed in depth in Chapter 11.

Reconciling Individualism and Communitarianism

Again, Figure 5.4 represents essentially a *vicious* circle, since one value is tied to the seemingly opposing value in such a way that they avoid each other's pathologies. It is a mistake to believe that individualists do not care for communities. Individualistic Americans are joiners *par excellence* and have probably formed more voluntary associations than any other culture. From Mothers Against Drunk Driving to the Michigan Militia, Americans form groups very readily. But the "voluntary association" is a giveaway, because it states that in the beginning was the voluntary individual and then the group was formed from such people. In communitarian Japan, by contrast, the individual alone is not regarded as a mature state. The word for a mature individual translates as "person-among-others." In the beginning is the group: How can I as an individual serve the group better? From that competence I derive my status.

But putting either the individual or the community first does not preclude a country from encompassing both values. Consider the following crucial incident.

WHO MADE A SERIOUS MISTAKE?
The Group That Was Not Willing to Tell the Truth

Jean Safari was investigating a serious error made by a Japanese worker at the Japanese subsidiary of a US multinational. A component had been inserted upside down and the entire batch had been pulled out of production to be reworked. The cost of this was high.

Jean asked the Japanese plant director about which employee had made the error. Had she been identified? What action was being taken against her? She was amazed when the director claimed not to know. "The whole work group has accepted responsibility," he told her. "As to the specific woman responsible, they have not told me, nor did I ask. Even the floor supervisor does not know, and if he did, he would not tell me either."

But if everyone is responsible, then in effect no one is, Jean argued. They are simply protecting each other's bad work.

"This is not how we see it." The plant manager was polite but firm. "I understand the woman concerned was so upset she went home. She tried to resign. Two of her coworkers had to coax her back again. The group knows she was responsible and she feels ashamed. The group also knows that she is new and that they did not help her enough, or looked out for her or saw to it that she was properly trained. This is why the whole group has apologized. I have their letter here. They are willing to apologize to you publicly."

"No, no. I don't want that," said Jean. "I want to stop it happening again . . ." She wondered what she should do.

Should Jean insist on knowing who the culprit was? Should the culprit be punished?

It is a fallacy to believe that because the group will not reveal who made the error the perpetrator of that error escapes without sanction. It depends whether the group supports or opposes high quality and high productivity. If the group supports management objectives so that the community is united, those "letting the group down" will experience shame in a shame culture. There is abundant evidence that the perpetrator of this error has already experienced shame. She went home rather than face her coworkers. The issue of the extent to which other team members should have helped her learn is also something on which the team has the best information. In a Japanese context, it is best left to them.

Reconciliation has occurred. While the individualist assumption is that individuals who make a mistake should be punished for it and therefore become a better team member, communitarian logic is the reverse: through team membership we support individuals so that they become better individual workers. If a mistake is made, only the immediate group needs to know this. As well as avoidance of shame, the reconciliation lies in the fact that the group has taken care of the individual's mistake and no extra punishment is required.

Test Yourself

In order to measure the degree to which the individual and the group are reconciled we have asked several thousand participants to answer a series of questions that have been captured in our separate dilemma database. Again, two answers represent the either/or type of answer, while two alternatives are reconciled answers. One starts with the individual and includes the group, while the other starts with the group and then reconciles the individual. What would be your choice?

Several managers were discussing whether close cooperation or fierce competition was the most salient mark of the successful enterprise. Below are four statements:

1. Competition is the supreme value of any successful economy or company. Attempts by major parties to cooperate usually end in collusion against one or more of them.

2. Competition is the supreme value of any successful economy or company, because this involves serving customers better than our rivals, so assuring the public interest.

3. Cooperation among stakeholders is the supreme value because this shared aim makes companies fiercely competitive toward outsiders, thereby fulfilling personal interests.

4. Cooperation among stakeholders is the supreme value. Personal rivalry and competing for self-advancement are seriously disruptive of effective operations.

Allocate "1" to the approach you prefer and "2" to your second choice. Similarly, indicate what you believe would be favored by your closest colleagues at work.

Answer 1 affirms competitive individualism and rejects communitarian cooperation, while answer 4 is the exact opposite. Answer 2 starts by affirming competitive individualism, but by connecting it to communitarian cooperation it reconciles it into an integrity which we might call "co-opetition." Answer 3 suggests the same end result, but the spiral is now anti-clockwise, from the cooperating group to the competing individual.

In Figure 5.5 the results of earlier competitions are cooperatively integrated before a new phase of competition begins.

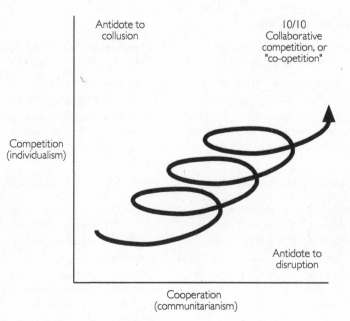

FIGURE 5.5. Competition or Cooperation?

The following tables highlight differences between individualist and communitarian approaches and give some tips for achieving reconciliation between the two views.

Recognizing the Differences

INDIVIDUALISM	COMMUNITARIANISM
• More frequent use of "I" form.	• More frequent use of "we" form.
• Decisions made on the spot by representative.	• Decisions referred back to organization by delegate.
• People ideally achieve alone and assume personal responsibility.	• People ideally achieve in groups that assume joint responsibility.
• Vacations taken in pairs, even alone.	• Vacations in organized groups or with extended family.

Tips for Reconciliation

COMMUNITARIANS DOING BUSINESS WITH INDIVIDUALISTS	INDIVIDUALISTS DOING BUSINESS WITH COMMUNITARIANS
• Prepare for quick decisions and sudden offers not referred to HQ.	• Show patience for time taken to consent and to consult.
• Negotiator can commit those who sent him or her and is very reluctant to go back on an undertaking.	• Negotiator can only agree tentatively and may withdraw an undertaking after consulting with superiors.
• The toughest negotiations were probably already done within the organization while preparing for the meeting. You have a tough job selling them the solution to this meeting.	• The toughest negotiations are with the communitarians you face. You must somehow persuade them to cede points that the multiple interests in your company demand.
• Conducting business alone means that this person is respected by his or her company and has its esteem.	• Conducting business when surrounded by helpers means that this person has high status in his or her company.
• The aim is to make a quick deal.	• The aim is to build lasting relationships.

Differences in Managing and Being Managed

INDIVIDUALISTS	COMMUNITARIANS
• Try to adjust individual needs to organizational needs.	• Seek to integrate personality with authority within the group.
• Introduce methods of individual incentives like pay-for-performance, individual assessment, managing-by-objectives.	• Give attention to *esprit de corps*, morale, and cohesiveness.
• Expect job turnover and mobility to be high.	• Have low job turnover and mobility.
• Seek out high performers, heroes, and champions for special praise.	• Extol the whole group and avoid showing favoritism.
	• Hold up superordinate goals for all to meet.

6

Feelings and Relationships

Fons Trompenaars and Charles Hampden-Turner

IN RELATIONSHIPS between people, reason and emotion both play a role. Which of these dominates will depend upon whether we are *affective*, that is, we show our emotions (in which case we probably get an emotional response in return), or whether we are emotionally *neutral* in our approach.

Neutral Versus Affective Cultures

Members of cultures that are affectively neutral do not telegraph their feelings but keep them carefully controlled and subdued. In contrast, in cultures high in affectivity people show their feelings plainly by laughing, smiling, grimacing, scowling, and gesturing; they attempt to find immediate outlets for their feelings. We should be careful not to overinterpret such differences. Neutral cultures are not necessarily cold or unfeeling, nor are they emotionally constipated or repressed. The amount of emotion we show is often the result of convention. In a culture in which feelings are controlled, irrepressible joy or grief will still signal loudly. In a culture where feelings are amplified, they will have to be signaled more loudly still in order to register at all. In cultures where everyone emotes, we may not find words or expressions adequate for our strongest feelings, since they have all been used up.

A workshop exercise under this heading asks participants how they would behave if they felt upset about something at work. Would they express their feelings openly? Figure 6.1 shows the relative positions of a representative sample of countries on the extent to which exhibiting emotion is not

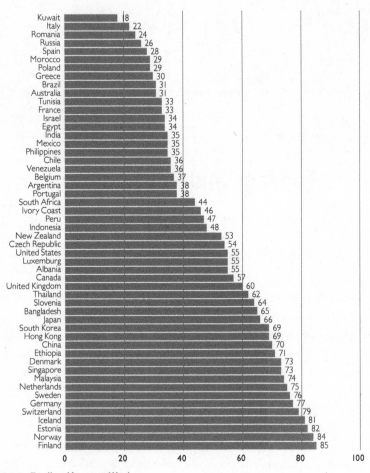

FIGURE 6.1. Feeling Upset at Work

acceptable. It is least acceptable in Finland and Norway, where our database shows a score of close to 85 percent on the neutral orientation. There are considerable variances between European countries, with Finland the most neutral (85 percent) and Romania, Italy, and Spain the least (28 percent, 24 percent, and 22 percent, respectively).

Note that Asian Hong Kong, Japan, South Korea, and Singapore all score much higher than Philippines or India and Indonesia; there is no general pattern by continent.

Typically, reason and emotion are of course combined. In expressing ourselves we try to find confirmation of our thoughts and feelings in the response of our audience. When our own approach is highly emotional, we are seeking a *direct* emotional response: "I have the same feelings as you on this subject." When our own approach is highly neutral, we are seeking an *indirect* response: "Because I agree with your reasoning or proposition, I give you my support." On both occasions approval is being sought, but different paths are being used to this end. The indirect path gives us emotional support contingent upon the success of an effort of intellect. The direct path allows our feelings about a factual proposition to show through, thereby "joining" feelings with thoughts in a different way.

Consider a scene in which the Italian office of MCC has made a proposal to allow the sales personnel to decide as a group whether they wish to have individual incentives or to share bonus payments among the whole team, while identifying the persons responsible for winning the bonus. You will recall that this was the idea Mr. Bergman, the Dutch representative, called "crazy" in Chapter 5.

Raising his voice, Mr. Pauli, Gialli's colleague, asked: "What do you mean, a crazy idea? We have carefully considered the pros and cons, and consider that it would greatly benefit the buyer."

"Please, don't get overexcited," pleaded Mr. Johnson. "We need to provide solid arguments and should not get sidetracked by emotional irrelevancies."

Before Bergman had a chance to explain why he thought it was a crazy idea, the two Italian colleagues left the room for a time-out. "This is what I call a typical Italian reaction," Mr. Bergman remarked to his colleagues. "Before I even had a chance to give my arguments as to why I think the idea is crazy, they walk out."

The other managers were squirming uncomfortably in their chairs. They did not know what to think. Mr. Johnson got up and left the room to talk to the Italians.

It is easy for British, Americans, or northwest Europeans to sympathize with Johnson or Bergman about "excitable" Italians. After all, the incentive system either works or it does not. This will not change however strongly we feel. It is a matter of trial and observation. According to this approach neutrality is a means to an end. The time to get emotional is when the incentives work or fail to work, at which point pleasure or disappointment are appropriate. After all, control of our feelings is a sign of civilization, is it not?

Such explanations show that we can offer good reasons for any cultural norm. The Italians were angry because they identified emotionally with their sales team and knew intuitively that working hard for each other as well as for customers was the motivation of an excellent salesperson. They felt as they knew their sales force would feel about the emotional rewards for hard work. Mr. Bergman's "reasonable judgment" was not relevant to Italians. Since when is the intrinsic pleasure found in work a matter of "fact" anyway? It is deeply personal and cultural. As Pascal wrote: "The heart has its reasons which reason knows not of." But then he was a Frenchman.

And what about the verdict of the Prime Court in Italy in late 1996, which indicates that husbands are allowed to beat their spouses if they are in a passionate mood and as long as it is done infrequently. The Italian judge did find compelling evidence that the husband had hit his wife so hard that she had to be hospitalized, and there was no "systematic and conscious brutality." The victim, Anna Mannino, was very pleased with the final verdict since she found her partner a "model husband." She had never accused him. The hospital did!

Degrees of Affectivity in Different Cultures

The amount of visible "emoting" is a major difference between cultures. We may think that a Frenchman who curses us in a traffic accident is truly enraged, close to committing violence. In fact, he may simply be getting his view of the facts in first and may expect an equal stream of vituperation from us in return. He may, indeed, be further from violence as a result of this expression. There are norms about acceptable levels of vehemence, and these can be much higher in some countries than in others.

Americans, for example, tend to be on the expressive side. Perhaps this is because with so many immigrants and such a large country they have had to break down social barriers again and again. The habit of using diminutives ("Chuck" instead of Charles, "Bob" instead of Robert), "smile" buttons, welcome wagons, and the speed with which cordial and informal relationships are made all testify to the need to resocialize in new neighborhoods several times in a lifetime.

This is a very different experience from life in smaller countries like Sweden, the Netherlands, Denmark, Norway, and so on. There it may be harder to avoid than to meet those of your generation with whom you grew up. Friendships tend to start early in life and last many years, so the need to be effusive with relative strangers is much less.

There is a tendency for those with norms of emotional neutrality to dismiss anger, delight, or intensity in the workplace as "unprofessional." Mr. Pauli at MCC has obviously "lost his cool," a judgment that assumes the desirability of a cool exterior to begin with. In fact, Pauli probably regards Bergman as emotionally dead, or as hiding his true feelings behind a mask of deceit. As we shall see in Chapter 7 when we go on to discuss how specific, as opposed to diffuse, emotions can be, there are really two issues wrapped up in the question of emotional display. Should emotion be *exhibited* in business relations? Should it be *separated* from reasoning processes lest it corrupt them?

Americans tend to *exhibit emotion, yet separate it* from "objective" and "rational" decisions. Italians and south European nations in general tend to *exhibit and not separate*. Dutch and Swedes tend *not to exhibit and to separate*. Once again, there is nothing "good" or "bad" about these differences. You can argue that emotions held in check will twist your judgments despite all efforts to be "rational." Or you can argue that pouring forth emotions makes it harder for anyone present to think straight. Similarly you can scoff at the "walls" separating reasons from emotions, or argue that because of the leakage that so often occurs, these should be thicker and stronger.

North Europeans watching a south European politician on television disapprove of waving hands and other gestures. So do the Japanese, whose saying "Only a dead fish has an open mouth" compares with the English "Empty vessels make the most noise."

Beware Humor, Understatement, or Irony

Cultures also vary on the permissible use of humor. In Britain or the USA we often start our workshops with a cartoon or anecdote that makes a joke about the main points to be covered. This is always a success. Hence one of the first workshops in Germany was launched, with some confidence, with a cartoon deriding European cultural differences. Nobody laughed; indeed, the audience was taking notes and looked puzzled. As the week went by, however, there was a lot of laughter in the bar, and eventually even in the sessions. It was simply that laughter was not permissible in a professional setting between strangers.

The British use humor a lot to release emotions dammed up behind the "stiff upper lip." They also regard understatement as funny. If a Briton speaks of being "underwhelmed" by someone's presentation, or regarding it with "modified rapture," that is a way of *controlling* emotional expression, while at the same time triggering emotional release in the form of laughter.

The individual thereby has it both ways. A Japanese superior will similarly rebuke an incompetent subordinate by exaggerated deference: "If you could see your way to kindly troubling yourself in a matter so minor, I would be in your debt." In affective language, this translates as "Do it or else."

Unfortunately, understatements of this kind, along with throwaway lines and jokes, are almost always lost on foreigners, even if they speak the language well enough for normal discourse. Humor is language-dependent and relies on a very quick sense of the meaning of words. "She was a good cook, as cooks go, and as cooks go she went." This is funny only if you are familiar with the colloquialism "as (something) goes," meaning "compared with other (somethings)," in which case "went" takes you by surprise. Not only is it hard for foreigners to release emotion in this way, but they are unlikely to grasp that understatements are actually intended ironically. They are more likely to see the English or Japanese as being opaque, as usual. Any statement that means the opposite of what it literally states may be hard on foreign managers and should be avoided. If insiders all laugh, the foreigner feels excluded, deprived of the emotional release the rest have enjoyed.

Intercultural Communication

There are a variety of problems of communication across cultural boundaries that arise from the differences between affective and neutral approaches. In our workshops we frequently ask the participants to describe the concept of intercultural communication. They list instruments—language, body language—and more general definitions like the exchange of messages and ideas. Communication is of course essentially the *exchange of information*, be it words, ideas, or emotions. Information, in turn, is the *carrier of meaning*. Communication is possible only between people who to some extent share a system of meaning, so here we return to our basic definition of culture.

Verbal Communication

Western society has a predominantly verbal culture. We communicate with paper, film, and conversation. Two of the bestselling computer programs in the Western world, word processing and graphics, have been developed to support verbal communication. We become nervous and uneasy once we stop talking. But we have very different styles of discussion. For the Anglo-Saxons, when person A stops talking, B starts. It is not polite to interrupt.

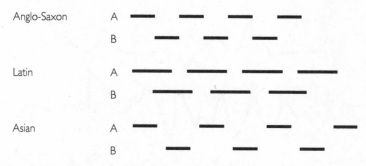

FIGURE 6.2. Styles of Verbal Communication

The even more verbal Latins integrate slightly more than this; B will fre-quently interrupt A and vice versa to show how interested each is in what the other is saying.

The pattern of silent communication shown in Figure 6.2 for oriental languages frightens the Westerner. The moment of silence is interpreted as a failure to communicate. But this is a misunderstanding. Let us reverse the roles; how can the Westerner communicate clearly if the other person is not given time to finish his or her sentence, or to digest what the other has been saying? It is a sign of respect for the other person if you take time to process the information without talking yourself.

Tone of voice. Another cross-cultural problem arises from tone of voice. Figure 6.3 (see next page) shows typical tonal patterns for Anglo-Saxon, Latin, and oriental languages. For some neutral societies, ups and downs in speech suggest that the speaker is not serious. But in most Latin societies this "exaggerated" way of communicating shows that you have your heart in the matter. Oriental societies tend to have a much more monotonous style; self-controlled, it shows respect. Frequently, the higher the position a person holds, the lower and flatter his or her voice.

A British manager posted to Nigeria found that it was very effec-tive to raise his voice for important issues. His Nigerian subordinates saw this unexpected explosion by a normally self-controlled manager as a sign of extra concern. After success in Nigeria he was posted to Malaysia. Shouting there was a sign of loss of face; his colleagues did not take him seriously and he was transferred.

The spoken word. The most obvious verbal process is the spoken word. Regardless of rhythm, pace, or humor, this needs to be taken

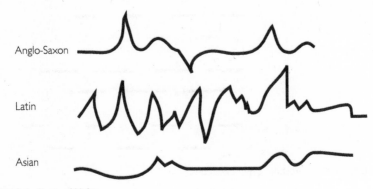

FIGURE 6.3. Tone of Voice

into consideration. English-speaking nations have the enormous advantage of 360 million native speakers and 1.5 billion who understand their language altogether. However, as we all know, even the English and Americans are "separated" by a common language that is used quite differently in different contexts and has some serious differences in the meanings of individual words. English speakers also face an enormous disadvantage, which is that it is very difficult to ever speak another language; speakers of other languages will allow you only so much accent before switching to English themselves. Yet to express yourself in another language is a necessary, if not a sufficient, condition for understanding another culture.

Nonverbal Communication

Research has shown that at least 75 percent of all communication is nonverbal. This figure is the minimum for the most verbal cultures of all. In Western societies *eye contact* is crucial to confirm interest. However, the amount differs sharply from society to society. An Italian visiting professor at Wharton arrived on campus and was surprised to be greeted by a number of students. His expressive Italian nature drove him eventually to catch one of them and ask him if he knew who he was. The student said he was afraid he did not. "So why did you greet me?" the professor asked. The student answered, "Because it seemed like you knew me, sir." The professor realized that in the USA eye contact between strangers is supposed to last only for a split second.

Leonel Brug, a retired colleague at the Trompenaars Hampden-Turner Group, was brought up in both Curaçao and Suriname. As a boy he would try to avoid eye contact, whereupon his Curaçao grandmother would slap him in the face (in some cultures body talk is very effective) and say, "Look me in the face." Respecting an elder involves eye contact. Leonel learned fast, and when in Suriname looked his other grandmother straight in the face to show respect. She slapped him too; respectful kids in Suriname do not make eye contact.

Touching other people, the space it is normal to keep between you, and assumptions about privacy are all further manifestations of affective or neutral cultures. Never help an Arab lady out of a bus; it might cost you your contract.

Reconciling Neutral and Affective Cultures

Overly neutral or affective (expressive) cultures have problems doing business with each other. The neutral person is easily accused of being ice-cold with no heart; the affective person is seen as out of control and inconsistent. When such cultures meet, the first essential is to recognize the differences and to refrain from making any judgments based on emotions or the lack of them.

The power of reconciliation can be shown if we see what happens when seemingly opposing values are disconnected. Emotions that are expressed without any "neutral" brake easily verge on the uncontrolled "neurotic." An overly neutral person may become an iceman who dies of a heart attack because of unexpressed emotions.

The traditional wooden roller-coaster ride has been a major attraction of amusement parks for nearly 100 years. In the last decade promoters have tried to give even greater thrills with "white-knuckle rides." The engineering of such rides requires the design engineer to provide a series of accelerations and twists to excite with just enough respite to recover before the next thrill. Western joyriders scream and wave their arms to participate in the spirit of the experience.

Supported by modern electronics and safety features, this is now big business, and specialist manufacturers from the USA and Europe have sought to export their offerings. One Californian company installed several of its rides in Japan. In spite of a well-proven design, Japanese riders continued to receive head injuries. Observation revealed that the Japanese riders were more likely to keep their heads low or forward in a semi-bowed posture, thereby striking their heads on the bar designed to hold them in place, rather than taking a more upright, arm-waving position. Expensive modifications were required that prevented head injuries—to the point where safety legislation in Japan requires design solutions to take regard of their relative neutrality. Their neutrality did not, of course, mean that they were not experiencing the thrill! It is just that they were trying to control it by lowering their heads.

Test Yourself

Consider the following question:

In a meeting you feel very insulted because your business counterpart tells you that your proposal is insane. What is your response?
1. I will not show that this person has hurt/insulted me, because that would be seen as a sign of weakness and would make me more vulnerable in the future.
2. I will not show that I am hurt because that would spoil our relationship. This will allow me later to tell the counterpart how much I was hurt by his or her comment so he or she might learn from it. I rather show my emotions when the counterpart has more chance to improve our business relationship.
3. I will show clearly that I am insulted so that my counterpart gets the message. I believe the clarity of my message will allow me to be able to control even greater emotional upset in the future.
4. I will show clearly that I am insulted so that my counterpart gets the message. If business partners cannot behave themselves properly they have to bear the consequences.

Indicate with "1" the approach you prefer and with "2" your second choice. Similarly, indicate with "1" the approach you believe would be favored by your closest colleagues at work, and "2" the approach you believe would be his or her second choice.

Obviously, answer 1 indicates that you prefer to be neutral and reject affectivity in response. Answer 4 clearly reflects a preference for emotional outbursts regardless of their consequences for the relationship. Answer 2 supports the neutral point of departure in order to show emotions more effectively in the future. Answer 3 takes an expressive point of departure in order to stabilize future emotional interactions.

The following tables highlight differences between neutral and affective orientation and give some tips for achieving reconciliation between the two views.

Recognizing the Differences

NEUTRAL ORIENTATION	AFFECTIVE ORIENTATION
• Do not reveal what they are thinking or feeling.	• Reveal thoughts and feelings verbally and nonverbally.
• May (accidentally) reveal tension in face and posture.	• Transparency and expressiveness release tension.
• Emotions often dammed up will occasionally explode.	• Emotions flow easily, effusively, vehemently, and without inhibition.
• Cool and self-possessed conduct is admired.	• Heated, vital, animated expressions are admired.

Tips for Reconciliation

AFFECTIVELY ORIENTED PEOPLE DOING BUSINESS WITH NEUTRALLY ORIENTED PEOPLE	NEUTRALLY ORIENTED PEOPLE DOING BUSINESS WITH AFFECTIVELY ORIENTED PEOPLE
• Ask for time-outs from meetings and negotiations where you can patch each other up and rest between games of poker with the "impassive ones."	• Do not be put off your stride when they create scenes and get histrionic; take time-outs for sober reflection and hard assessments.
• Put as much as you can on paper beforehand.	• When they are expressing goodwill, respond warmly.
• Their lack of emotional tone does not mean they are disinterested or bored, only that they do not like to show their hand.	• Their enthusiasm, readiness to agree, or vehement disagreement does not mean that they have made up their minds.
• The entire negotiation is typically focused on the object or proposition being discussed, not so much on you as persons.	• The entire negotiation is typically focused on you as persons, not so much on the object or proposition being discussed.

Differences in Managing and Being Managed

NEUTRALLY ORIENTED PEOPLE	AFFECTIVELY ORIENTED PEOPLE
• Avoid warm, expressive, or enthusiastic behavior. This is interpreted as lack of control over their feelings and inconsistent with high status.	• Avoid detached, ambiguous, and cool demeanor. This will be interpreted as negative evaluation, as disdain, dislike, and social distance. You are excluding them from "the family."
• If you prepare extensively beforehand, you will find it easier to "stick to the point," that is, the neutral topics being discussed.	• If you discover whose work, energy, and enthusiasm has been invested in which projects, you are more likely to appreciate tenacious positions.
• Look for subtle indications that the person is pleased or angry and amplify their importance.	• Tolerate great "surfeits" of emotionality without getting intimidated or coerced and moderate their importance.

7

How Far We Get Involved

Fons Trompenaars and Charles Hampden-Turner

Closely related to whether we show emotions in dealing with other people is the degree to which we engage others in *specific* areas of life and single levels of personality or *diffusely* in multiple areas of our lives and at several levels of personality at the same time.

Specific Versus Diffuse Cultures

In specific-oriented cultures a manager *segregates out* the task relationship she or he has with a subordinate and insulates this from other dealings. Say a manager supervises the sale of integrated circuits. Were she to meet one of her sales reps in the bar, on the golf course, on vacation, or in the local DIY superstore, almost none of her authority would diffuse itself into these relationships. Indeed, she might defer to the sales rep as a more skilled DIY practitioner, or ask advice on improving her golf game. Each area in which the two encounter each other is considered apart from the other, a *specific* case.

However, in some countries every life space and every level of personality tends to permeate all others. *Monsieur le directeur* is a formidable authority wherever you encounter him. If he runs the company, it is generally expected that his opinions on *haute cuisine* are better than those of his subordinates. His taste in clothes and value as a citizen are all permeated by his directorship, and he probably expects to be deferred to by those who know him in the street, the club, or a shop. Of course reputation always leaks to some extent into other areas of life. This extent is what we measure for specificity (small) versus diffuseness (large).

Kurt Lewin,[1] the German-American psychologist, represented the personality as a series of concentric circles with "life spaces" or "personality levels" between. The most personal and private spaces are near the center. The most shared and public spaces are at the outer peripheries. As a German-Jewish refugee in the USA, Lewin was able to contrast U-type (American) life spaces with G-type (German) life spaces. These are illustrated in Figure 7.1.

Lewin's circles show Americans, in the U-type circle, as having much more public than private space, segregated into many specific sections. The American citizen can have a standing and reputation at work, in the bowling club, at the Parent-Teachers' Association, among fellow computer hackers, and in the local chapter of the Veterans of Foreign Wars. Colleagues who enter any of these spaces are not necessarily close or lifetime buddies. They may not feel free to call on you if the subject is not computers or bowling. One reason why the American personality is so friendly and accessible (illustrated by the dotted lines) is that being admitted into one public layer is not a very big commitment. You "know" the other for limited purposes only.

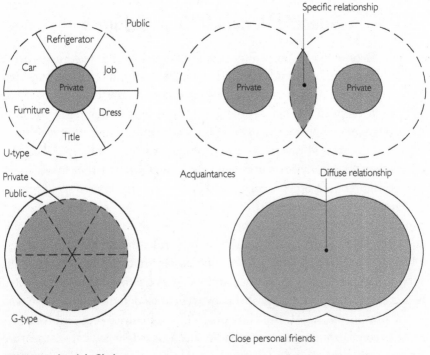

FIGURE 7.1. Lewin's Circles

Contrast this with the G-type circle. Here access to life spaces is guarded by a solid line. It is harder to enter and you need the other's permission. The public space is relatively small. The private spaces are large and *diffuse*, which means that once a friend is admitted, this lets him or her into all, or nearly all, your private spaces. Moreover, your standing and reputation crosses over these spaces. Herr Doktor Muller is Herr Doktor Muller at his university, at the butcher's, and at the garage; his wife is also Frau Doktor Muller in the market, at the local school, and wherever she goes. She is not simply joined diffusely to her husband but to his job and title. In the USA, in contrast, the British author has been introduced at a reception following a graduation ceremony as Dr. Hampden-Turner, but at a party for much the same people a few hours later as Charles Hampden-Turner. He has also been introduced as "I want you all to meet my very good friend Charles . . . (what's your surname?)" In the USA a title is a *specific* label for a *specific* job in a *specific* place.

For all these reasons Germans may be thought of by Americans as remote and hard to get to know. Americans may be thought of by Germans as cheerful, garrulous, yet superficial, who let you into a very small corner of their public life and regard you as peripheral.

Borders and barriers between "life spaces" have physical dimensions as well. The Dutch author remembers arriving as a student at the Wharton School in Philadelphia, Pennsylvania. Bill, a new American friend, rushed to help him move in. In gratitude for his hard work on the hot summer day, I asked him to stay for a while and have a beer. I went to wash up and came back to get him a beer out of the refrigerator. I did not need to; he had already opened the refrigerator and was helping himself. For him, a refrigerator was my public space into which I had invited him. To me and most of my Dutch compatriots, it was definitely private space. A few days later I was struck by a similar event. I was inquiring about transportation across town when Denise, a fellow student, tossed me her car keys and said to call her when I was finished with my errand. I could not believe it. To me, a car was certainly private space. Have you ever tried to borrow a German acquaintance's Mercedes?

In the USA, where people are relatively mobile, furniture, cars and so on can be semi-public. People will hold garage sales and yard sales: exhibiting very personal items on tables in a yard for all not only to see, but to purchase. They may be as open with intimate personal experiences. It is not rare to be regaled at a party with confessions of sexual incompatibility from a complete stranger. You even suspect he has forgotten your name by the time his story is finished. An American cartoon by Jules Feiffer has the anti-hero Bernard Mergendeiler explain to his audience:

> "I met this *marvelous* girl. I've told all my friends and colleagues at work. I go up to strangers in the street and tell them about her. I've told nearly *everyone*—except her. Why give her the advantage?"[2]

Clearly this character's public spaces overwhelm his private one. He confesses in the first to avoid communication in the second.

The situation in France or Germany is quite different. You have only to note the high hedges and shuttered windows to appreciate French concern for large private spaces. If you are invited to dinner in a French home, that invitation extends to only the rooms in which that hospitality occurs. If you start wandering around the house you may offend. If your hostess goes into her study to find a book you are discussing, and you follow her, that may be considered a trespass into her private domain.

The concentric circles are not simply in the mind, but refer to spaces in which we live.

The concepts of the specific and the diffuse help us to make sense of the dispute being described in the MCC head office, which involved Mr. Johnson (American), Mr. Bergman (Dutch), and Messrs. Gialli and Pauli (Italian). Both Mr. Johnson and Mr. Bergman, while not in agreement on permissible levels of emotional expression (Mr. Johnson being more affective), *are* in agreement on the separation of reason from emotion. Americans and Dutch both believe that there are specific times, places, and spaces for being reasonable and specific times, places, and spaces for being affective. To their perplexity and dismay the Italians have "thrown a tantrum" in the middle of a meeting on serious, professional issues.

Let us continue the story.

As the representative from the head office, Mr. Johnson felt very responsible for the developments at the meeting. The Italians' behavior seemed strange to him. Mr. Bergman just wanted to discuss an important aspect of the consistency of the reward system, and they did not even give him a chance to explain his position. Moreover, the Italians had refused to put any solid arguments on the table themselves.

When Johnson entered Mr. Gialli's room he said: "Paolo, what's the problem? You shouldn't take this too seriously. It's just a business discussion."

"Just a business discussion?" Gialli asked with unconcealed rage. "This has nothing to do with a business discussion. It is typical for that Dutchman to attack us. We have our own ways of being effective, and then he calls us crazy."

"I didn't hear that," Johnson said. "He simply said that he found your group bonus idea crazy. I know Bergman, and he didn't intend that to refer to you."

"If that's so," answered Gialli, "why is he behaving so rudely?"

Johnson realized how deeply his Italian colleagues had been offended. He went back to Bergman, took him aside, and told him about his conversation with Gialli. "Offended!" said Bergman. "Let them have the self-control to respond to professional arguments. I don't understand why they are so hotheaded anyway. They know we have done extensive research on this. Let them listen first. You have to remember that these Latins never want to be bothered with facts."

The Italian reaction is of course quite understandable if you grasp that their feelings about group bonuses as opposed to individual bonuses, their sympathy with their sales force and customers, and the proposal they put forward are *one diffuse whole*. To call "the idea" crazy is to call *them* crazy and to question their ability to represent the cultural views of fellow Italians. It offends them deeply. Their ideas are not separated from themselves. If they "thought of it" and if it represents "Italian thinking" then the proposition is an extension of their personal honor.

One problem with the overlap between U-types and G-types is that the U-type sees as impersonal something the G-type sees as highly personal. Italian views on the effectiveness of group bonuses are tied to their diffuse sense of private space. It is not "just a business discussion" taking place in a realm apart from their private selves, but a discussion touching on what it means to be a feeling, thinking Italian. You cannot criticize Italians as "generators of a crazy idea" without profoundly affecting their whole system. When Americans "let in" a German, French, or Italian colleague into one compartment of their public space and show their customary openness and friendliness, that person may assume that they have been admitted to diffuse private space (see Figure 7.2, next page). The space where the private zone of one culture overlaps with the public zone of the other culture can therefor be seen as a danger zone.

They may expect the American to show equivalent friendship in all life spaces and be offended if he or she comes to their town without contacting them. They may also be offended by criticism as a professional, which they take to be an attack by a close friend.

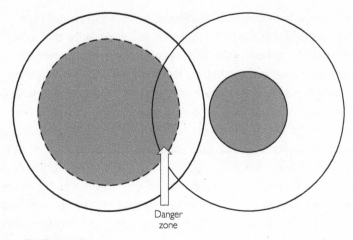

Danger zone

FIGURE 7.2. The Danger Zone

Losing Face

Specific cultures, with their small areas of privacy clearly separated from public life, have considerable freedom for direct speech. "Do not take this personally" is a frequent observation. In relationships with diffuse people this approach can be an insult. American and Dutch managers find it particularly easy to insult their opposite diffuse partners (see Mr. Johnson's problems with the Italians, above). This is because they do not understand the principle of losing face, which is what happens when something is made public that people perceive as being private. The importance of avoiding loss of face in diffuse cultures is why so much more time is taken to get to the point; it is necessary to avoid private confrontation because it is impossible for participants not to take things personally. I try to avoid asking a Dutch audience for criticism after one of my workshops; the experience is much the same as being machine-gunned. Afterward, however, they tend to ask the corpse for the next date it will be available. In contrast, English and French managers will make a few mild suggestions in a context of positive congratulation, never to be heard from again.

At an international university at which I was teaching, a Ghanaian student wrote a paper for me that I was unable to grade at more than 4 out of 10, a fail. All scores were posted on a noticeboard. The student said that this would be a public insult to him, impossible for me as a respected professor to perpetrate, although he agreed with the mark. What I should do was to mark the paper "I" (incomplete) for the board, while feeding the actual grade into the system.

National Differences

National differences are sharp under the headings of specificity and diffuseness. The range is illustrated well by responses to the following situation.

A boss asks a subordinate to help him paint his house. The subordinate, who does not feel like doing it, discusses the situation with a colleague.

    A. The colleague argues: "You don't have to paint if you don't feel like it. He is your boss at work. Outside he has little authority."

    B. The subordinate argues: "Despite the fact that I don't feel like it, I will paint it. He is my boss, and you can't ignore that outside work either."

In specific societies, where work and private life are sharply separated, managers are not at all inclined to assist. As one Dutch respondent observed: "House painting is not in my collective labor agreement." Figure 7.3 (see next page) shows the proportion of managers that would not paint the house, around 70 percent or higher in the UK, the USA, Switzerland, and most of northern Europe; 64 percent of Japanese would not either, but in the diffuse Asian societies of China and India and South American societies of Peru and Brazil the majority would. (Surprised by the Japanese score, we re-interviewed some Japanese respondents. They replied that it most probably had to do with the fact that the Japanese would never wait till the boss asks, which illustrates the relativity of empirical data.) The range of differences is not so steeply graded as when we looked at the basic cultural divides of Chapters 3 and 4, but it is nevertheless clearly a source of deep potential incomprehension.

Negotiating the Specific-Diffuse Cultural Divide

Doing business with a culture more diffuse than our own feels very time-consuming. Some nations refuse to do business in a mental subdivision called "commerce" or "work" that is kept apart from the rest of life. In diffuse cultures, everything is connected to everything. Your business partner may wish to know where you went to school, who your friends are, what

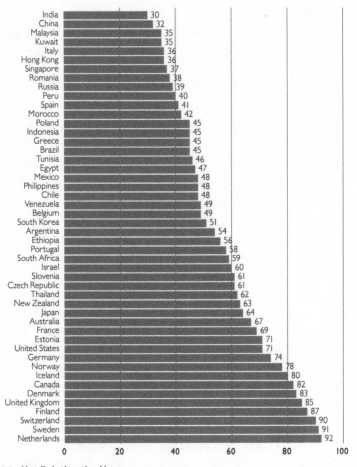

FIGURE 7.3. Not Painting the House

you think of life, politics, art, literature, and music. This is not "a waste of time" because such preferences reveal character and form friendships. They also make deception nearly impossible. As with the example in Chapter 1 of the Swedish company that beat an American company with a technically superior product for a contract with an Argentinian customer, the up-front investment in building relationships in such cultures is as important, if not more so, than the deal. The Swedes invested a whole week in the selling trip, the first five days of which were not related to the business at all. They just shared the diffuse life spaces of their hosts, talking about common interests. Only *after* a "private space" relationship had been established were the Argentinians willing to talk business. And that had to include several life spaces, not just one. In contrast, the Americans invested only two days in the trip, knowing they had a superior product and presentation, and were turned down.

It is really a question of priority. Do you start with the specific and neutral proposition and later get to know those interested in that proposition? Or do you start with people you can trust because you have invited them into multiple life spaces and then move on to business? Both approaches make good sense to those living in that culture, but each plays havoc with the other. The American team found themselves continually interrupted by "personal" questions and "social distractions," and when the corporate jet arrived on schedule to take them home, they had not adequately covered the business agenda. The Argentinians, to the Americans, seemed unable or unwilling to stick to the point. The Argentinians, for their part, found the Americans too direct, impersonal, and pushy. They were surprised by the Americans' apparent belief that you could use logic to force someone to agree with you.

In other words, specificity and diffuseness are about strategies for getting to know other people.

The diagram on the left of Figure 7.4 shows the typically diffuse strategy common in Japan, Mexico, France, and much of southern Europe and Asia. Here you "circle around" the stranger, getting to know him diffusely, and come down to the specifics of the business only later when relationships of trust have been established. On the right you get "straight to the point," to the neutral, "objective" aspects of the business deal, and *if* the other remains interested then you "circle around" getting to know them in order to facilitate the deal.

Both approaches claim to save time. In the diffuse approach you do not get trapped in an eight-year relationship with a dishonest partner because you detect any unsavory aspects early on. In the specific approach you do not waste time wining and dining a person who is not fully committed to the specifics of the deal.

Diffuse, high context
(from general to
specific)

Specific, low context
(from specific to
general)

FIGURE 7.4. Circling Around

Specific and diffuse cultures are sometimes called *low and high context*. Context has to do with how much you have to know before effective communication can occur, how much shared knowledge is taken for granted by those in conversation with each other, how much reference there is to tacit common ground. Cultures with high context like Japan and France believe that strangers must be "filled in" before business can be properly discussed. Cultures with low context like the USA or the Netherlands believe that each stranger should share in rulemaking, and the fewer initial structures there are the better. Low-context cultures tend to be adaptable and flexible. High-context cultures are rich and subtle, but carry a lot of "baggage" and may never really be comfortable for foreigners who are not fully assimilated. There is growing evidence, for example, that westerners working for Japanese companies are never wholly "inside." It is similarly hard to feel fully accepted within the richness of French culture with its thousands of diffuse connections.

There is a tendency for specific cultures to look at objects, specifics, and things before considering how these are related. The general tendency for diffuse cultures is to look at relationships and connections before considering all the separate pieces. The configuration is circular (see Figure 7.5).

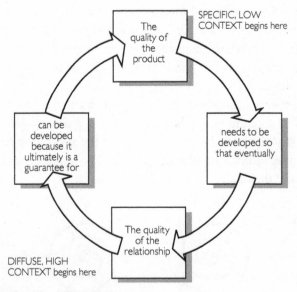

FIGURE 7.5. The Specific–Diffuse Circle

The Effect of Specific-Diffuse Orientation on Business

That Americans choose MBO (management by objectives) and pay-for-performance as favorite devices to motivate employees testifies in part to their specific orientation. In MBO you first agree on the "objectives," that is, the specifics.

Supervisor A agrees with subordinate B that B will work toward agreed objectives in the coming quarter and that evaluation of his or her work will take as a benchmark the objectives agreed to. Good objectives satisfactorily achieved will make for a productive relationship between A and B. What could be fairer or more logical? Why would the whole world not agree to do this?

This system does not appeal to diffuse cultures because they approach the issue from the opposite direction. It is *the relationship between A and B that increases or reduces output, not the other way around.* Objectives or specifics may be out of date by the time evaluation comes around. B may not have performed as promised yet done something more valuable in altered circumstances. Only strong and lasting relationships can handle unexpected changes of this kind. Contracts and small print face backward in such cultures.

Japanese corporate cultures, for example, use terms unfamiliar to Westerners that are clearly aimed at putting the diffuse before the specific. They speak of "acceptance time," the time necessary to discuss proposed changes before these are implemented. They speak of *nemawashi*, literally binding the roots of shrubs and trees before transplanting them. This refers to extensive consultations before implementing changes. All these constitute "the circling around before coming to the point" that we saw in Figure 7.4.

Pay-for-performance is not very popular in diffuse cultures because it arbitrarily severs relationships. It says "you are solely responsible for what you sold this month" when, in fact, other salespeople may have helped you and your superiors may have inspired you or instructed you to act in more effective ways. To claim most or all of the rewards for yourself denies the importance of relationships, including feelings of affection and respect for superiors and peers with whom you have diffuse contacts and shared private life spaces.

Expressions like "do not mix business with pleasure" and "don't talk shop" testify to the desire in some cultures to keep specific life spaces separate from each other. Arguably it is harder to coerce people or subordinate them if their lives are honeycombed with separate compartments. In this situation only one area of somebody's life can be dominated and they can call on the resources they have in other areas. Diffuse cultures have "all their eggs in one basket." Again, we are talking about *relative* not absolute separation. There is always a kind of wall between life spaces in most cultures.

Diffuse cultures tend to have lower turnover and employee mobility because of the importance of "loyalty" and the multiplicity of human bonds. They tend not to "headhunt" or lure away employees from other companies with high (specific) salaries. Takeovers are rarer in diffuse cultures because of the disruption caused to relationships and because shareholders (often banks) have longer-term relationships and cross-holdings in each other's companies and are less motivated by the price of shares.

Pitfalls of Performance Evaluation

Specific cultures find it much easier to criticize people without devastating the whole life space of the target of that criticism. There are at least two tragic corporate cases where criticism during performance evaluations by Western superiors led to their murder by outraged targets.

In one case a Dutch doctor whose job was to evaluate a Chinese subordinate in the company clinic had a "frank discussion" of the latter's shortcomings. In his view these could easily be remedied by the company's training courses. Yet to the Chinese doctor who had worked closely with the Dutch doctor, and whom he regarded as a "father figure," the criticism was a savage indictment, a total rejection, and a betrayal of mutual confidence. The next morning he knifed his critic to death. It is easy to imagine the Dutch ghost protesting that he had never said his Chinese colleague was not a great fellow; it was only his medicine he was worried about.

In a second case a British manager who fired an employee in Central Africa was later poisoned, with the seeming connivance of the other African employees. The fired man had a large number of hungry children and had stolen meat from the company cafeteria. In a diffuse culture "stealing" is not easily separable from domestic circumstances, and the Western habit of separating an "office crime" from a "problem at home" is not accepted.

We must be careful, however, not to regard diffuse cultures as "primitive." Japanese corporations give bigger salaries to workers with larger families, help in the search for housing, and often provide recreation facilities, vacations, and consumer products at favorable prices. Another pair of questions we use to test for cultural diffuseness is the following.

A. Some people think a company is usually responsible for the housing of its employees. Therefore, a company has to assist an employee in finding housing.

B. Other people think the responsibility for housing should be carried by the employee alone. It is so much to the good if the company helps.

Figure 7.6 shows the percentage of managers who do not think that housing is a company's responsibility. Only 45 percent of Japanese managers think that it is not, as opposed to 85 percent of Americans. The great

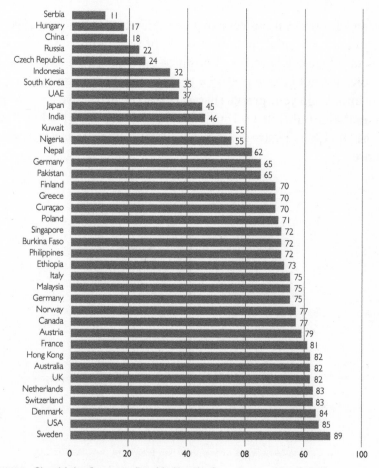

FIGURE 7.6. Should the Company Provide Housing?

majority of all north European managers do not expect company help, in most Asian countries the majority do. The exception is Singapore, where Western principles have become much more widespread. It is also interesting to note the impact of Communist regimes on the various European countries that appear at the top of the chart.

Japanese consumers may reject Western imported goods because their value is specific; Japanese corporations produce goods with benefits diffused through their society. So we buy more than a Honda motor scooter; we "buy" economic and social development for our society, a highly diffuse concept.

The Mix of Emotion and Involvement

There are of course various combinations of levels of emotion or affectivity (high to low, or neutral) with its "reach" or scope (diffusing several life spaces or remaining specific). A business partner can be emotional and expressive yet not be involved *with you*. He may be cool and neutral, yet deeply involved in your private spaces. He can be expressive and involved, or neutral and uninvolved. Four combinations are described by Talcott Parsons,[3] which as Figure 7.7 shows yield four different sorts of primary response.

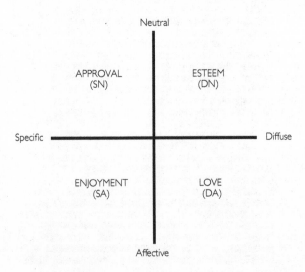

Source: Talcott Parsons, *The Social System*. New York: *The Free Press*, 1951.

FIGURE 7.7. The Emotional Quadrant

In diffuse-affective (DA) interactions the expected relational reward is *love,* a strongly expressed pleasure diffusing many life spaces. In diffuse-neutral (DN) interactions the expected reward is *esteem,* a less strongly expressed admiration also spread over many life spaces. In specific-affective (SA) interactions the expected reward is *enjoyment,* a strongly expressed pleasure specific to a certain occasion or performance. In specific-neutral (SN) interactions the expected reward is *approval,* a job, task, or occasion-specific expression of positive, yet neutral approbation. Of course these four quadrants might also contain negative evaluations: *hate* (DA), *disappointment* (DN), *rejection* (SA), and *criticism* (SN). It is important to remember that love and enjoyment have their mirrors in hate and rejection, while more neutral cultures do not risk such extreme mood swings.

We have tried to measure the relative national preferences for love, esteem, enjoyment, and approval by using the following question, which is taken from some earlier work by L. R. Dean:

Which of the following four types of people do you prefer to have around you? Review these descriptions carefully, then circle the one that most closely relates to your preference and the one that represents your second preference.[4]

A. People who completely accept you the way you are and feel responsible for your personal problems and welfare (combines diffuse and affective: love).

B. People who do their work, attend to their affairs, and leave you free to do the same (specific and neutral: approval).

C. People who try to improve themselves and have definite ideals and aims in life (diffuse and neutral: esteem).

D. People who are friendly, lively, and enjoy getting together to talk or socialize (specific and affective: enjoyment).

Figure 7.8 shows how a number of nationalities score in this exercise. We see that a typical American approach is quite close to the North European combining Specificity with Neutrality. This is in great contrast with the Latin cultures, such as Spain, Italy and Mexico who prefer to combine Diffuseness with Affectivity. Once again there are no clear rules by continent, although if we try to picture the most important regional cultural differences, we get the division shown in Figure 7.9.

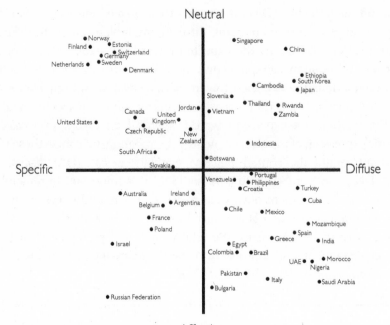

FIGURE 7.8. What Type of People Do You Prefer Around You?

American (West Coast) enthusiasms tend to be for specific issues and causes and belong as it were in separate boxes—that is, saving the redwoods, rebirthing, nanotechnology, virtual reality, and so on. DA cultures spill over between life spaces. Dishonor to a family member disgraces the family and must be avenged. You may not be able to work in the same company as a person with whom your uncle has a feud going back 10 years.

On one occasion a Dutch and a Belgian manager disagreed on a fiscal issue in politics. The Dutch manager let the disagreement stand, in a separate compartment as he saw it, and tried to get on with other business. But for the Belgian their disagreement colored everything. The Dutch manager could not be a trusted partner if his views on the fiscal issue were so mistaken. The Dutchman's desire to move on to other business was a slight to the Belgian's feeling of profound disturbance in their relationship. Their business dealings were broken off.

North Europeans, especially Scandinavians, are somewhat less specific than Americans, but are more disapproving of overt emotion. Like the Japanese, however, they sanction alcohol to loosen inhibitions. The lack of

Neutral

USA (East Coast),
Scandinavia,
Northern Europe

APPROVAL,
DISAPPROVAL
(around specific
causes)

Japan, SE Asia,
East Africa

DEEP
RESPECT/ESTEEM,
DISRESPECT

Specific ——————————————————— Diffuse

USA (West Coast),
Canada

SYMPATHY,
ENJOYMENT
OUTRAGE
(around specific
causes)

Latin, Arab,
South America,
Southern Europe

LOVE, HATE

Affective

FIGURE 7.9. Regional Cultural Differences

explicit emotion does not mean that people do not feel for each other. It means that a "soft pedal" is used to communicate emotions, but these small signs can, of course, speak volumes to the recipient who understands how to read them.

Reconciling Specific-Diffuse Cultures

This is perhaps the area in which balance is most crucial, from both a personal and a corporate point of view. The specific extreme can lead to disruption, and the diffuse extreme to a lack of perspective; a collision between them results in paralysis. It is the interplay of the two approaches that is the most fruitful, recognizing that privacy is necessary, but complete separation of private life leads to alienation and superficiality; that business is business, but stable and deep relationships mean strong affiliations.

The need for interplay is shown by the following case.

It was in the late 1980s and early 1990s that merger mania hit the airline industry. John Perrish of British Airways was sitting at his desk wondering what to do in the latest discussions on the alliance with US Air. As a marketing manager he was worried that the results of passenger studies would jeopardize the long-term development of an airline serving the global passenger. The studies revealed that American passengers were increasingly less willing to pay high ticket prices. Competition between American airlines was a price rather than a quality issue.

In Europe business-class travel was still characterized by high prices and competition was aimed at legroom, quality of meals, and flexibility of changing routes. It seemed that the service was seen in dramatically different ways by American and European passengers. The globalization that would result from the alliance would force both partners to rethink what a true global client expects.

Peter Butcher, John's counterpart at US Air, could not resist making cynical comparisons and often said: "John, you might say that we in the USA tend to serve our passengers as a 'piece of meat' that needs to travel from NY to LA, and in Europe people are willing to include their stomach for an extra $300 during a one-hour flight." Indeed, at BA passengers are served a hot breakfast on a flight from London to Amsterdam that is no longer than 40 minutes. John's reply was as biting: "I remember I once had a first-class flight from Detroit to Chicago of just over an hour. It took off at 6.30 a.m., and around 7, long after our seatbelts were loosened, I wondered when breakfast would be served. I couldn't smell anything. I asked the flight attendant when I could expect a breakfast. I took her by surprise with that question. Two minutes later she came back with a big smile asking: 'Sir, we have pretzels or potato chips; which do you prefer?' I said that a cup of coffee would do."

When clients' expectations are so diverse around the world, how would you advise John and Peter to approach their global marketing campaign?

It is obvious that American passengers and the airlines serving them share a perception of a very specific relationship. You are a person who needs to go from A to B in a safe, reliable, and inexpensive way. Period. In Europe and Asia the involvement is perceived as going beyond safety and reliability. When flying with Singapore Airlines, for example, we can see a mutual need to involve the whole person. This diffuse relationship is expressed by excellent service, food, and a general attitude of *service*. In much of the USA and on some airlines in Europe neither client nor airline feels the need to get involved beyond a safe and fast trip for as low a price as possible. It is up to the client to decide.

However, in the case of BA and US Air it was not as simple. To serve global clients they first needed to decide what level of integration was necessary. KLM and Northwest Airlines, for example, decided to integrate their schedules and parts of their financial and booking systems. But KLM's service was still quite different from that on Northwest Airlines.

What do you do when the alliance goes beyond the technicalities and includes the service on board? A compromise is not desirable, because not many passengers like hot pretzels or lukewarm breakfasts. SAS tried by introducing a business class to leave the choice to the passenger. But what about serving the global customer? The challenging question becomes: How could the excellence of our specific services increase the quality of the holistic approach to the passenger? The reconciling graph could be as shown in Figure 7.10.

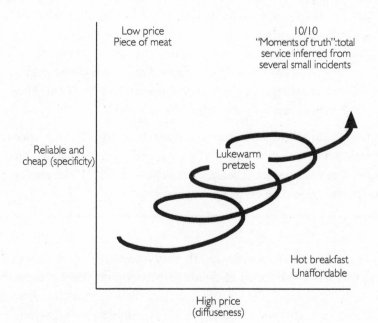

FIGURE 7.10. Moments of Truth

Test Yourself

Consider the following question:

A group of managers and financial analysts were arguing about whether profitability or ongoing stakeholder relationships, most especially between company and customers, formed the best way of monitoring organizational effectiveness. The following positions were advanced:

1. Feedback within close customer relationships is the timeliest advice about corporate effectiveness. Its value is its inclusivity. Profits measure what is taken out of a relationship, not what is staked or contributed.

2. Feedback within close customer relationships is the most timely advice about corporate effectiveness. Because customers generate the funds used to pay profits, the quality of these relationships anticipates profitability.

3. Profitability or shareholder value is the prime criterion of corporate effectiveness, because it distils in one precise and unambiguous measure the vitality and value of all activities by other stakeholders.

4. Profitability or shareholder value is the prime criterion of corporate effectiveness, because it proclaims in one precise and unambiguous measure that labor works for capital and business exists to enrich individual owners.

Indicate with "1" the approach you prefer and with "2" your second choice. Similarly, indicate with "1" the approach you believe would be favored by your closest colleagues at work, and with "2" the approach you believe would be his or her second choice.

This question reveals quite clearly four alternative approaches to the criteria that need to be used to define organizational effectiveness. If you think an organization is primarily a money-making machine you would opt for answer 4. Answer 1 rejects specificity, while answer 2 is a reconciliation starting from a diffuse point of departure. Answer 3 reconciles the diffuse responsibility starting from a specific standpoint of profitability or shareholder value.

The following tables highlight differences between specific and diffuse orientation and give some tips for achieving reconciliation between the two views.

Recognizing the Differences

SPECIFIC ORIENTATION	DIFFUSE ORIENTATION
• Direct, to the point, purposeful in relating	• Indirect, circuitous, seemingly "aimless" forms of relating
• Precise, blunt, definitive, and transparent	• Evasive, tactful, ambiguous, even opaque
• Principles and consistent moral stand independent of the person being addressed	• Highly situational morality depending upon the person and context encountered

Tips for Reconciliation Doing Business With

DIFFUSELY ORIENTED INDIVIDUALS DOING BUSINESS WITH SPECIFICALLY ORIENTED PEOPLE	SPECIFICALLY ORIENTED INDIVIDUALS DOING BUSINESS WITH DIFFUSELY ORIENTED PEOPLE
• Study the objectives, principles, and numerical targets of the specific organization with which you are dealing.	• Study the history, background, and future vision of the diffuse organization with which you expect to do business.
• Be quick, to the point, and efficient.	• Take time and remember there is more than one way to skin a cat.
• Structure the meeting with time, intervals, and agendas.	• Let the meeting flow, occasionally nudging its process.
• Do not use titles or acknowledge skills that are irrelevant to the issue being discussed.	• Respect a person's title, age, background, and connections, whatever issue is being discussed.
• Do not be offended by confrontations; they are usually not personal.	• Do not get impatient when people are indirect or circuitous.

Differences in Managing and Being Managed

SPECIFICALLY ORIENTED PEOPLE	DIFFUSELY ORIENTED PEOPLE
• Management is the realization of objectives and standards with rewards attached.	• Management is a continuously improving process by which quality improves.
• Private and business agendas are kept separate from each other.	• Private and business issues interpenetrate.
• Conflicts of interest are frowned upon.	• Consider an employee's whole situation before you judge him or her.
• Clear, precise, and detailed instructions are seen as assuring better compliance, or allowing employees to dissent in clear terms.	• Ambiguous and vague instructions are seen as allowing subtle and responsive interpretations through which employees can exercise personal judgment.
• Begin reports with an executive summary.	• End reports with a concluding overview.

8

How We Accord Status

Fons Trompenaars and Charles Hampden-Turner

ALL SOCIETIES give certain of their members higher status than others, signaling that unusual attention should be focused upon such people and their activities. While some societies accord status to people on the basis of their achievements, others ascribe it to them by virtue of age, class, gender, education, and so on. The first kind of status is called *achieved* status and the second *ascribed* status. While achieved status refers to *doing*, ascribed status refers to *being*.

When we look at a particular person we are partly influenced by their track record (top Eastern Division salesman for five consecutive years). We may also be influenced by:

- Age (a more experienced salesperson)
- Gender (very masculine and aggressive)
- Social connections (friends in the highest places)
- Education (top scholar at the Ecole Polytechnique)
- Profession (electronics is the future)

While there are ascriptions that are not logically connected with business effectiveness, such as gender, skin color, or birth, there are some ascriptions that do make good sense in predicting business performance: age and experience, education, and professional qualifications. Education and professional qualifications, moreover, are related to an individual's earlier schooling and training and are therefore not unconnected with achievement. A culture may ascribe higher status to its better-educated employees in the belief that scholarly success will lead to corporate success. This is a generalized expectation and may show up as a "fast-track" or "management-trainee" program that points a recruit to the top of the organization.

With the issue of status in mind, let us get back to the trials of Mr. Johnson, who you may recall is struggling with a walkout by Italian managers. Mr. Gialli and Mr. Pauli left the room furious when their suggested modification to the pay-for-performance plan was called "a crazy idea" by Mr. Bergman from the Netherlands. In order to save the situation, Johnson has turned to shuttle diplomacy. Like a youthful Henry Kissinger (Johnson is only 35), he finds himself moving between the two parties to settle the dispute. He rapidly begins to feel less like Kissinger and more like Don Quixote.

The Italian managers were far from assuaged. One even referred unpleasantly to "the American cult of youth: mere boys who think they know everything." So when the Spanish HR manager, Mr. Munoz, offered to mediate, Johnson readily agreed. It occurred to him that Spanish culture might be closer to Italian culture, apart from the fact that Munoz was some 20 years his senior, so could hardly be accused of inexperience.

While hopeful that Munoz might succeed, Johnson was astonished to see him bring the Italians back into the conference room in minutes. Munoz was not, in Johnson's view, the most professional of HR managers, but he was clearly expert at mending fences. It was at once apparent, however, that Munoz was now backing the Italians' call for modifications to the pay-for-performance plan. The problem as he saw it, and the Italians agreed, was that under the current plan winning salespeople were going to earn more than their bosses. Subordinates, they believed, should not be allowed to undermine their superiors in this way. Mr. Munoz explained that back in Spain his sales force would probably simply refuse to embarrass a boss like this; or perhaps one or two, lacking in loyalty to the organization, might, in which case they would humiliate their boss into resignation. Furthermore, since the sales manager was largely responsible for the above-average performance of his team, was it not odd, to say the least, that the company would be rewarding everyone except the leader? The meeting broke for lunch, for which Johnson had little appetite.

As we can see, different societies confer status on individuals in different ways. Mr. Munoz carried more clout with the Italians for the same reason that Johnson had less: they respected age and experience much more than the specific achievements that had made Johnson a fast-tracker in the company. Many Anglo-Saxons, including Mr. Johnson, believe that ascribing status for reasons other than achievement is quite archaic and inappropriate to business. But is achievement orientation really a necessary feature of economic success?

Status by Achievement and Economic Development

Most of the literature on achievement orientation sees it as part of "modernization," the key to economic and business success. The theory goes that once you start rewarding business achievement, the process is self-perpetuating. People work hard to assure themselves of the esteem of their culture and you get *The Achieving Society*, as David McClelland, the Harvard professor, defined his own culture in the late 1950s.[1] Only nations setting out upon an empirical investigation of "what works best," and conferring status on those who apply it in business, can expect to conduct their economies successfully. This is the essence of Protestantism: the pursuit of justification through works that long ago gave achievers a religious sanction—and capitalism its moving spirit.

According to this view, societies that ascribe status are economically backward because the reasons they have for conferring status do not facilitate commercial success. Catholic countries ascribing status to more passive ways of life, Hinduism associating practical achievements with delusion, and Buddhism teaching detachment from earthly concerns are all forms of ascribed status that are thought to impede economic development. Ascription has been seen as a feature of countries either late to develop or still underdeveloped. In fact, ascribing status has been considered "dangerous for your economic health."

To measure the extent of achieving versus ascribing orientations in different cultures, we used the following statements, inviting participants to mark them on a five-point scale (1 = strongly agree, 5 = strongly disagree).

A. The most important thing in life is to think and act in the ways that best suit the way you really are, even if you do not get things done.

B. The respect a person gets is highly dependent on their family background.

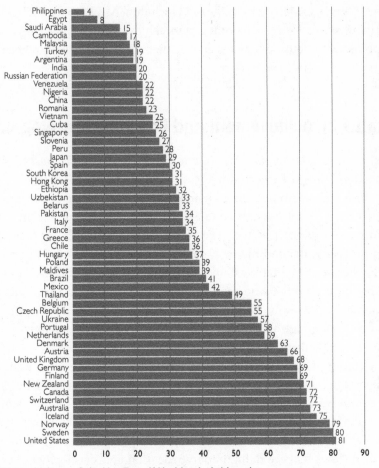

FIGURE 8.1. Acting as Suits You Even If Nothing Is Achieved

Figures 8.1 and 8.2 show the percentage of participants who disagree with each of these statements. The countries in Figure 8.1 where only a minority disagree with "getting things done" are broadly speaking ascriptive cultures—very broadly speaking—because there are in fact less than 18 societies (one-third of the 54 presented), English-speaking and Scandinavian countries, where there is a majority in favor of getting things done even at the expense of personal freedom to live as you feel you should. The USA is clearly a culture in which status is mainly achieved, as shown by Figure 8.2: 91 percent of Americans disagree that status depends mainly on family background. A number of societies that are ascriptive in the first figure (Slovenia, for example) do in fact show majorities against the proposition that status is

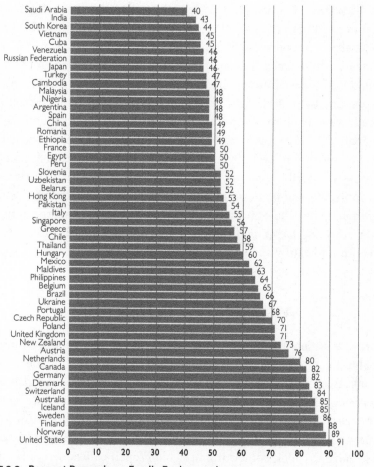

FIGURE 8.2. Respect Depends on Family Background

largely dependent on family; aspects of ascription vary greatly from country to country.

Both figures show that there is a correlation between Protestantism and achievement orientation, with Catholic, Buddhist, and Hindu cultures scoring considerably more ascriptively. There is, incidentally, no correlation between support for achievement or ascription and the age, gender, or education of respondents across our database as a whole, although there is for these factors in some societies.

A second glance at the scores shows that there are growing difficulties with the thesis that an achievement orientation is the key to economic success. In the first place, Protestant cultures are no longer growing faster than

Catholic or Buddhist ones. Catholic Belgium, for example, has a slightly higher GDP per head than the more Protestant Netherlands. Catholic France and Italy have been growing faster than the UK or parts of Protestant Scandinavia. Japan, South Korea, Taiwan, Singapore, and Hong Kong are influenced by Buddhism and Confucianism. It is certainly not evident that Japan's habit of promoting by seniority has weighed its corporations down beneath piles of dead wood. In short, there is no evidence that either orientation belongs to a "higher" level of development, as modernization theorists used to claim.

What appears to be happening is that some very successful business cultures are ascribing status to people, technologies, or industries that they anticipate will be important to their future as an economy, with the result that these people and sectors receive special encouragement. In other words, ascribing *works with* achieving by generating social and economic momentum toward visualized goals.

Ascription and Performance

Andrew, a British manager and trained geologist, had been working for a French oil company for 20 years and was still confused by one aspect of his colleagues' behavior. He found that his fellow French geologists would simply not tolerate outside criticism of their profession. Initially he would get puzzled looks and frowns if he admitted he did not know the answer to some technical question in front of laypeople. Once when he said he would have to "look something up," his French colleagues were overtly annoyed with him. He was confused because in his view geologists are frequently asked questions for which they do not have answers right at hand, or for which there is no answer. But his French fellows would chide him for admitting this publicly. They believed he was letting his profession down.

This experience is supported by research undertaken at INSEAD business school in France by André Laurent.[2] He found that French and Italian managers were much more emphatic about "knowing all the answers" than managers from many other cultures.

Notice, though, the effect that ascription has on performance. The French geologists are determined to live up to their ascribed status, which, in turn, can lead to higher performance. Hence, it can be a self-fulfilling prophecy: through living up to the status ascribed to them, they "deserve" the status that is given to them before they actually earn it. In practice, then, achieving and ascribing status can be finely interwoven.

The European Union is a very good example of an ascribed self-fulfilling prophecy; its importance and power in the world was proclaimed before it had achieved anything.

The interweaving of ascribing and achieving orientations is a feature of the world's leading economies, China, Japan and Germany. Both cultures tend to confine achieving *as individuals* to school. Thereafter, managers are supposed to cooperate. Achievement becomes less a task for individuals jostling each other for advantage than for whole groups, led by those who excelled earlier and individually.

We must bear these distinctions in mind when we examine the data presented earlier. Ascribing and achieving can be exclusive of each other, but are not necessarily so. Your achieving can drive your ascribing, as when you "land winners." Or ascribing can drive achieving, as when key industries are first targeted and then won by "national champions."

The belief that electronic equipment made by Olivetti, Bosch, Siemens, or Alcatel is more important to the EU than enhanced expertise in distributing hamburgers or bottling colas is not entirely mistaken. You can ascribe greater importance to supposedly "key" industries on the basis of bad judgment or of good judgment. It is at least arguable that an economy needs to master electronics if it seeks to maintain competitiveness in manufacturing since machines are increasingly monitored, controlled, and retooled electronically. You have a choice, then, of ascribing status to electronics *before* the achievements of manufacturing lapse, or *afterward*. A culture that insists on waiting for dire results before changing course may handicap itself. Intelligent anticipation requires ascribing importance to certain projects, just as joint ventures, strategic alliances, and partnerships require us to value a relationship *before* it proves successful.

Achievement- and Ascription-Oriented Cultures' Negotiations

It can be extremely irritating to managers from achieving cultures when an ascriptive team of negotiators has some éminence grise hovering in the background to whom they have to submit any proposals or changes. It is not even clear what this person does. He will not say what he wants, but simply expects deference not just from you but from his own team, which is forever watching him for faint signs of assent or dissent. It is, of course, equally upsetting for ascriptive cultures when the "achieving team" wheels in its aggressive young men and women who spout knowledge as if it were a kind of ammunition before which the team opposite is expected to surrender. It is rather like having to play a game with a toddler and a toy gun; there is a lot of noise coming from someone who is of no known authority or status.

Indeed, sending whiz kids to deal with people 10 to 20 years their senior often insults the ascriptive culture. The reaction may be: "Do these people think that they have reached our own level of experience in half the time? That a 30-year-old American is good enough to negotiate with a 50-year-old Greek or Italian?" Achievement cultures must understand that some ascriptive cultures, the Japanese especially, spend much on training and in-house education to ensure that older people actually are wiser for the years they have spent in the corporation and for the sheer number of subordinates briefing them. It insults an ascriptive culture to do anything that prevents the self-fulfilling nature of its beliefs. Older people are held to be important *so that* they will be nourished and sustained by others' respect. A stranger is expected to facilitate this scheme, not challenge it.

Consider a Japanese-Dutch negotiating session. When Dutch experts in finance, marketing, and human resources meet their Japanese opposite numbers, the Dutch approach is to try to clarify facts and determine who holds the decision-making power. To the Dutch, the Japanese will appear evasive and secretive, not revealing anything. For the Japanese, these are not "facts" so much as mutual understandings between their leaders and themselves, which the Dutch seem to be prying into. This may come across as disrespectful. Anyway, it is for the leader of the negotiating team to say what these relationships are if he or she chooses to.

At a conference on a Japanese-Dutch joint venture held in Rotterdam, a Japanese participant fell ill. A member of the Dutch delegation approached Mr. Yoshi, another Japanese delegate with fluent English and outstanding technical knowledge, and asked if he would replace the sick man in a particular forum. Mr. Yoshi demurred, and the Dutchman was annoyed at the lack of a straight response. Several minutes later the leader of the Japanese delegation, Mr. Kaminaki, announced that Mr. Yoshi would replace the sick man because Mr. Kaminaki was appointing him to the task. It was made very clear whose decision that had been.

The Translator's Role

In this and other negotiations it often becomes clear that the translator from an ascriptive culture behaves "unprofessionally" according to the standards of achieving cultures. According to British, German, North American,

Scandinavian, and Dutch values, the translator is an achiever like any other participant, and the height of his or her achievement should be to give an accurate, unbiased account of what was said in one language to those speaking the other language. The translator is supposed to be neutral, a black box serving the interests of modern language comprehension, not the interests of either party who may seek to distort meanings for their own ends.

In other cultures, however, the translator is doing something else. A Japanese translator, for example, will often take a minute or more to "translate" an English sentence 15 seconds long. And there is often extensive colloquy between the translator and the team he or she serves about what the opposite team just said. Japanese translators are interpreters, not simply of language but of gesture, meaning, and context. Their role is to support their own team and possibly even to protect them from confrontational conduct by the Western negotiators. They may protect superiors from rudeness and advise the team how to counter opposition tactics. The "translator" is very much on the ascribing team's side, and if the achievement-oriented team seeks flawless, if literal, translation they should bring their own translator. This may not actually improve relationships because Asian teams are quite used to speaking among themselves in the belief that foreigners do not understand. If you bring someone fluent in their tongue, they will have to withdraw in order to confer. Your "contribution" to mutual understanding may not be appreciated.

The Role of Titles

The use and mention of titles with business cards and formal introductions can be complex. Both authors carry three kinds of cards to introduce themselves. In the Middle East and Southern Europe formal titles received for formal education are diffused through several different contexts to elevate my status. In Britain, however, presenting yourself as "doctor" may suggest a rather too academic bent for a business consultant. It may not be considered relevant for a consultant to have a PhD, and if attention is drawn to it, the status claimed is not necessarily legitimate. Achievement in a university may even disqualify a person from likely achievement in a corporation.

We might expect a similar situation in the USA, another achievement-oriented, yet specific society. However, the "inflation" of qualifications in the USA makes it legitimate to draw attention to higher degrees from good universities, provided it is relevant to the task at hand. Typically the specialty is mentioned: MBA, Sociology, and so on.

In diffuse cultures it is important to *tie in* your status with your organization. Indeed your achievement as an individual will be discounted compared with the status your organization ascribes to you. It is therefore important to say not just that you are chief, but what you are chief of: marketing, finance, human resources, and so on. Many a deal has been lost because the representative was not seen to have high status back home. Ascriptive cultures must be assured that your organization has great respect for you and that you are at or near the top.

Relationship with the Mother Company

In the value system of individualist, achievement-oriented cultures, the specific "word" of the representative pledges the company to any commitment made. The individual has delegated authority to use personal judgment. In ascriptive cultures, the individual, unless head of the organization, almost never has the personal discretion to commit the company without extensive consultations. An individual from an ascriptive culture may not really believe that the achieving representative has this authority either. Hence agreements are tentative and subject to back-home ratification. It is partly for this reason that your title and power "back home" is important to the ascriptive negotiator. How can you deliver your company if you are not high in its status hierarchy? If you send an impetuous, though clever youth, you cannot be very serious. It is important to send senior people if you are visiting an ascriptive culture, even if they are less knowledgeable about the product. It could also be important to ask for senior people in the ascriptive culture to attend in person and meet their opposite numbers. The closer you get to the top, the more likely it is that promises made in negotiations will be kept.

Signs of Ascriptive Status Are Carefully Ordered

We are now beginning to see why pay-for-performance and bonuses to high achievers whatever their rank can be upsetting to ascriptive cultures. The superior is *by definition* responsible for increased performance, so relative status is unaffected by higher group sales. If rewards are to be increased, this must be done proportionately to ascribed status, not given to the person closest to the sale. If the leader does something to reduce his own status, *all his subordinates are downgraded as a consequence.*

A British general manager upon arrival in Thailand refused to take his predecessor's car. The Thai finance manager asked the new GM what type of Mercedes he would like, then. The GM asked for a Suzuki or a Mini, anything that could be handled easily in the congested traffic in Bangkok.

Three weeks later the GM called the finance manager and asked about prospects for the delivery of his car. The Thai lost his reserve for a moment and exclaimed: "We can get you a new Mercedes by tomorrow, but Suzukis take much, much longer." The GM asked him to see what he could do to speed up the process. After four weeks the GM asked to see the purchase order for the car. The purchasing department replied that, because it would take so long to get a small car, they had decided to order a Mercedes.

The GM's patience had run out. At the first management meeting he brought the issue up and asked for an explanation. Somewhat shyly, the predominantly Thai management team explained that they could hardly come to work on bicycles.

In this case the status of each member was interdependent. Had the British GM ordered an even more expensive car, all the other managers might have moved up a notch. In ascriptive societies you "are" your status. It is as natural to you as your birth or formal education (rebirth) through which your innate powers were made manifest. Ascribed status simply "is" and requires no rational justification, although such justifications may exist. For example, a preference for males, for greater age or social connections is not usually justified or defended by the culture ascribing importance to older men from "good" families. That does not mean it is irrational or without competitive advantage, however; it simply means that justifications are not offered and not expected. It has always been so, and if this means a major effort to educate staff as they age, that is all the better, but it is *not* the basis for preferring older people in the first place.

Achievement-oriented organizations justify their hierarchies by claiming that senior people have "achieved more" for the organization; their authority, justified by skill and knowledge, benefits the organization. Ascription-oriented organizations justify their hierarchies by "power to get things done." This may consist of power *over* people and be coercive, or power *through* people and be participative. There is high variation within ascriptive cultures, and participative power has well-known advantages. Whatever form power takes, the ascription of status to people is intended to be exercised as power, and that power is supposed to enhance the effectiveness of the organization. The sources of ascribed status may be multiple, and trying to alter it by promotion on the grounds of achievement can be hazardous.

An achievement-oriented Swedish manager was managing a project in Pakistan. A vacancy needed to be filled, and after careful assessment the Swedish manager chose one of his two most promising Pakistani employees for promotion. Both candidates were highly educated, with PhDs in mechanical engineering, and in Pakistan both were known authorities in their field. Although both had excellent performance records, Mr. Kahn was selected on the basis of some recent achievements.

Mr. Saran, the candidate not chosen, was very upset by the turn of events. He went to his Swedish boss for an explanation. However, even an explanation based on the specific needs of the business did not calm him. How could this loss of face be allowed?

The Swedish manager tried to make the engineer understand that only one of the two could be promoted because there was only one vacancy. One of them was going to be hurt, even though they were both valued employees. He made no progress. The reason, as he eventually learned, was the fact that Mr. Saran received his PhD two years before Mr. Khan from the same American university. Saran was expected to have more status than his colleague because of this. His family would never understand. What was this Western way of treating ascribed status so lightly? Should not more than just the achievements of the past months be considered?

It is important to see how different the logics of achievement and ascription are and not consider either as worthless. In achieving countries people are evaluated by how they performed the allocated function. Relationships are functionally specific; I relate to you as, say, a sales manager. The justification of my role lies in the sales records. Another person in that role must be expected to be compared with me and I with that person. Success is universally defined as increased sales. My relationship to manufacturing, R&D, planning, and so on is instrumental. I either sell what they have developed, manufactured, and planned, or I do not. I *am* my functional role.

In ascribing cultures, status is attributed to those who "naturally" evoke admiration from others, that is, older people, highly qualified people, and/or people skilled in a technology or project deemed to be of national importance. To show respect for status is to assist the person so distinguished to fulfill the expectations the society has of him or her. The status is generally independent of task or specific function. The individual is particular and not easily compared with others. His or her performance is partly determined by the loyalty and affection shown by subordinates and that they, in turn, display. He or she *is* the organization in the sense of personifying it and wielding its power.

Achievement-oriented corporations in Western countries often send young, promising managers on challenging assignments to faraway countries without realizing that the local culture will not accept their youthfulness and/or gender however well they achieve. A young (age 34), talented female marketing manager had worked for an American company in both the USA and Britain. She was so successful in her second year there that she was named the most promising female manager in Britain. This vote of confidence influenced her decision to accept an offer to transfer as director of marketing to her company's operation in Ankara, Turkey. She knew she had always been able to win the support and trust of her subordinates and colleagues.

The first few weeks in Ankara were as usual in a new job, getting to know the local business, the staff, and how to get things done. Luckily, she knew one of the marketing managers, Guz Akil, who had been her marketing assistant in London. They had worked very well together.

Working as hard as she could over the first few months, she found her authority gradually slipping away. The most experienced Turk, Hasan (aged 63), informally but consciously took over more and more of her authority, getting things done where her own efforts were frustrated, although his marketing knowledge was only a fraction of her own. She had to watch him exercise influence that most often led to unsatisfactory results. Through Guz she learned that the head office complied with this arrangement, communicating more and more through Hasan, not her. She also heard that 10 years earlier an American male manager the same age as she had been withdrawn for his inability to command local managers effectively. He was now working very effectively indeed for a competitor back in the USA.

When presenting this case in a workshop in San Francisco, pointing out the dangers of a universalist system for personnel planning, one female manager expressed concern. "You should not linger on this issue. You are advising us to discriminate on the basis of gender and age, or allow our overseas subsidiaries to do so. In this country you could get sued for that."

Indeed cultural preferences often have the force of law as well as custom. Refusal to send young women managers to Turkey because they are young and female is probably illegal, yet to send them is to confront them with difficulties that they may not have the capacity to surmount, through no fault of their own. The more they achieve, the more they seem to subvert the ascription process. A better tactic can be to make a young female an assistant or adviser to indigenous managers. She will make up for any deficits in knowledge they have, while using local seniority to get things done. Such a posting could be paid and evaluated in the same way as being chief in an achievement-oriented culture, perhaps with a bonus for culture shock. You cannot replace Turkish with American cultural norms if you seek to be effective in Turkey. This will not be effective in the long run, and in the short run can be very expensive.

Toward Reconciliation

Despite far greater emphasis on ascription or achievement in certain cultures, they do in my view develop together. Those who "start" with ascribing usually ascribe not just status but future success or achievement and thereby help to bring it about. Those who "start" with achievement usually start to ascribe importance and priority to the people and projects that have been successful. Hence all societies ascribe and all achieve after a fashion. It is once again a question of where a cycle starts.

The need for reconciliation becomes paramount when one needs to lead a multicultural team. Suppose your team consists of a Swede who believes in bottom-up processes. Your French team member believes it should be more directive and top-down, the American participant has a strong confidence in the effectiveness of management by objectives (give me the goal and freedom to attain it), and the Chinese has preference for management by subjectives (do anything that pleases the boss). What leadership style do I need to apply?

We have looked at many leadership models, and most of them are culturally biased.[3] The one that would work in every culture is Greenleaf's original idea of servant leadership, best defined as enabling others to perform better. It is not by accident that most religious leaders were serving (from Jesus Christ to Mohammed) and that we all admire political leaders such as Gandhi and Mandela, because they were serving their societies. Look at Figure 8.3 to see the expressions of the reconciliation.

FIGURE 8.3. Reconciling Achievement Versus Ascription

It was in 1985 that Belly Electronics (BE) started to manufacture in South Korea. The fast-changing prices in consumer electronics had forced the San Francisco—based company to decentralize its production facilities. After some quite serious starting losses BE began to recover, and late in 1989 it could report some promising profits. Early in 1991 margins came under pressure because of Thai and Vietnamese competition. BE decided to reengineer its business processes following its major competitors in the region.

For the first time BE flew in experienced US managers from the Bay Area. Their approach was consistent and had made them managers of the year in BE for similar turnaround projects in California and Massachusetts. On the basis of a continuous improvement program Korean managers were put under pressure to "get their act together." Something said by the first US manager is still remembered in Seoul: "Ladies and gentlemen, we are on a burning platform. Figures tell us there is not much time left. Competitors in the region are doing much better than us; in fact, comparative research shows that in terms of quality our benchmark companies in California and Thailand are outperforming us by 35 percent on quality and 42 percent on quantity per worker. I therefore give you six months to get the numbers up and then to become a profit-generating company. Let us show that we are a worthwhile company in BE by achievements and not just promises."

After very disappointing results a second US manager was flown in, but his similar approach made no difference. Interviews with the key Korean players were not helpful. Loss after loss was defended by: "We are trying, but it is not easy in Korea. Fierce competition explains a lot. But we need to stop turnover of personnel so we can trust each other more."

Jerome Don was asked to come to the rescue of BE-Korea. He was known for turning companies around with great skill in both South America and Asia. He started by telling Korean managers that his predecessors were quite right in their approach: "We are on a burning platform, but I ask you to help us to save this facility because it is so important to BE. I'll give you three years to get your act together, and I'll help you whenever you need me."

Within six months BE-Korea was profitable. Quality went up, and morale resulted in 60 percent lower staff turnover. Mr. Don did not know exactly what happened, but he had done the same in South America and now in Asia.

Why was Jerome Don successful in Korea, while his predecessors had not been?

The initial actions by the American managers were counterproductive. In the great American tradition the turnaround managers started at the top of Figure 8.3 and focused on the reward that people could get for their achievements. The Koreans became even more nervous than they had been before the intervention, because basic trust seemed to be lacking. They were afraid to be judged on their past performance.

Jerome Don gave his Korean colleagues three years to get their act together. By doing so he intuitively ascribed status to the Korean organization. This gave the Koreans the trust they needed because they were feeling that they were respected for who they were based on their years at BE. This made them work even harder. From ascribed status comes achievement.

Test Yourself

Consider the following:

> There are different grounds for according status to employees based on what people have succeeded in doing or on what qualities are attributed to them by the social system.
>
> Consider these statements:
>
> 1. Status should lie in the permanent attributes of employees, i.e., their education, seniority, age, position, and the level of responsibility ascribed. Status should not change according to occasion or just because of recent successes. It reflects intrinsic worth, not the latest forays.
> 2. Status should lie in the permanent attributes of employees, i.e., their education, seniority, age, position, and the level of responsibility ascribed. Such status tends to be self-fulfilling, with achievement and leadership resulting from what the corporation values in you and expects of you.
> 3. Status is a matter of what the employee has actually achieved, his or her track record. Yet over time this deserved reputation becomes a permanent attribute, allowing success to be renewed and enabling even more achievement to occur.

4. Achievement or success is the only legitimate source of status in business. The more recent the achievement, the better and more relevant it is to current challenges. Achievement gets its significance from the humble nature of the individual's birth and background, and from beating the odds.

Indicate with "1" the approach you believe would be favored by your closest colleagues at work, and with "2" the approach which you believe would be that person's second choice.

If you chose 2 or 3 you have expressed a belief in reconciling achieved and ascribed status. Answer 2 affirms socially ascribed status that leads to achievement and success (the Korean case was based on a similar principle). Answer 3 affirms achieved status that is believed to lead to social ascription. In both cases the integrity lies in the self-fulfilling sense of self-worth. Answers 1 and 4 respectively reject achieved and ascribed status.

The following tables highlight differences between achievement and ascription orientation and give some tips for achieving reconciliation between the two views.

Recognizing the Differences

ACHIEVEMENT ORIENTATION	ASCRIPTION ORIENTATION
• Use of titles only when relevant to the competence you bring to the task.	• Extensive use of titles, especially when these clarify your status in the organization.
• Respect for superiors in hierarchy is based on how effectively they perform their job and how adequate their expertise is.	• Respect for superior in hierarchy is seen as a measure of your commitment to the organization and its mission.
• Most senior managers are of varying age and gender and have shown proficiency in specific jobs.	• Most senior managers are male, middle-aged, and qualified by their background.

Tips for Reconciliation

ASCRIPTION-ORIENTED INDIVIDUALS DOING BUSINESS WITH ACHIEVEMENT-ORIENTED PEOPLE	ACHIEVEMENT-ORIENTED INDIVIDUALS DOING BUSINESS WITH ASCRIPTION-ORIENTED PEOPLE
• Make sure your negotiation team has enough data, technical advisors, and knowledgeable people to convince the other company that the project, jointly pursued, will work.	• In order to convince the other company that you consider this negotiation important, make sure your negotiation team consists of enough older, senior officials, as well as others with formal titles.
• Respect the expertise and information of your counterparts even if you suspect they are short of influence back home.	• Respect the status and influence of your counterparts, even if you suspect they lack experience. Do not make them feel foolish.
• Use the title that reflects how competent you are as an individual.	• Use the title that reflects your degree of influence in your organization.
• Do not underestimate the need of your counterparts to do better or do more than is expected. To challenge is to motivate.	• Do not underestimate the need of your counterparts to make their ascriptions come true. To challenge is to subvert.

Differences in Managing and Being Managed

ACHIEVEMENT-ORIENTED PEOPLE	ASCRIPTION-ORIENTED PEOPLE
• Respect for a manager is based on knowledge and skills.	• Respect for a manager is based on seniority.
• Management by objectives and pay-for-performance are effective tools.	• Management by objectives and pay-for-performance are less effective than direct rewards from the manager.
• Decisions are challenged on technical and functional grounds.	• Decisions are only challenged by people with higher authority.

9

How We Manage Time

Fons Trompenaars and Charles Hampden-Turner

I F ONLY because managers need to coordinate their business activities, they require some kind of shared expectations about time. Just as different cultures have different assumptions about how people relate to one another, so they approach time differently. This chapter is about the relative importance cultures give to the past, present, and future. Does an achievement-oriented culture believe that the future must be better than the past or present, since it is there that aspirations are realized? Does a relationship-oriented culture, on the other hand, see the future as threatening, likely to loosen current bonds of affection? How we think of time has its own consequences.

As well as cultural differences about the past, present, and future, there are additional factors (what we might call subcomponents of the time dimension). These subcomponents include:

- Whether time is sequential (a series of linear passing events) or synchronic (in which we can work on tasks in parallel).
- The magnitude of time horizon—the duration of thinking time. Is a business plan for the next 3 months, 3 years, or 30 years?
- Clock or event time? Do we get the job done in the scheduled time or deliver a better job a little later?

These are all interrelated so that ideas about the future and memories of the past both shape present action.

The Concept of Time

Primitive societies may order themselves by simple notions of "before" and "after" moons, seasons, sunrises, and sunsets. For educated societies the concept of time is increasingly complex. Running through all our ideas of time are two contrasting notions: time as a line of discrete events, minutes, hours, days, months, years, each passing in a never-ending succession, and time as a circle, revolving so that the minutes of the hour repeat, as do the hours of the day, the days of the week, and so on.

In the Greek myth the Sphinx, a monster with the face of a woman, the body of a lion, and the wings of a bird, asked all wayfarers on the road to Thebes: "What creature is it that walks on four legs in the morning, two legs at noonday, and three legs in the evening?" Those unable to answer she ate. Oedipus, however, answered "man," and the Sphinx committed suicide. He had grasped that this riddle was a metaphor for time. Four legs was a child crawling, two legs the adult, and three legs an old person leaning on a stick. By thinking in a longer sequence about time, the riddle was solved. He had also understood that within the riddle time orientations had been compressed or synchronized, and that language allows us to do this.

Anthropologists have long insisted that how a culture thinks of time and manages it is a clue to the meanings its members find in life and the supposed nature of human existence. Kluckhohn and Strodtbeck[1] identified three types of culture: present-oriented, which is relatively timeless, without tradition, and ignores the future; past-oriented, mainly concerned to maintain and restore traditions in the present; and future-oriented, envisioning a more desirable future and setting out to realize it. It is chiefly people falling into the latter category who experience economic or social development.

Time is increasingly viewed as a factor that organizations must manage. There are time-and-motion studies, time-to-market, and just-in-time, along with ideas that products age or mature, and have a life cycle similar to that of human beings. Uniquely in the animal kingdom, humankind is aware of time and tries to control it. Human beings think almost universally in categories of past, present, and future, but do not give the same importance to each. Our conception of time is strongly affected by culture because time is an idea rather than an object. How we think of time is interwoven with how we plan, strategize, and coordinate our activities with others. It is an important dimension of how we organize experience and activities.

When we create instruments to measure time, we shape our experience of it. We can differentiate between duration and succession and make fine distinctions within the compass of astronomical time, the time taken for the earth to revolve around the sun. We can think of time as fixed in this way by the motion of the earth, or we can think of time as experienced subjectively; on a jet aircraft, the position of the plane is sometimes shown on a map of the earth. We appear to be crawling very, very slowly toward our destination.

The experience of time means that we can consider a past event now (out of sequence as it were), or envision a future event. In this way past, present, and future are all compressed. We can consider what competitive move to make today based on past experience and with expectations of the future. This is an interpretative use of time.

Time has meaning not just to individuals but to whole groups or cultures. Emile Durkheim, the French sociologist, saw it as a social construct enabling members of a culture to coordinate their activities.[2] This has important implications in a business context. The time agreed for a meeting may be approximate or precise. The time allocated to complete a task may be vitally important or merely a guide. There may be an expectation of mutual accommodation as to the exact time when a machine and its microprocessor are ready to be assembled, or there may be a penalty clause of thousands of dollars a day imposed by one party upon another. Intervals between inspections may be indicators of a manager's level of responsibility. Is he or she left for three months or three years to get on with the job? Organizations may look ahead a long way, or get obsessed by the monthly reporting period.

Orientations to Past, Present, and Future

Saint Augustine pointed out in his *Confessions* that time as a subjective phenomenon can vary considerably from time in abstract conception. In its abstract form we cannot know the future because it is not yet here, and the past is also unknowable. We may have memories, partial and selective, but the past has gone. The only thing that exists is the present, which is our sole access to past or future. Augustine wrote: "The present has, therefore, three dimensions . . . the present of past things, the present of present things and the present of future things."

The idea that at any given moment the present is the only real thing, with the past and future ceasing to be or yet to come, must be qualified by the fact that we think *about* past and future in the present. However imperfect our ideas about past or future, they influence our thinking powerfully. These subjective times are ever-present in our judgment and our decision-making. Although our lives may be consciously oriented to the future success of the enterprise, past experiences have deeply affected our perceptions of that future, as does our present mood. There is a potentially productive tension between the three, along with the ever-pressing question as to whether the future can benefit from past and present experiences (although companies, it is often remarked, have no memory). All three time zones unite in our actions. It is as true to say that our expectations of the future determine our present, as to say our present action determines the future; as true to say that our present experience determines our view of the past, as to say that the past has made us what we are today. This is not simply juggling terms but describing how we think. We can make ourselves miserable in the present if a long expected payment is delayed to the future. We can discover in the present a fact that makes what we did in the past far more justifiable. In fact, an important part of creativity is to assemble past and present activities, plus conjectures about the future, in new combinations.

Different individuals and different cultures may be more or less attracted to past, present, or future orientations. Some live entirely in the present, or try to. "History is bunk," as Henry Ford put it, and inquiry into things past is best forgotten. Some dream of a world that never was and seek to create it from their own imaginings and yearnings, or they may seek the return of a golden age, a Napoleonic legend reborn, a new frontier similar in its challenges to the Wild West. They believe the future is coming to them, as a destiny, or that they alone must define it. Others live in a nostalgic past to which everything attempted in the present must appeal.

Sequentially and Synchronically Organized Activities

We have seen that there are at least two images that can be extracted from the concept of time. Time can be legitimately conceived of as a line of sequential events passing us at regular intervals. It can also be conceived of as cyclical and repetitive, compressing past, present, and future by what these have in common: seasons and rhythms. At one extreme, then, is the person who conceives of time as a dotted line with regular spacing. Events are organized by the number of intervals before or after their occurrence. Everything has its time and place as far as the sequential thinker is concerned. Any change or turbulence in this sequence will make the sequential person more uncertain. Try jumping into a line in Britain. You will find that orderly sequence has very stern defenders. Everyone must wait his or her turn; first come, first served. It is part of "good form." In London the Dutch author once saw a long line of people waiting for a bus when it started pouring with rain. They all stood stolidly getting soaked, even though cover was close by, lest they lose their sequential order. They preferred to do things right rather than do the right thing. In the Netherlands you could be the Queen, but if you are in a butcher's shop with number 46 and you step up for service when number 12 is called, you are still in deep trouble. Nor does it matter if you have an emergency; order is order.

Going from A to B in a straight line with minimal effort and maximum effect is known as efficiency. It has a major influence on the conduct of business in northwest Europe and North America. The flaw in this thinking is that "straight lines" may not always be the best way of doing something; it is blind to the effectiveness of shared activities and cross-connections.

In a butcher's shop in Italy the Dutch author once saw the butcher unwrap salami at the request of one customer and then shout: "Who else for salami?" The sequential idea is not entirely absent. People still pay in turn when they are finished, but if a customer has all she wants, she might as well pay and leave earlier than someone wanting additional cuts. The method serves more people in less time.

At a butcher's shop in Amsterdam or London, the butcher calls a number, unwraps, cuts, and rewraps each item the customer wants, and then calls the next number. Once one of us ventured the suggestion: "While you have the salami out, cut a pound for me too." Customers and staff went into shock. The system may be inefficient, but they were not about to let some wise guy change it.

The synchronic method, however, requires that people track various activities in parallel, rather like a juggler with six balls in the air with each being caught and thrown in rhythm. It is not easy for cultures that are not used to it. Edward T. Hall, the American anthropologist,[3] described what we call synchronic as *polychronic*, putting emphasis on the number of activities run in parallel. There is a final, established goal, but numerous and possibly interchangeable stepping-stones to reach it. A person can "skip between stones" on the way to the final target.

In contrast, the sequential person has a "crucial path" worked out in advance with times for the completion of each stage. They hate to be thrown off this schedule or agenda by unanticipated events. In *The Silent Language*

Hall revealed that Japanese negotiators would make their major bids for a concession *after* their American partners were confirmed on their return flights from Tokyo. Rather than risk their schedules, Americans would often concede to the Japanese demands.

Synchronic or polychronic styles are extraordinary for those unused to them. The Dutch author once purchased an airline ticket from a woman at a ticket counter in Argentina who, while making out the ticket (correctly), was talking on the telephone to a friend and admiring her coworker's baby. People who do more than one thing at a time can, without meaning to, insult those who are used to doing only one thing.

Likewise, people who do only one thing at a time can, without meaning to, insult those who are used to doing several things. A South Korean manager explained his shock and disappointment upon returning to the Netherlands to see his boss:

> "He was on the phone when I entered his office, and as I came in he raised his left hand slightly at me. Then he rudely continued his conversation as if I were not even in the room with him. Only after he had finished his conversation five minutes later did he get up and greet me with an enthusiastic, but insincere, 'Kim, happy to see you.' I just could not believe it."

To a synchronic person, not being greeted spontaneously and immediately, even while still talking on the telephone, is a slight. The whole notion of "sequencing" your emotions and postponing them until other matters are out of the way suggests insincerity. You show how you value people by "giving them time" even if they show up unexpectedly.

Sequential people tend to schedule very tightly, with thin divisions between time slots. It is rude to be even a few minutes late because the whole day's schedule of events is affected. "I'm running late . . ." the scheduler will complain, as if he were himself a train or airline. Time is viewed as a commodity to be used up, and lateness deprives the other of precious minutes in a world where "time is money."

Synchronic cultures are less insistent upon punctuality, defined as a person arriving at the agreed moment of passing time increments. It is not that the passage of time is unimportant, but that several other cultural values vie with punctuality. It is often necessary to "give time" to people with whom you have a particular relation (see the discussion of universalism versus particularism in Chapter 4). It may be required that you show affective pleasure on meeting a friend or relation unexpectedly (see the discussion of the affective versus the neutral approach in Chapter 6). Your schedule is not an excuse for passing them by. Your mother, fiancée, or friend could be seriously offended. Raymond Carroll, the French anthropologist, tells of an American girl who left a note for her French lover.[4] Could he let her know if he wanted to see her this evening, as if not she would like to make other plans? The Frenchman was offended. Her schedule should not get in the way of their spontaneously affective and particular relationship. People prominent in a hierarchy must also be "given time" if encountered (see status by achievement versus status by ascription in Chapter 8). For all such reasons, meeting times may be approximate in synchronic cultures. The range is from 15 minutes in Latin Europe to part or all of a day in the Middle East and Africa. Given the fact that most of those with appointments to meet are running other activities in parallel, any waiting involved is not onerous and late arrival may often even be a convenience, allowing some time for unplanned activities.

Even the preparation of food is affected by time orientations. In sequential, punctual cultures, exactly the right quantity of food will usually be prepared, and in such a way that it might spoil or get cold if the guests are not on time. In synchronic cultures, there is usually more than enough food in case more guests drop by unexpectedly, and it is either not the kind that spoils or else is cooked as wanted.

Measuring Cultural Differences in Relation to Time

The methodology used to measure approaches to time in this book comes from Tom Cottle, who created the "Circles Test."[5] The question asked was as follows:

> Think of the past, present, and future as being in the shape of circles. Please draw three circles on the space available, representing past, present, and future. Arrange these circles in any way you want that best shows how you feel about the relationship of the past, present, and future. You may use different size circles. When you have finished, label each circle to show which one is the past, which one the present, and which one the future.

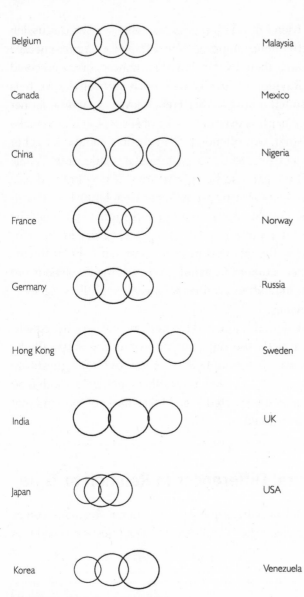

FIGURE 9.1. Past, Present, and Future

Cottle ended up with four possible configurations. First, he found absence of zone relatedness. Figure 9.1 shows that this last approach is characteristic of the Belgians, who see a smaller overlap. In this they are not dissimilar to the British, who have a rather stronger link with the past but see it as relatively unimportant, whereas the Belgians view all three aspects of time as equally important. Both are quite different from the Japanese, for whom all three aspects overlap considerably; they share this view with the Malaysians. The Venezuelans and Russians seem to have quite some focus on the past and don't feel any relationship between past, present and future. What drawing the figure in two dimensions does not reveal is that half of our Japanese respondents see the three circles as concentric and stacked on top of one another.

The above interpretations and inferences derived from these circles diagrams is facilitated by taking in to account other discriminating questions from our surveys and the other aspects of the time dimension as discussed below.

Time Horizon

The circles test measured how different cultures assign different meanings to past, present, and future. We have used another test developed by Cottle to see whether people share a short-term or a long-term time horizon.[6] The Duration Inventory inquires into how people perceive the boundaries separating time zones as well as the extension of these zones. We have paraphrased the Inventory in order to make it shorter, since we are concerned with only one of the 58 items in the questionnaire.

The question is as follows:

Consider the relative significance of the past, present, and future. You will be asked to indicate your relative time horizons for the past, present, and future by giving a number:

> 7 = years
>
> 6 = months
>
> 5 = weeks
>
> 4 = days
>
> 3 = hours
>
> 2 = minutes
>
> 1 = seconds

My past started . . . . . . ago, and ended . . . . . . ago.

My present started . . . . . . ago, and ended . . . . . . from now.

My future started . . . . . . from now, and ended . . . . . . from now.

We have taken the average of each of the six scores and calculated an average score per country, for which very significant differences can be found (see Figure 9.2). The longest horizon is found in Hong Kong and the shortest in the Philippines.

Our time horizon significantly affects how we do business. It is obvious that the relatively long-term vision of the Japanese contrasts with the "quarterly thinking" of the Americans. This was shown in a striking way when the Japanese were trying to buy the operations of Yosemite National Park in California. The first thing they submitted was a 250-year business plan. Imagine the reactions of the Californian authorities: "Gee, that is 1,000 quarterly reports."

The long Swedish horizon is explained by their long winters. There are only a few months in which you have to plan for the whole year.

However, there are some striking differences between long-term past orientation, the perceived extension of the present, and a long-term view of the future. A selection of scores are presented in Figures 9.3 and 9.4.

7 = year   I = seconds

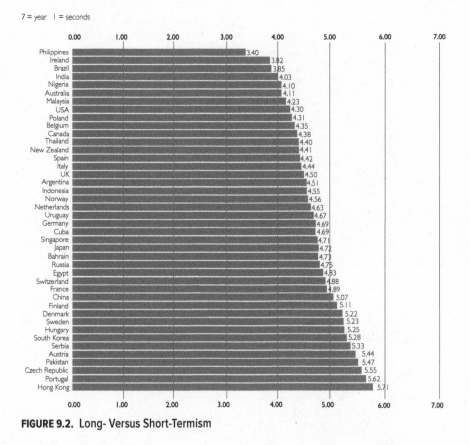

FIGURE 9.2. Long- Versus Short-Termism

The duration questionnaire also allowed us to check the overlap between time zones, which is the degree of synchronicity. Correlations found are high and significant compared to the overlap of the circles discussed earlier.

Time Orientations and Management

Business organizations are structured in accordance with how they conceive of time. Corporations have whole departments given over to planning, to scanning the environment for new trends, to getting production out faster, to shortening the time-to-market, that is, the time interval between a customer demanding a product and that product being designed, manufactured, and delivered. Strategies, goals, and objectives are all future-oriented. Joint

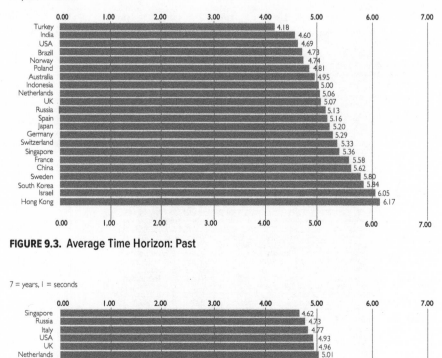

FIGURE 9.3. Average Time Horizon: Past

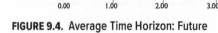

FIGURE 9.4. Average Time Horizon: Future

ventures and partnerships are agreements about how the future should jointly be engaged. "Motivation" is about what we can give to a person now so that he or she will work better in the future. Progress, learning, and development all assume an augmentation of powers over time, as does the habit of paying senior people more for the experience supposedly accumulated over time. When orientations to time differ within corporations spanning different cultures, confusion can occur. Let us return to the sorrows of young Mr. Johnson of MCC. A good lunch makes even the most fundamental intercultural misunderstandings seem like ripples on a lake.

Johnson had asked that the group reconvene at 2:00 p.m. precisely because they had a tight agenda for the afternoon.

At 1:50 p.m. most participants returned to the meeting room. At 2:05 p.m. Johnson started pacing restlessly up and down. Munoz and Gialli were still down the hall making telephone calls. They came in at 2:20 p.m. Johnson said, "Now, gentlemen, can we finally start the meeting." The Singaporean and African representatives looked puzzled. They thought the meeting had already started.

The first point on the agenda was the time intervals determining bonuses and merits. All except the American, Dutch, and other northwest European representatives complained that these were far too frequent. To Johnson and his Dutch and Scandinavian colleagues, the frequency was obviously right. "Rewards must closely follow the behavior they are intended to reinforce, otherwise you lose the connection." In response, manager from Singapore said:

> "Possibly, but this go-for-the-quick-buck philosophy has been losing us customers. They don't like the pressure we put on at the end of the quarter. They want our representatives to serve them, not to have private agendas. We need to keep our customers long-term, not push them into buying so that one salesperson can beat a rival."

The American view of the future is that the *individual* can direct it by personal achievement and inner-directed effort. This is why Johnson, backed by Dutch and Scandinavian managers, is keen to give pay-for-performance at regular intervals. Yet because the individual achiever cannot do very much about the *distant* future—there are simply too many events that could occur—the USA's idea of the future is short-term, something controllable from the present. Hence the accusation of "going for the quick buck" and the great importance given to the next quarterly figures. If the future is to be better, it is by steadily increasing increments of sales and profits. There is no excuse, ever, for not doing better now, since success now causes greater successes in the future.

It is interesting to compare the French respondents with the Americans. In French culture the past looms far larger and is used as a context in which to understand the present. Past, present, and future overlap synchronically so that the past informs the present, and both inform the future. The Dutch author was once visiting the futuristic La Défense in Paris. As my French colleague was delayed, I picked up a brochure at the reception desk. It was about the company's achievements during the 1980s. I read it with interest and, as my colleague was further delayed, I asked the receptionist for a more recent one. She handed me the same brochure I had just read. She said it had been printed only two months ago and was the most recent available. Future opportunities for this company were very apparently connected to the success of the past.

Human Relations and Orientations to Time

Different orientations are also reflected in the quality of human bonds within an organization, and between the corporation and its partners. Any lasting relationship combines past, present, and future with ties of affection and memory. The relationship is its own justification and is enjoyed as a form of durable companionship extending both far back and far forward. Cultures that think synchronically about time are more we-oriented (communitarian) and usually more particularist in valuing people known to be special.

The cultures concerned with sequential time tend to see relationships as more instrumental. The separation between time intervals seems also to separate means from ends, so that higher pay is the means toward still higher performance and my customer's purchase is the means by which I will receive a higher bonus. The relationship is not entered into for its own sake but in order to enhance the income of each party and the profit of the organization. The future looms large because present activity is but a means for realizing it. The important result is in the (near-term) future. Gratification is postponed because it will soon be greater.

Whether relationships unmediated by calculation of future gain are not closer and more amenable to dialogue is of course a very interesting question. Given the sheer complexity of modern business and the mounting volume of information that must be communicated, the durable, synchronic relationship in which the past, present, and future of the partners are bound together in coevolution may be becoming a more effective way to manage. Certainly the idea that synchronic cultures are somehow "primitive" because their schedules are looser is not borne out. Sequential cultures where human resources are seen as a variation on physical plant, equipment, and cash are more likely to have we–them relationships or, to quote Martin Buber, I–it.[7]

Time Orientation and Authority

In nations in which the past looms large and where time orientations overlap, status is more likely to be legitimized by ascription based on durable characteristics such as age, class, gender, ethnicity, and professional qualification. Past qualifications, for example at *les grandes* écoles, explain present eminence and promising futures, all of which are closely connected and synchronized.

On the other hand, when a person's career in Hollywood is "only as good as the last performance," the future is a sequence of episodes of relative success and failure. People will unburden themselves of relationships and dependencies not useful in the next stage of their career, just as the original American immigrants cut off their roots. The authority of the individual will depend upon the latest achievement; those on the up today may be gone tomorrow. Yet the authority of the individual can easily be challenged and assessed. What did they do in the most recent time interval? We find a reflection of this in the project-group organization pioneered by NASA and popular in North America and northwest Europe. Different parts of the organization are identified by and rewarded according to the fortunes in the future of the project being undertaken. Successes grow incrementally; failures are pruned back. Within the group those contributing most to the project are also rewarded accordingly.

Policies of Promotion and Performance Evaluation

Sequential or synchronic cultures, and those concerned more with the past or with the future, may assess and promote differently. In sequential cultures the supervisor asks how the employee has performed over the previous interval. The more that employee can be held responsible for a rise or fall in fortune the better, and the supervisors will be tempted to minimize their own roles, or that of their relationship with the employee, since this does not help the employee to see his or her own recent achievement separated out as an increment of gain or loss. In more synchronic organizations, on the other hand, the employee may be favorably assessed and promoted for the positive relationship established with the supervisors, who see that relationship developing over time and accumulating knowledge and mutuality. The supervisors gladly acknowledge their role in making the subordinate's career, as in the master–apprentice system in Germany.

Managing Change in a Past-Oriented Culture

The English author was recently in Ethiopia with a Dutch manager who was terribly frustrated by his unsuccessful efforts to organize a Management of Change seminar with Ethiopian managers. They all kept harking back to a distant and wealthy era in Ethiopian civilization and would not incorporate any developmental principles that were not based in this past. After a discussion with the Ethiopian colleagues, we decided to study some Ethiopian history books, looking at them from the perspective of modern management. What had Ethiopia done right in that period to make its cities and trade so flourishing? The company also had a rich history within Ethiopia, and these records too were studied. The Dutch manager posed the challenge anew. The future was now seen as a way of recreating some of the greatest glories of the past; suddenly, the Management of Change seminar had captured everyone's enthusiastic support.

This is not a remote case applicable only to Ethiopia. All change includes continuity; that is, staying the same in *some* respects so as to preserve your identity. Many cultures decline to change at the behest of Western consultants unless the ways in which they will preserve their identity are made clear to them. Synchronic cultures carry their pasts through the present into the future and will refuse to consider changing unless convinced that their heritage is safe.

A large American telecommunications company introduced a technically superior product on the world market. It planned to focus specifically on increasing sales in Latin America, where it had not been very successful previously. The only serious competitor was a French company that had an inferior product, but whose after-sales support was reputedly superior.

The Americans went to great pains to prepare their first presentation in Mexico. "Judgment day" would begin with a video presentation of the company and its growth potential in the medium-long term. After this the vice president of the group would personally give a presentation to the Mexican minister of communications. Also meticulously planned was the two-hour lunch. Knowing Mexican culture, they believed this was where the battle would be fought. The afternoon session was reserved for questions and answers. The company jet would then be ready to leave Mexico City in the last departure slot. It was tight, efficient, and appreciated, right?

Wrong; the Mexican team threw off the schedule right away by arriving one hour late. Then, just as the Americans were introducing the agenda for the day, the minister was called out of the room for an urgent phone call.

He returned a while later to find that the meeting had gone on without him. The Mexicans were upset that the presentation had proceeded, that the after-sales service contract was separate from the sales contract, and that the presentation focused only on the first two years after installation rather than the longer-term future together.

The French, on the other hand, prepared a loosely structured agenda. They determined some of the main goals to be attained by the end of the two-week visit. The timing, the where, and the how were dependent on factors beyond their control, so they left them open. A long presentation on the historical background of the French state-owned company was prepared for the minister and his team. It had done business with Mexico's telephone system as early as 1930 and wanted to reestablish a historic partnership. As far as the French were concerned, the after-sales service, which extended indefinitely, was part of the contract. It was the French who received the order for a product known in the industry to be technologically less sophisticated.

What had gone wrong for the Americans? The main mistake was creating a tight, sequential agenda that was almost inevitably thrown off by Mexican officials who had deliberately built slack into their procedures and pursued agendas that were multiple and (to the Americans) distracting. The belief that the technologically superior product *should* win the contract is part of the original cultural bias in which each episode within a sequence is separated out. The Mexicans were interested in the product only as part of an ongoing relationship, an issue that the synchronic French were also careful to stress. Similarly the Americans separated the after-sales service contract from the rest, presumably because it occurred at a later period. French and Mexican culture see these time intervals as joined.

The French emphasis on the historic renewal of French–Mexican bonds was also effective with a culture that identifies with Spain and has deep European roots. American sequencing strikes synchronic cultures as aggressive, impatient, and seeking to use customers as stepping-stones to personal advantage. If the relationship is genuinely to last, what is the hurry? Because the Mexicans did not agree that technological perfection was the key issue, they did not want to be on the receiving end of a detailed presentation timed to end just before the American departure. They wanted to experience a relationship they could partly control. In synchronic time, the demeanor of the American corporation during the presentation presaged its conduct in the future, and the Mexicans did not like it.

However, the biggest advantage the French had was their willingness to spend two weeks dedicated to an agreement and leave it up to their hosts to use those two weeks in a flexible program aimed at synchronizing mutual efforts, rather than trying to agree a schedule in advance. For the French and Mexicans, what was important was that they get to the end, not the particular path or sequence by which that end was reached. Similarly, the details of the equipment were less important to the Mexicans than the responsiveness of the supplier, since they could not know what problems might surface in the future. All they could really ask for, given this concern, was someone willing to alter a schedule to their convenience, and that the French showed they could do.

Moreover, the Americans had a narrower definition of how the negotiation should end. There should come a deadline when the Mexicans would say yes. For the French, and synchronic cultures generally, there is no real "end" because the partnership continues. Instead of the *efficiency* of getting from A to B in the shortest possible time, there is the *effectiveness* of developing closer relationships long-term. The Americans also made one more serious mistake. Anticipating that the Mexicans would be late returning from lunch, as they had been several times, the Americans caucused for half an hour among themselves. This failed to show respect for the buyer. You "give them time" by waiting for them to join you. You do not use that time yourself in a way that makes you unavailable should they enter the room. A "readiness to synchronize" must be shown, as opposed to a mere delay in the sequence.

Planned Sequences or Planned Convergence?

In sequentially organized cultures planning consists largely of forecasts, that is, of extending existing trend lines into the future and seeing this as "more of the same." Strategies consist of choosing desirable goals and then discovering by analysis the most logical and efficient means of attaining them. It is commonly believed that present and future are causally linked so that rewards now produce future achievements, which produce greater achievements, which produce greater rewards. Deadlines are important because they signal the end of one link in a causal chain and the beginning of the next and keep you "on schedule."

In our Culture for Business app we have measured the degree of sequentialism and synchronism by the following question:

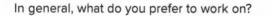

In general, what do you prefer to work on?

One project at a time _____⬤_____ More than one

The scores in Figure 9.5. speak for themselves, where the Bulgarians score the most synchronic (drawing the circle to the right), while the Icelanders prefer single-tasking (drawing the circle to the left).

Planning varies considerably between sequential and synchronic cultures. In sequential planning it is vital to get all the means or stages right and completed on time. "In Britain," an Italian female researcher told me,

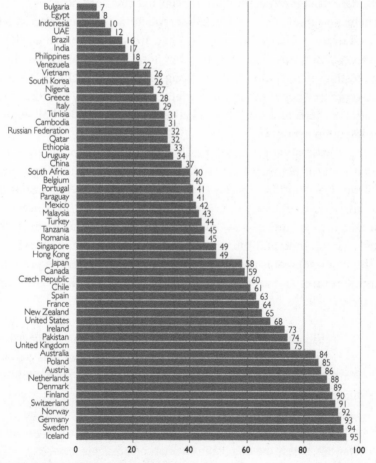

FIGURE 9.5. Sequential Versus Synchronic

"everything needs to be planned from start to finish. When the environment changes, everything needs to be recalculated from the start." For the more synchronic Italians the goals are what is most important, and the more paths you can devise to their realization, the better you fare against unforeseen events that block one path or another.

The 1990 Mundialito (Football World Cup) in Italy was an interesting example of Italian organization. The challenge was to complete the championships by a certain date on which the finals would be staged. To the dismay of the British and other northwest Europeans, the Italians would periodically reorganize the entire program to bring about this result. To the surprise of these other cultures, though, the Italians were able to pull it off. The 1992 Olympic Games in Spain had many similarities with Italian planning. In Atlanta in 1996 it seemed that the sequential Americans had much more trouble in adapting to unexpected circumstances.

There is accumulating evidence that sequential planning processes work less well in turbulent environments. They are too brittle, too easily upset by unforeseen events. The fact that they tend to concentrate on the near future testifies to the vulnerability of long sequences. Synchronic plans tend to converge or "home in" upon predetermined targets, taking into consideration fusions and lateral connections *between* trends that sequential planning often overlooks.

A most interesting example of a shift by a major corporation to a synchronic style of planning was the adoption by the Shell International Petroleum Corporation of *scenario planning*. In this exercise, scenarios for three alternative futures are written as if the writer was a contemporary commentator explaining how business had reached that point. In other words, past, present, and future are synchronized within the imagination, and three developments are traced from the past through the present into diverging futures and are written up as stories or narratives. For example, a scenario for 2003:

> "In retrospect it was inevitable that California would be the launching pad for the electric car. So polluted had the Los Angeles area grown, that the world's strictest emission standards, originating in the 1980s, led to partly electric cars in 1995 and the fully electric car eight years later. Slowly the pall began to lift. The final breakthrough was the '1,000 mile electric' with batteries that were rechargeable overnight. Was this, at last, the end of the internal combustion engine?"[8]

In this type of planning we see sequential and synchronic thinking combined. It proves possible to reestablish forecasts within the scenarios, so that each "synchronic scene" has a different sequence of events.

Once again we find that differences in cultural orientation are not truly alternatives but are capable of being used in conjunction. The wise cross-cultural manager perceives *all* the ways preferred by different cultures. In scenario planning, sequencing and synchronizing work together.

Reconciling the Sequential and the Synchronic

It is frequently suggested that synchronic people are difficult to do business with because they tend to ignore deadlines and are imprecise in appointments. Take the following example.

> Jan Kuipers, a Dutch manager of a wholesale distributor of Italian *haute couture*, was getting very worried about late delivery times to his Dutch clients. The short Dutch summer did not allow delivery of high-priced goods a week late, which was the average delay from the Italian group. Kuipers had tried many ways of solving the problem but with no result. He tried to order early, but the Italians were not impressed. He tried to have them sign a contract so that they would take back the clothes unconditionally. Kuipers was now fighting the Italian transport firm because the fashion partner denied any responsibility. What would you advise him to do to solve the late delivery problem?

The Italian designers in Milan were giving a signal by consistently delivering late. It meant that they had no respect for the relationship. Italians are able to deliver on time, but they prefer to follow the subjective time of the relationship than the objective time of the clock. While the Dutch, like Germans and Americans, would follow the clock, Italians are very much concerned about delivering in time for you. Jan Kuipers went to Milan and befriended the head of logistics. He discovered that in the Italians' view the contract intended to ensure on-time delivery was a reason for delivering even later. The problem never recurred.

We have learned from the Japanese that the best way to speed up the sequence is to synchronize it "just in time."

Test Yourself

Consider the following problem:

> Some managers are arguing about the best ways of improving cycle time and getting products to market when they are needed.
>
> There were four possible views:
>
> 1. It is crucial to speed up operations and shorten time to market. Time is money. Enemies of tighter schedules and faster deliveries do too much talking and relating to each other.
> 2. It is crucial to speed up operations and shorten time to market. The faster jobs are done the sooner you can "pass the baton" to colleagues/customers in the relay race.
> 3. Just-in-time synchronization of processes and with customers is the key to shorter cycle times. The more processes overlap and run simultaneously the more time is saved.
> 4. Just-in-time synchronization of processes and with customers is the key to shorter cycle times. Doing things faster results in exhaustion and rushed work.
>
> Indicate with "1" the approach you believe would be favored by your closest colleagues at work, and with "2" the approach you believe would be his or her second choice.

Answers 1 and 4 show approval of respectively high-speed sequences and just-in-time synchronicity, but reject the opposite orientation. Answer 2 approves of high-speed sequences and connects it to synchronic processes. Answer 3 approves of just-in-time synchronicity connected to high-speed sequences.

The following tables highlight differences between past, present, and future orientation and between sequential and synchronic orientation and give some tips for achieving reconciliation between the views.

Recognizing the Differences

PAST	PRESENT	FUTURE
• Talk about history, origin of family, business, and nation.	• Activities and enjoyments of the moment are most important.	• Much talk of prospects, potentials, aspirations, future achievements.
• Motivated to recreate a golden age.	• Plans are not objected to, but rarely executed.	• Planning and strategizing done enthusiastically
• Show respect for ancestors, predecessors, and older people.	• Show intense interest in present relationships, the "here and now."	• Show great interest in the youthful and in future potentials.
• Everything is viewed in the context of tradition or history.	• Everything is viewed in terms of its contemporary impact and style.	• Present and past are used, even exploited, for future advantage.

Tips for Reconciliation Doing Business With

PRESENT AND FUTURE-ORIENTED INDIVIDUALS DOING BUSINESS WITH PAST AND PRESENT-ORIENTED PEOPLE	PAST AND PRESENT-ORIENTED INDIVIDUALS DOING BUSINESS WITH FUTURE-ORIENTED PEOPLE
• Emphasize the history, tradition, and rich cultural heritage of those you deal with as evidence of their great potential.	• Emphasize the freedom, opportunity, and limitless scope for that company and its people in the future.
• Discover whether internal relationships will sanction the kind of changes you seek to encourage.	• Discover what core competence or continuity the company intends to carry with it into the envisaged future.
• Agree to future meetings in principle but do not fix deadlines for completion.	• Agree to specific deadlines and do not expect work to be complete unless you have set such deadlines.
• Do your homework on the history, traditions, and past glories of the company; consider what reenactments you might propose.	• Do your homework on the future, the prospects, and the technological potentials of the company; consider mounting a sizeable challenge.

Recognizing the Differences

SEQUENTIAL ORIENTATION	SYNCHRONIC ORIENTATION
• Only engage in one activity at a time.	• Engage in more than one activity at a time.
• Time is tangible and measurable.	
• Keep appointments strictly; schedule in advance and do not run late.	• Appointments are approximate and subject to "giving time" to significant others.
• Relationships are generally subordinate to schedule.	• Schedules are generally subordinate to relationships.
• Strong preference for following initial plans.	• Strong preference for following where relationships lead.

Differences in Managing and Being Managed

SEQUENTIALLY ORIENTED PEOPLE	SYNCHRONICALLY ORIENTED PEOPLE
• Employees feel rewarded and fulfilled by achieving planned future goals as in management by objectives.	• Employees feel rewarded and fulfilled by achieving improved relationships with supervisors/customers.
• Employees' most recent performance is the major issue, along with whether their commitments for the future can be relied upon.	• Employees' whole history with the company and future potential is the context in which their current performance is viewed.
• Plan the career of an employee jointly with him or her, stressing landmarks to be reached by certain times.	• Discuss with the employee his or her final aspirations in the context of the company; in what ways can these be realized?
• The corporate ideal is the straight line and the most direct, efficient, and rapid route to your objectives.	• The corporate ideal is the interacting circle in which past experience, present opportunities, and future possibilities interact.

10

How We Relate to Nature

Fons Trompenaars and Charles Hampden-Turner

THE LAST dimension of culture we shall consider in this book concerns the role people assign to their natural environment. This, like the other dimensions, is at the center of human existence. Man has from the beginning been besieged by natural elements: wind, floods, fire, cold, earthquakes, famine, pests, and predators. Survival itself has meant acting *against* and *with* the environment in ways to render it both less threatening and more sustaining. Constant action was originally an inescapable necessity.

Man's economic development can be viewed as a gradual strengthening of his devices to keep nature at bay. In the course of human existence there has been a shift from a preponderant fear that nature would overwhelm human existence to the opposite fear that human existence may overwhelm and degrade nature, so that, for example, a genetic storehouse of incredible richness in the Amazon rain forest may be bulldozed to oblivion before we have even discovered it.

Controlling Nature or Letting It Take Its Course

Societies that conduct business have developed two major orientations toward nature. They either believe that they can and should *control* nature by imposing their will upon it, as in the ancient biblical injunction "multiply and subdue the earth," or they believe that man is part of nature and must *go along* with its laws, directions, and forces. The first of these orientations we shall describe as *inner-directed*. This kind of culture tends to identify with mechanisms; that is, the organization is conceived of as a machine that obeys the will of its operators. The second, or *outer-directed*, tends to see an organization as itself a product of nature, owing its development to the nutrients in its environment and to a favorable ecological balance.

The American psychologist J. B. Rotter, working in the 1960s, developed a scale designed to measure whether people had an *internal locus of control*, typical of more successful Americans, or an *external locus of control*, typical of relatively less successful Americans, disadvantaged by their circumstances or shaped by the competitive efforts of their rivals.[1] The questions he devised we used in building our cultural databases to assess our respondents relationship with natural events, and the answers suggest that there are some very significant differences here between geographical areas. These questions all take the form of alternatives; leaders and managers were asked to select the statement they believed most reflected reality. The first of these pairs is as follows.

A. It is worthwhile trying to control important natural forces, like the weather.

B. Nature should take its course and we just have to accept it the way it comes and do the best we can.

Figure 10.1 shows the percentage of respondents who chose A, that is, the inner directors. No country produces a totally internalized reaction to this statement; the highest score is only 83 percent, but we see considerable variations between countries and, again, no marked pattern by continent. Only 23 percent of Japanese believe it is worth trying to control the weather, as few as 37 percent of Chinese, only 18 percent of Swedes, but 51 percent of the Polish. The Italian, Swiss, and Danish are above the middle of the range, but by no means among the top scorers. If the alternatives are made to appear more personally related, however, we get a different result. Figure 10.2 shows the percentage of respondents who chose A when asked to choose between the following:

A. What happens to me is my own doing.

B. Sometimes I feel that I do not have enough control over the directions my life is taking.

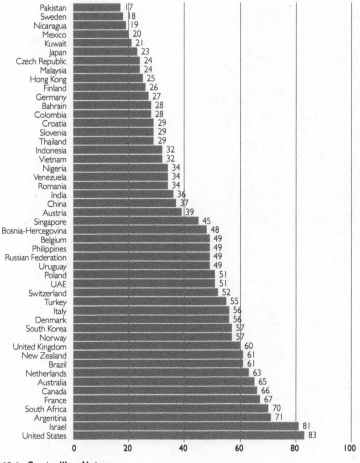

FIGURE 10.1. Controlling Nature

    On this basis a number of countries appear almost completely internalized; in the USA, for instance, 83 percent of managers believe they control their own destinies, as do 67 percent of the French. Most European countries score high, in fact, though not the Russians, on whom 65 years of Communism may have had some effect. Similarly the Japanese now rank much lower than the Chinese, although in Japan as in Singapore managers are far less likely to believe in internal control than they are in North America or Europe.

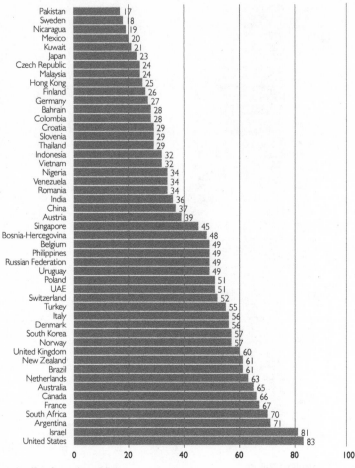

FIGURE 10.2. The Captains of Fate

Control and Success

The extremes of possible relationships between humankind and nature are perhaps best instanced by contrasting the ancient Greeks with twentieth-century Americans. For the Greeks the world was ruled by natural godlike forces: beauty (Aphrodite), truth (Apollo), justice (Athena), passion (Diony-sus). These forces would contend for human allegiance and were often in conflict, leading to tragedy. Virtue was to achieve *harmonia*, or harmony, among the natural forces acting through you. Those who wanted their own will to triumph, like Oedipus or Jason, were frequently confounded in a struggle with their fates. The post–Industrial Revolution society, on the other hand, has made heroes of entrepreneurs, whose struggles to tame nature are not expected to end in tragedy. This is especially the American view, shaped by the experience of discovering a new continent of immense size and small indigenous population and turning a wilderness into a new nation. Success is identified with control over outside circumstances.

However, internal versus external loci of control do not necessarily distinguish the successful from the less successful in non-American cultures. There are ways of adapting to external influences that can prove economically effective. To accept direction from customers, market forces, or new technologies can be more advantageous than opposing these with your own preferences. The "obvious" advantages (to Americans) of being inner-directed may not be obvious at all to managers in Japan or Singapore, and will be at least less obvious in Italy, Sweden, or the Netherlands, for example. Outer-directed need not mean God-directed or fate-directed; it may mean directed by the knowledge revolution or by the looming pollution crisis, or by a joint venture partner. The ideal is to fit yourself advantageously to an external force.

In the original American concept of internal and external sources of control, the implication is that the outer-directed person is offering an excuse for failure rather than a new wisdom. In other nations it is not seen as personal weakness to acknowledge the strength of external forces or the arbitrariness of events.

In outer-directed behavior the reference point lies outside of people. A good example is the history of the Sony Walkman, already described in Chapter 1. In an interview, Akio Morita of Sony explained that he conceived of the notion of the Walkman while he was searching for a way to enjoy music without disturbing others. This is in sharp contrast to the normal motivation for using a Walkman in northwest Europe and North America, where most users do not want to be disturbed by other people. In our continuing research in marketing (see, for example, *Marketing Across Cultures*)[2] we find this same construct for consumers wanting an iPod and now iPad and the role of headphones for MP3 players and streaming sounds.

The preponderant inner-directedness of North America and parts of northwest Europe may help to explain why we have to go out of our way to teach "customer orientation" and "scanning the business environment." To outer-directed cultures, like Japan and Singapore, this comes so naturally that they do not need to teach it. It is also noteworthy that outer-directedness does *not* preclude rivalry or competition but rather can help to give it form and style. To be directed by a customer or by the force of an opponent, as in Indo (Japanese wrestling) and judo, is not to lack combativeness but to use another's powers in a more effective combination or harmony (*wa*). The word *do* in *judo*, *Indo*, *kendo*, and *Bushido* means "way of." You follow the way of the sword (kendo) or the warrior (Bushido), their practices and disciplines, until they become part of your nature. You may, as a result, be a more formidable competitor, not less. Like a surfer you respond to the waves and keep your balance where others lose theirs.

In contrast to many Eastern sports, in which the opponent's force is harnessed to your own, Western sports like American football or baseball idealize the zero-sum game, the clash of opposites, the rivalry of inner-directed wills, one-on-one—"If you can't beat 'em, join 'em." Even negotiations are "won" or "lost" depending on how much of what you originally wanted was gained, while compromise reduces the moral stature of all concerned.

Our Western contention that Asians "steal our ideas" is also shaped by our proprietary notions about what comes from *inside* of us and is therefore "ours." Asians may regard Western technologies as part of the environment, like fruit on a tree, which wise people pick and incorporate into themselves. Moreover concepts such as *kaizen*, refinement, have very high cultural prestige. To take something from the external environment and then refine or improve it is not "copying" but celebrating that environment, letting the finest forces shape your character. Even when the forces are violent and humiliating, such as devastation, surrender, and occupation by Americans, the Japanese prove masters at adapting to external circumstances and emerging on top. As they like to say, "a crisis is an opportunity."

Inner-Directed Mechanism: The Renaissance Ideal

The Western world is heavily influenced by Copernican and Newtonian views of the universe as a vast perpetual motion machine that God wound up and left for his faithful to discover. To discover the laws of this universe, laws of time and motion, was to worship its Creator. To understand the laws of the mechanism, it was necessary to predict and control the operation of nature's machinery, that is, to internalize natural law and then show that nature obeyed you. Against this background, to be inner-directed has become proof of scientific veracity. We hypothesize and deduce, and the principle is correct if the predicted result follows. Enlightened man is the master mechanic, the driver with his hand on the throttle.

While the early physicists left the description of man to religious authorities, this division of labor broke down in the seventeenth and eighteenth centuries. Man, too, became a machine, using reason to drive a somewhat reluctant body to obey rational dictates. According to Jacques Ellul, the earlier belief in magic was now replaced by *technique*, applied not simply to external nature but to man's head and body. "Technique," writes Ellul, "is the translation into action of man's concern to master things by means of reason, to account for what is subconscious, make quantitative what is qualitative, make clear and precise the outlines of nature, take hold of chaos, and order it."[3]

After the Renaissance, then, nature became objectified so that manipulation could be more easily demonstrated over passive entities. Quantification and measurement became central to science, including social science.

The Modern View of Nature: The Cybernetic Cosmology

While for the Greeks nature was a living organism and for the Renaissance it was a machine potentially controllable by human reason, in modern system dynamics or cybernetics both these views are transcended into a more inclusive concept of a living system that both nurtures the individual and can be developed by individuals dependent upon that system.[4] There is a shift from trying to seize control *over* nature to identifying with its ecological self-regulation and natural balance. The manager *intervenes* but is not the *cause* of what occurs; the systems of organizations and markets have their own momentum that we can influence but not drive. As the world fills up with economic actors and forces, we are simultaneously more influenced by external forces, yet more determined to create our own space among these. Figure 10.3 summarizes these changing views.

FIGURE 10.3. Changing View of Nature

ERA	KIND OF NATURE	PRODUCTIVE FUNCTIONS	PHILOSOPHIES	FOCUS OF CONTROL
Primitive	Organic nature	Arts: to form	Natural; natural world	External control
Renaissance	Mechanism nature	Techniques: to transform	Mechanical; technical world	Internal control
Modern	Cybernetic nature	Applied sciences: to develop	Scientific; social world	Reconciliation of internal and external control

How Important Is a Culture's Orientation to Nature?

Orientations to nature have much to do with how we conduct our day-to-day lives and manage businesses. Cultures may seek to master nature, accept and be subjugated by it, or live in the most effective harmony with it. Nature is both controllable by man and liable to show sudden reversals of relative strength, becoming man's master, not slave. Neither situation is very stable nor very desirable, since a subjugated nature may fail to sustain man on earth.

A relationship closely analogous to man and nature is that of organization and markets. A product may succeed not simply because we will it to, or because the special features designed into it delight customers. It may succeed for reasons *other than those that come from inside of us*, reasons that have to do with the way *other* people in the environment think rather than we ourselves. Are we then willing to take direction from customers, where this is not our original direction? Are we willing to change our minds when it becomes clear that customers' preferences are different from our own?

One powerful example of outer-directedness is the theory of evolution. According to evolutionary biologists, it is the environment that decides which creatures fit and which do not, so by extension markets decide, not managers. The business world does not see the survival of the fittest, driven by mechanisms determined to fight each other, but the survival of those best able to form a nurturing relationship with external niches and conditions. It may be for this reason that some outer-directed cultures are among the world's better economic performers. While the belief that the environment is all-powerful in deciding the future can lead to fatalism or resignation, the belief that we are all responsible can lead to scapegoating, blaming the victim, and a lack of compassion for those who have suffered misfortune.

An important aspect of inner-directedness is the notion of business *strategy*, which is a plan designed in advance to wrest competitive advantage from other corporations. The metaphor comes from the military sphere, and it is clear that either the organization prevails in its strategic intention or it is beaten by its environment. The seeming lack of interest in strategy per se by the Japanese and similar outer-directed cultures has been noted, and the whole "militaristic" concept of strategy criticized, by Henry Mintzberg. Mintzberg points out that, in any organization, those interfacing with customers have *already devised strategies for coping with day-to-day problems*.[5] The job of top management, therefore, is to take these emergent strategies and give recognition, status, and formal sanction to those that have proved most valuable. This is an outer-directed process for adopting strategies *already initiated* at the organization's grassroots and is a further example of the need to let the environment shape *you*.

Managing Between Different Orientations to Nature

Paradoxically, Western and inner-directed managers trying to impose uniform procedures and methods on foreign and outer-directed cultures often "succeed" better than they expect, just because at least some of those cultures are accustomed to being heavily influenced from external sources and taking their cue from the environment. But it is a mistake to assume that *accepting* guidance from outside is the same as internalizing it or using it successfully. Some outer-directed cultures do not like to debate or confront, but this does not mean that the directive is appropriate to their culture. The source of authority is seen as "natural" and will quickly be dissipated if the manager behaves in "unnatural" ways—for example, by imposing his or her will for its own sake rather than because of a natural endowment of wisdom to sustain and nurture the organism. Other-directed cultures often regard nature as *benign*. If, therefore, you behave in ways interpreted as hostile, your "natural powers" will be forfeit.

At a Gabon subsidiary of a French oil company, the Dutch author discovered that a change management program initiated by headquarters was failing miserably. The French managers, when interviewed, could not really explain what was going on. The Gabonese seemed to agree completely with the drafted mission statement. They even accepted the operational steps that had been discussed and planned at length. But when the plan had to be put into action, nothing happened. The employees behaved precisely as before. After careful inquiry it turned out that the Gabonese did indeed endorse the change but did not believe that it was for them as individuals to direct its implementation. The signal had to come from their French superiors who alone had the natural authority to command action. When no command came, no action was taken. The idea that self-directed change would emerge from reasoned principles was *not* culturally shared.

It was the same with the pay-for-performance program initiated by MCC. Such a program assumes that each employee can behave in ways that increase the sales of computers, that he or she can personally induce greater effort and hence greater sales. This assumption was questioned by an Asian manager.

Mr. Djawa from Indonesia raised two objections to Mr. Johnson:

"Pay-for-performance does not work in our sales territories. It leads to customers being overloaded with products they never wanted and do not need. Furthermore, when things are not going well for our people, it is a mistake to hurry them or blame them. There are good times and bad times. Paying them for performance does not change inevitable trends."

This did not impress Johnson and his Western colleagues. "We want to develop something at HQ that will motivate everyone. Are you saying that linking reward to success has no influence at all? Surely you must agree there is some connection." Mr. Djawa said:

"It certainly has effects, but these tend to be swamped by economic booms and busts. Moreover the customer needs to be assisted and protected from these fluctuations. It is not wise to push customers into buying more than they should. We need to ride out bad times together, and then take joint advantage of good times."

Many of Mr. Djawa's Eastern and Latin colleagues concurred. Mr. Johnson was exasperated. "Why don't some of you suggest a method that *does* work?"

Here the Indonesians, seeing themselves as relatively more controlled by external forces, seek to join with customers and each other to "ride out the inevitable waves." They can be motivated, but in directions consistent with their culture, and that is to make skillful adjustments to the ups and downs that they experience as "natural" and not caused by their own greater or lesser determination to prosper. They seem to regard the turbulence of their environment as a sufficient challenge to the members of their organization, without needing to attribute blame to those caught in a downturn or reward those caught in an upturn. To do either would sap group morale by adding to the arbitrariness of events and tempt sales personnel to put their own advantage ahead of the customers'.

In contrast, the mechanistic view of man sees the salesperson cutting through the waves like a ship heading for its own planned destination and not being diverted from its path by poor weather. The test of good engineers or MBAs is to do things right the first time and have their judgment vindicated by results. The good company promises "to put you in the driver's seat." Ideal mechanisms obey the will of their operators and enable them to overcome natural obstacles to achieve personal goals.

Is Modern Management a Battle Between Private Agendas?

One problem with the inner-directed person seeking mastery over nature is that *everyone else* may come to stand for "nature." We all want power, but can achieve it only if others are viewed as means to our ends. By definition we cannot *all* direct the environment from within ourselves, since we ourselves constitute great parts of that environment. The invitation to others to "participate" is largely vitiated if, in fact, you are trying to steer them toward a conclusion you arrived at before the discussion began. Yet the relentlessly inner-directed manager has no other option. He or she is obliged to define social relationships objectively, as if moving pieces on a chess board. This is what Chris Argyris calls "Model I behavior," behavior designed to motivate the employee into doing what the manager formulated earlier.[6] Mr. Johnson, too, uses motivation in this sense, a method of persuading salespeople to sell more in any or all circumstances and regardless of what they say or want, or what their cultures believe in.

The Hay method of evaluation of personnel is similarly inner-directed in identifying managers with their function. In this system it is not the employee who is being evaluated, but the efficiency with which he or she completes a task assumed to be directed from within the supervisor, within the organization. It is this that gives authority its reason and legitimacy. Suppose the company exists to turn natural raw materials into products. It requires these functions to be fulfilled by a division of labor. It hires people who agree to fill these functions. They are directed by a chief executive officer who personifies the organization's inner-directed purpose. People trying to fulfill these functions are then paid according to the complexity and difficulty of the function, how well they have discharged it, and how well they used their own (inner-directed) judgment. This is all logical, neat, and obvious, yet it treats physical and social environments as if they were objects and is not the way large parts of the world economy think. It is also blind to some of the most obvious social facts, that during a conversation both parties may change their minds and transform their joint thought processes into something new and better.

Reconciling Internal and External Control

For some considerable time there has been discussion in the business world about whether one should be led by technology push or market pull when developing new products. In an internally controlled culture people prefer to focus on technological innovation. What this can lead to we have seen at Mercedes-Benz. In the early 1990s this car manufacturer became the victim of its own successful technology push in the 1980s. With the S-class—indubitably the best car at the time—it managed to find a new, supremely exclusive market: a market without customers. In an externally controlled culture people focus mainly on the market. This also has its limitations. The client is not always fully aware of its wishes. Sometimes listening to the client takes so long that a product is redundant as soon as it enters the market. Again, we may observe the power of reconciling the two cultures. The *push* of the technology may determine the choice of the clients to whom one wants to listen. The *pull* of the market may provide direction for the development of the technology.

An additional challenge today is the speed in which markets and technologies are changing. If an organization is pushing technology, you often see that it launches the fully tested product too late. If an organization is drawn by the latest needs of the market, often products are launched too early and lead to complaining clients. As we will discuss in Chapter 19 the solution is found in the *minimum viable product*[7] that is good enough to be launched and open enough for fast learning and thus improvement.

We all make mistakes in life. Some three weeks ago the Dutch author asked his wife if he could borrow her car—a Mitsubishi Space Wagon—to pick up some loudspeakers in town. He had to stop for a pedestrian crossing. Just after coming to a stop he heard a noise indicating that he had been hit by a car from behind. He stepped out and saw that the length of our impressive Japanese car had diminished by at least 20 percent. Psychologically it felt as though the whole back of the car had disappeared in the crash. Pulling away from his car was a Volvo 200 series, better known as "the tank." Not a scratch could be seen on this vehicle even when examined closely. The driver emerged with one hand covering a severe cut on his head. He apologized almost routinely: "There is not much left of your car, sir," he said, "but are you OK?" The Dutch author was fine, because he had hardly felt the collision.

The externally controlled Japanese evidently apply martial arts to safety. Japanese cars are designed to take the energy out of their opponent to their advantage. The Volvo and BMWs of this world seem to operate like an American football player. If I am stronger than you, I'll win and be safe. The end result, however, was that the driver of the Japanese car did not feel the collision while the Volvo driver took it all.

The newest safety designs are built to reconcile flexibility and strength. The similarity with the Dutch poldering system is striking. Dikes are built to stop the water with great strength. If the pressure becomes too great, doors are opened to relieve the pressure. In turn the next diking system takes the second overflow.

And doesn't your organization struggle to achieve a balance between technology push and market pull? Intuitively we know that if we push the technology to its extreme we might end up in the ultimate niche market, best defined as that part of the market with no clients. But what if we just follow what clients' desire? We might not deliver fast enough and be at their mercy. The most effective organizations are those that are better at connecting the push of the technology to the pull of the market. Isn't it curious that the Americans are superior both in marketing techniques and in developing innovative products, yet the Japanese wiped out the US consumer electronics industry? The Japanese seem to be very good at connecting what has been developed elsewhere. They also apply martial arts to essential economic laws.

Figure 10.4 shows that too much inner-directedness can lead to the lack of a market. Conversely an overly developed customer focus risks leaving the organization at the mercy of market forces. Inner- and outer-directedness have to be reconciled.

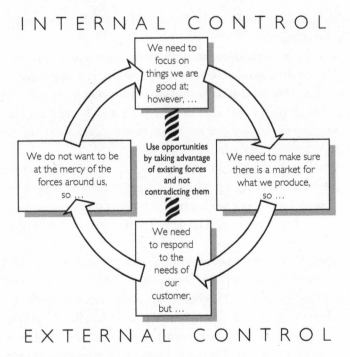

FIGURE 10.4. Reconciling Internal and External Control

Test Yourself

Several senior strategists were discussing whether strategy should be devised at the top of the corporation and "cascaded down" to be implemented locally, or emerge from the grassroots and successful interfaces with customers. The following views were expressed:

1. No one dealing with customers is without a strategy of sorts. Our task is to find out which of these strategies work, which don't, and why. Devising our own strategy in the abstract and imposing it downwards only spreads confusion.

2. No one dealing with customers is without a strategy of sorts. Our task is to find out which of these strategies work and then create a master strategy from proven successful initiatives by commending and combining the best.

3. To be a leader is to be the chief devisor of strategy. Using all the experience, information, and intelligence we can mobilize, we devise an innovative strategy and cascade it down to be vigorously implemented.

4. To be a leader is to be the chief devisor of strategy. Using all the experience, information, and intelligence we can mobilize, we create a broad thrust, leaving it to subordinates to fit these to customer needs.

Indicate with 1 the approach you believe would be favored by your closest colleagues at work, and with 2 the approach you believe would be his or her second choice.

Answer 1 affirms an outer-directed strategy and rejects inner-direction, while answer 3 represents the opposite. Answer 2 affirms a connection between an outer-directed strategy and an inner-directed strategy, while answer 4 affirms the opposite connection.

Summary

Cultures vary in their approaches to the given environment, between belief that it can be controlled by the individual and belief that the individual must respond to external circumstances. We should not, however, make the error of assuming that inner-direction and outer-direction are exclusive options. All cultures necessarily take *some* notice of what is inside or outside. To fail to do so would lead inner-directed cultures into a headlong rush to disaster, while outer-directed cultures would try to please everyone and dissipate their energies by overcompliance.

Inner-directed managers are never happier than when they have won over other people to their own way of thinking. This is the ideal they strive for, but it is one that may be deemed aggressive and uncouth in outer-directed cultures. Leaders in these stress how much they have learned from their mistakes and from others' objections or criticisms. One reason staff suggestions enrich several Asian organizations and participation is so high is because listening rather than declaiming is seen as the more admirable trait. Such cultures do not clash openly. To negate what someone else is saying is to ride roughshod over nature. The alternative is to take the proposal on board and alter its import subsequently if it remains unpopular.

The word "feedback" is an interesting one in Western management jargon. It recognizes the need to periodically correct an ongoing thrust or function. But *rarely is feedback considered as important as the original direction.* Indeed feedback is the means by which the original direction is *maintained.*

To participate fully in an outer-directed culture, inner-directed managers must accept that feedback can alter the whole direction of the organization. They must listen to the customers and aim to fill their need as opposed to win their allegiance.

Major change can come from both outside and inside. Once again we see that culture is about where a circle "starts" or where a manager conceives of change originating. To conceive of the organization as an open system operating within a larger system allows both inner-directed and outer-directed orientations to develop.

The following tables highlight differences between internal and external orientation and give some tips for achieving reconciliation between the two views.

Recognizing the Differences

INTERNAL ORIENTATION	EXTERNAL ORIENTATION
• Often dominating attitude bordering on aggressiveness toward the environment.	• Often flexible attitude, willing to compromise and keep the peace.
• Conflict and resistance mean that you have convictions.	• Harmony and responsiveness, that is, sensibility.
• Focus is on self, function, own group, and own organization.	• Focus is on "other," that is customer, partner, colleague.
• Uncomfortable when environment seems "out of control" or changeable.	• Comfortable with waves, shifts, cycles, if these are "natural."

Tips for Reconciliation

EXTERNALLY ORIENTED INDIVIDUALS DOING BUSINESS WITH INTERNALLY ORIENTED PEOPLE	INTERNALLY ORIENTED INDIVIDUALS DOING BUSINESS WITH EXTERNALLY ORIENTED PEOPLE
• Playing "hardball" is legitimate to test the resilience of an opponent.	• Softness, persistence, politeness, and long, long patience will get rewards.
• It is most important to "win your objective."	• It is most important to "maintain your relationship."
• Win some, lose some.	• Win together, lose apart.

Differences in Managing and Being Managed

INTERNALLY ORIENTED PEOPLE	EXTERNALLY ORIENTED PEOPLE
• Get agreement on and ownership of clear objectives.	• Achieve congruence among various people's goals.
• Make sure that tangible goals are clearly linked to tangible rewards.	• Try to reinforce the current directions and facilitate the work of employees.
• Discuss disagreements and conflicts openly; these show that everyone is determined.	• Give people time and opportunity to quietly work through conflicts; these are distressing.
• Management by objectives works if everyone is genuinely committed to directing themselves toward shared objectives and if these persist.	• Management by environments works if everyone is genuinely committed to adapting themselves to fit external demands as these shift.

11

Cross-Cultural Competence

Assessment and Diagnosis

Fons Trompenaars and Peter Woolliams

I N THIS chapter we introduce a new approach to measuring intercultural competence that overcomes many of the limitations of other methods, including our own earlier frameworks: the Intercultural Awareness Profiler and the Culture for Business app.

The world of business is changing ever more rapidly due to the internalization of business and migration of people from their fatherlands. Yet we still observe that the major instruments and methods used for evaluating and assessing staff and the performance of their business units owe their origins to an Anglo-Saxon philosophy and are still dominated by an Anglo-Saxon or US signature. Competency lists abound, and to date there appears to be a disagreement in the literature over which competencies leaders should possess. These lists overlap competencies, however, they do not converge.[1] In addition, researchers offer different methodologies that are not easily comparable. Finally and most important, much of the available literature related to intercultural competence is prescriptive rather than resulting from research, or is drawn from a US perspective.

One might conjecture that there is a bountiful supply of diagnostic instruments to determine individual or company-based cross-cultural profiles and competence. Not surprisingly, we can all observe how each is promulgated by its originators claiming their own is the best. These varying authors usually claim degrees of "reliability," but this is not the same as them being "valid." And are they seeking to measure what we should be measuring to inform the HR function and corporate strategy to improve business performance in 2020 and beyond?

On critical evaluation one finds that most are not free of cultural bias and are stuck in the time warp of focusing on cultural differences—and not how to assess (and thereby develop) the competence to deal with cultural differences. We had developed our own series of instruments over the last 20 years that have sought to assess different aspects of cultural competence. These have ranged from assessing fundamental awareness, cultural orientation, the propensity to reconcile differences, through to the competence to realize the business benefits of cultural differences—and in the context of both country and corporate cultural frameworks. As individual instruments they have served their purpose well. However, we have recognized limitations in earlier versions of some of our own cross-cultural frameworks and have been searching for solutions that overcome common problems faced by all consultants and researchers in the quest for intercultural competence.

Even without the complexity of the cultural context, confusion begins over the use of the term "competence." It is applied variously to denote the capacity in an individual but also as an element of a job role. The term "competence" has its origins in the research of the McBer Consultancy in the late 1970s in the USA as part of the initiative by the American Management Association to identify the characteristics that distinguish superior from average managerial performance.[2] The work was encapsulated in the seminal book *The Competent Manager*.[3] This has spawned a mass of literature and initiatives in organizational attempts to identify and construct the "competent" manager.

However, the term and its related concepts have become problematic as they have been taken and adapted to different environments. Boyatzis defined the term as "an underlying characteristic of a person."[4] It could be a motive, trait, skill, aspect of one's self-image or social role, or a body of knowledge that he or she uses. However, as Woodruffe[5] has pointed out, there is a mass of literature attempting to define the terms *motive, trait, skill*, and so on. This again opens the term to a multitude of interpretations. Woodruffe, for example, defines *competency* as "a set of behaviour patterns that the incumbent needs to bring to a position in order to perform its tasks and functions with competence."[6] Others have used the terms *skill* and *competence* interchangeably: "Perhaps the most fundamental implication of moving to a skill- or competency-based approach to management concerns the area of work design."[7] For Rhinesmith: "If mindsets and personal characteristics are the 'being' side of global management, then competences are the 'doing' side."[8] As a basis for management training needs analysis or organizational review and development, most authors fail to clarify which of these meanings they are ascribing to "competence."

Additionally, we have the challenge of how to design an instrument that covers the spectrum of cultural effects. When we begin to incorporate non-Western types of logic, such as yin-yang or Taoism, we soon realize that we have all been restrictive in basing any profiling on bimodal dimensions. For example, we were trying to place respondents along a scale with "individualism" at one end and "communitarianism" at the other. But in a multicultural environment, a highly individualized leader will agonize over the fact that many subordinates prefer to work with their team. Conversely, the group-oriented leader will fail because of an apparent fault of not recognizing the efforts of individuals. Thus we have a dilemma between the seemingly opposing orientations of individualism or communitarianism. Similarly, do we find undue criticisms of staff in a business unit or an excess of support? Someone criticized by authorities feels attacked, where support in absent, or indulged where criticism is withheld. Any instrument that seeks to be free of cultural bias needs to avoid being based on this type of Western Cartesian logic that forces us to say if it is "either . . . or."

With the above in mind, we have recently assembled our ICP (Intercultural Competence Profiler). The ICP is a multifunctional instrument that enables participants to assess their current intercultural competence or that of their organization or business unit. Unlike other competence tools, the ICP does not focus on a single basic area of cultural knowledge or behavior but addresses the complete spectrum from cross-cultural awareness through to the business benefits deriving from effective action in multicultural situations. It has been developed by combining our earlier frameworks based on our extensive research and intellectual property that originally addressed each area separately. Each component has been subject to rigorous research and testing with many PhD projects plus extensive application in many client situations across the world. Recently we have confirmed the reliability of the combined integrated instrument with a sample base that has included MBA students as well as senior managers and business leaders from our client base.

It comprises some 100 questions that are used in different combinations for several constructs to achieve the total profile. Ratings are not simply added and averaged for the different scales. In many cases the sectors are computed from the RMS quadrature* of competing questions to assess their mutual interaction.

The ICP Instrument

The daily life in the intercultural arena of each person involves judgments, decisions, and actions that, however minor in themselves, in the aggregate affect not only their own lives, but the future of our society. Similar decisions in other places affect us as a society and as individuals.

Our ICP is an attempt to describe and measure certain modes of thought, sensitivities, intellectual skills, and explanatory capacities that might *in some measure* contribute to the formation of an intercultural competence.

We distinguish four aspects of intercultural competence (Figure 11.1):

1. Recognition: How competent is a person to recognize cultural differences around him or her?
2. Respect: How respectful is a person about those differences?
3. Reconciliation: How competent is a person to reconcile cultural differences?
4. Realization: How competent is a person to realize the necessary actions to implement the reconciliation of cultural differences?

Recognition

The first competence of *recognizing cultural differences* focuses on the individual's ability to understand his or her condition in the community and the world and improves the ability to make effective judgments.

It includes the study of nations, cultures, and civilizations, including our own society and the societies of other peoples, with a focus on understanding how these are all interconnected and how they change, and on the individual's responsibility in this process. It defines some key elements of what we call a global consciousness—to flesh out some of the things we will need to know and understand if we are to cope with the challenges of an increasingly interdependent world.

---

* For example: a contributing component score might be the root mean square (Question A score × Question B score).

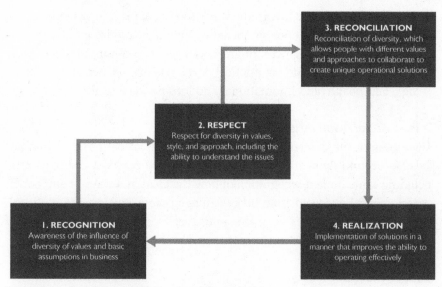

FIGURE 11.1. Four Aspects of Intercultural Competence

Operationally, we assume that it consists *partly* of the modes of thought, skills, and so on. But as conceived here a recognition competence is not a quantum, something you either have or don't have. It is a blend of many things, and any given individual may be rich in certain elements and relatively lacking in others. A very crucial part of intercultural awareness, as Eileen Sheridan found in her Delphi-based research,[9] is *self-awareness*.

In the competence of recognition, very much according to the description of Robert G. Hanvey,[10] we distinguish three main areas:

Worldly Consciousness
The worldly consciousness consists of:

Perspective consciousness. The recognition or awareness on the part of the individual that he or she has a view of the world that is not universally shared, that this view of the world has been and continues to be shaped by influences that often escape conscious detection, and that others have views of the world that are profoundly different from one's own. Perspective consciousness is an intricate part of the self-awareness assuming the road to discovering one-self is through the contrast with others.

"State of the planet" awareness. Awareness of prevailing world conditions and development, including emergent conditions and trends such as population growth, migrations, economic conditions, resources and physical environment, political developments, science and technology, law, health, and international and intranational conflicts.

Cross-Cultural Awareness

Awareness of the diversity of ideas and practices to be found in human societies around the world, of how such ideas and practices compare, and including some limited recognition of how the ideas and ways of one's own society might be viewed from other vantage points. Again, cross-cultural self-awareness is the result of this endeavor to compare oneself against others.

Global Dynamics

Part of intercultural competence is to be able to have a prime awareness that ultimately the world is a product of human interactions. According to Hanvey, it consists of:

Knowledge of global dynamics. Some modest comprehension of key trails and mechanisms of the world system, with emphasis on theories and concepts that may increase intelligent consciousness of global change.

Awareness of human choices. Some awareness of the problems of choice confronting individuals, nations, and the human species as consciousness and knowledge of the global system expands.

The questions we have developed to measure the recognition part of the ICP has many sources such as the ideas developed by Van der Zee and Brinkmann,[11] Lynn Rew, et al.,[12] and in particular Robert G. Hanvey in *An Attainable Global Perspective*[13].

For helping individuals to enhance their awareness we have developed two additional tools, The Intercultural Awareness Profiler and Culture for Business app (see Appendix A).

THE INTERCULTURAL AWARENESS PROFILER (IAP)

The IAP is a diagnostic, self-evaluation profiler that aims to increase a person's awareness of the influence of his or her own basic assumptions and how these may influence interactions in a business situation. This tool thus addresses the first R—Recognition in our 4-R model. It enables participants to perform a comprehensive personal analysis of their own cross-cultural orientation. The questionnaire uses a range of diagnostic questions to elicit personal cross-cultural orientations against the reference "Seven Dimensions of Culture" model discussed in this book. Further questions are used to subgroup participants according to their organization's culture, functional areas, and other variables. The analysis is then cross-referenced with the full cross-cultural database, which consists of 140,000 datapoints.

Each respondent receives a full personal cultural profile together with a personal report on their orientation and thereby individual advice for doing business and managing across cultures. The primary aim is to help managers structure their experiences to further rapid personal development to facilitate success in international business and/or diversity situations.

History of the IAP

The originals of the IAP date from between 1979 and 1982 when the Dutch author developed a multidimensional model of cultural differences as part of his PhD research at Wharton University, Pennsylvania. At the time, very little research had been done to explore the impact of culture on management. The original questionnaire consisted of 107 questions and was completed by 7,000 respondents. Since then, the questionnaire has been revised and rigorously tested. The current online IAP consists of 44 questions measuring a person's preferred orientation along the Seven Dimensions of Culture. In the extended version of 58 questions, it also provides a corporate culture profile.

It can be used as preparation for a workshop, thus maximizing participation in the workshop. Post-workshop use is aimed at the transfer and application of the learning to the work situation as well as to help support personal development, including personal coaching.

Participants benefit from the extensive research database that underpins this analysis. Understanding one's own cultural profile is key in enhancing job performance and bottom-line business results when working with other cultures.

When Is It Appropriate to Use the IAP?

When deciding to use the IAP as part of a training, teaching, coaching, or consulting intervention, it is important to remember that the IAP is not a psychological assessment. As a diagnostic tool, it has no predictive value and cannot measure a person's competence and should thus not be used in this manner. The IAP is not a stand-alone tool and should always be used in conjunction with training, coaching, or as part of a consulting process where a debriefing of the questionnaire is provided.

The IAP is appropriate for people who wish to increase their own intercultural awareness or to gain insight into their own preferred cultural orientations, such as:

- Managers who work in culturally diverse environments
- Expatriates
- Intact, culturally diverse teams
- Students

The completed IAP comes with a four-page report as shown in Figures 11.2 and 11.3.

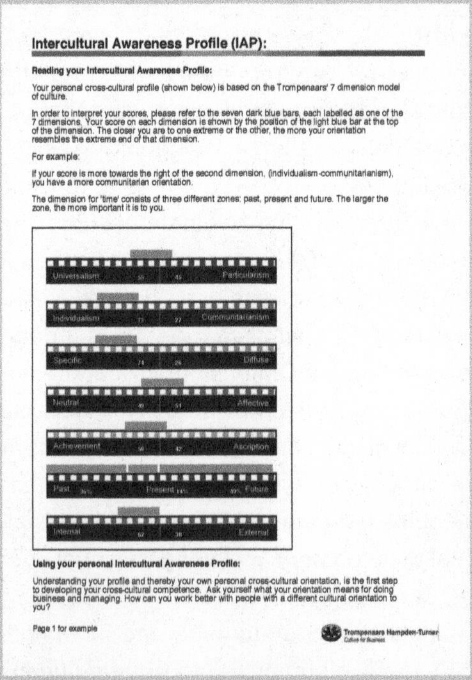

Intercultural Awareness Profile (IAP):

Reading your Intercultural Awareness Profile:

Your personal cross-cultural profile (shown below) is based on the Trompenaars' 7 dimension model of culture.

In order to interpret your scores, please refer to the seven dark blue bars, each labelled as one of the 7 dimensions. Your score on each dimension is shown by the position of the light blue bar at the top of the dimension. The closer you are to one extreme or the other, the more your orientation resembles the extreme end of that dimension.

For example:

If your score is more towards the right of the second dimension, (individualism-communitarianism), you have a more communitarian orientation.

The dimension for 'time' consists of three different zones: past, present and future. The larger the zone, the more important it is to you.

Using your personal Intercultural Awareness Profile:

Understanding your profile and thereby your own personal cross-cultural orientation, is the first step to developing your cross-cultural competence. Ask yourself what your orientation means for doing business and managing. How can you work better with people with a different cultural orientation to you?

Page 1 for example

Trompenaars Hampden-Turner
Culture for Business

FIGURE 11.2. Intercultural Awareness Profile (IAP)

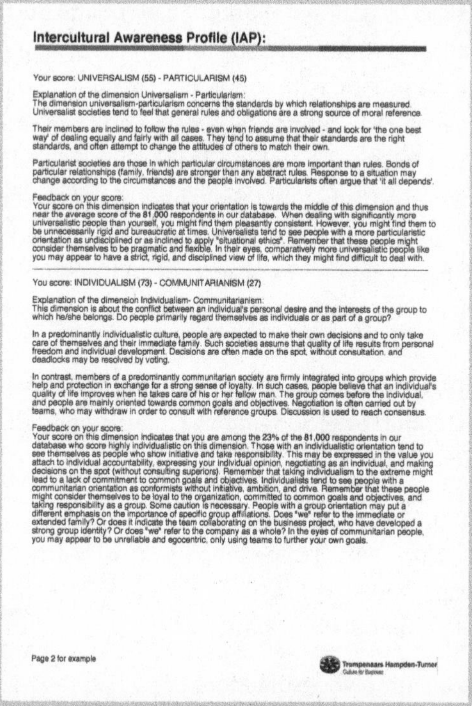

Intercultural Awareness Profile (IAP):

Your score: UNIVERSALISM (55) - PARTICULARISM (45)

Explanation of the dimension Universalism - Particularism:
The dimension universalism-particularism concerns the standards by which relationships are measured. Universalist societies tend to feel that general rules and obligations are a strong source of moral reference.

Their members are inclined to follow the rules - even when friends are involved - and look for 'the one best way' of dealing equally and fairly with all cases. They tend to assume that their standards are the right standards, and often attempt to change the attitudes of others to match their own.

Particularist societies are those in which particular circumstances are more important than rules. Bonds of particular relationships (family, friends) are stronger than any abstract rules. Response to a situation may change according to the circumstances and the people involved. Particularists often argue that 'it all depends'.

Feedback on your score:
Your score on this dimension indicates that your orientation is towards the middle of this dimension and thus near the average score of the 81,000 respondents in our database. When dealing with significantly more universalistic people than yourself, you might find them pleasantly consistent. However, you might find them to be unnecessarily rigid and bureaucratic at times. Universalists tend to see people with a more particularistic orientation as undisciplined or as inclined to apply "situational ethics". Remember that these people might consider themselves to be pragmatic and flexible. In their eyes, comparatively more universalistic people like you may appear to have a strict, rigid, and disciplined view of life, which they might find difficult to deal with.

You score: INDIVIDUALISM (73) - COMMUNITARIANISM (27)

Explanation of the dimension Individualism- Communitarianism:
This dimension is about the conflict between an individual's personal desire and the interests of the group to which he/she belongs. Do people primarily regard themselves as individuals or as part of a group?

In a predominantly individualistic culture, people are expected to make their own decisions and to only take care of themselves and their immediate family. Such societies assume that quality of life results from personal freedom and individual development. Decisions are often made on the spot, without consultation, and deadlocks may be resolved by voting.

In contrast, members of a predominantly communitarian society are firmly integrated into groups which provide help and protection in exchange for a strong sense of loyalty. In such cases, people believe that an individual's quality of life improves when he takes care of his or her fellow man. The group comes before the individual, and people are mainly oriented towards common goals and objectives. Negotiation is often carried out by teams, who may withdraw in order to consult with reference groups. Discussion is used to reach consensus.

Feedback on your score:
Your score on this dimension indicates that you are among the 23% of the 81,000 respondents in our database who score highly individualistic on this dimension. Those with an individualistic orientation tend to see themselves as people who show initiative and take responsibility. This may be expressed in the value you attach to individual accountability, expressing your individual opinion, negotiating as an individual, and making decisions on the spot (without consulting superiors). Remember that taking individualism to the extreme might lead to a lack of commitment to common goals and objectives. Individualists tend to see people with a communitarian orientation as conformists without initiative, ambition, and drive. Remember that these people might consider themselves to be loyal to the organization, committed to common goals and objectives, and taking responsibility as a group. Some caution is necessary. People with a group orientation may put a different emphasis on the importance of specific group affiliations. Does "we" refer to the immediate or extended family? Or does it indicate the team collaborating on the business project, who have developed a strong group identity? Or does "we" refer to the company as a whole? In the eyes of communitarian people, you may appear to be unreliable and egocentric, only using teams to further your own goals.

Page 2 for example

Trompenaars Hampden-Turner

FIGURE 11.3. Explanation of Scores in IAP

The IAP is not appropriate for use with students or people who have never worked before—a separate version of the IAP is available for students and spouses.

See: www.ridingthewavesofculture.com.

The Culture for Business App

To enhance the individual's power to recognize cultural differences we have developed a comprehensive app that informs the user about 144 countries.

The Culture for Business app is based on the Seven Dimension of Culture model and is supported by data collected in over 140 countries. The app provides employees with a better understanding of, and detailed information on, the differences across national cultures. It provides business travelers, international managers, or anyone who is interested in understanding other cultures specific tips for *meetings, management, and negotiations.* This app gives employees a better understanding of cultural differences as well as the reasons for these differences and thereby helps to increase users' cross-cultural management skills to connect different viewpoints and improve communication and cooperation capabilities.

The unique capability is that it is not just a list of tips that every user sees the same. The feedback is selected from the Trompenaars Hampden-Turner country database according to the magnitude of the cultural difference between the culture of the destination country and that of the user. Areas and topics of wider difference are given higher priority than others. There are over 140 countries available in this app, which is extended to cover generations, gender, and corporate culture.

The app retains our unique knowledge and expertise; and it is capable of being extended to include more countries and more features.

App features include:

- Offline and online use
- Personal score and tips in comparison with other countries
- Self-learning tool
- Consult for immediate insights

See: www.ridingthewavesofculture.com.

Respect

How respectful is a person about cultural differences? Respect serves as the basis for our attitudinal, cognitive, and behavioral orientation toward people that hold a diversity of values.

In our practices we have focused much of our work on helping people to recognize cultural differences. The risk of stopping at the level of awareness and recognition only is that one might be supported in one's (negative) stereotypes. Respect of those differences is crucial for one's competence to deal with cultural differences.

According to the *Webster's Dictionary*,[14] the noun *respect* is defined as the giving of particular attention, high or special regard, and expressions of deference. As a verb, *to respect* is to consider another worthy of esteem, to refrain from obtruding or interfering, to be concerned, and to show deference. A compositive definition of respect that reflects these characteristics is presented as follows.

Respect is a basic moral principle and human right that is accountable to the values of human dignity, worthiness, uniqueness of persons, and self-determination. As a guiding principle for actions toward others, respect is conveyed through the unconditional acceptance, recognition, and acknowledgment of the above values in all persons. Respect is the basis for our attitudinal, cognitive, and behavioral, orientation toward all persons with different values.

In our idea of competence to respect cultural differences, we use the three categories of respect identified by Kelly[15] as they are helpful for organizing the measurement of respect as an attitude. These categories are as follows.

Respect for Human Dignity and Uniqueness of a Person from Another Culture

This means that one would treat other persons the same no matter who they were (dignity and inherent worth). A well-developed competence means that one is open toward different working habits of others and tends to question the norms and values of one's own culture. In this case one has to see oneself through the eyes of others, and how one's own normal patterns of behavior are interpreted by others.

Respect for the Person's Rights to Self-Determination

In this second level of respect one considers another person's opinion when planning interactions or trying to elicit suggestions for a plan of action (self-determination). Competence means that one respects different goals or determinations of others; one is at ease with those who hold different views or values. Since one is not judging on first impressions, one tends to check and clarify meaning frequently.

Acceptance of Another Culture's Values

On the third level of respect we try to measure whether, if you had a choice, you would rather deal or not deal with a person from another culture. People with a highly develop competence tend to enjoy variety and diversity around themselves and are open to new ideas. In this case, one is seeking new insights and ways of understanding issues and accepts people who are different.

Reconciliation

The third competence of reconciliation deals with the capability of a person to deal with the differences that one both is aware of and respects. The competence is close to the creativity a person displays in combining values that are at first sight contradictory. We also determined that competency occurs when an individual recognizes cultural differences and ultimately reconciles them by transforming conflicting values into complementary values.[16] As a competent reconciler you have to inspire as well as listen. You have to make decisions yourself but also delegate, and you need to centralize your organization around local responsibilities. As a competent professional, you need to master your materials, and at the same time you need to be passionately at one with the mission of the whole organization. You need to apply your brilliant analytic skills to place these contributions in a larger context. You are supposed to have priorities and put them in a meticulous sequence, while parallel processing is in vogue. You have to develop a brilliant strategy and at the same time have all the answers to questions in case your strategy misses its goals.

We have looked at three levels of reconciliation, very much according to our seven dimensions of culture, which include five aspects of human relationships plus attitudes toward time and the environment.

Reconciling Aspects of Human Relationships

The first five dimensions of culture involve human relationships:

Standardization and adaptation. Do we have to globalize our approach, or do we just have to localize? Is it more beneficial for our organization to choose mass production than just focus on specialized products? Competent people find the solution in the "transnational organization" where the best local practices are being globalized on a continuous basis. "Mass customization" is the keyword for reconciling standardized production and specialized adaptations.

Individual creativity and team spirit. A second dilemma asks for a competence of the integration of team spirit with individual creativity and a competitive mindset. The competent person knows how to make an excellent team out of creative individuals. The team is stimulated to support brilliant individuals, while these individuals deploy themselves for the greater whole. This has been called co-opetition.

Passion and control. Is a competent person an emotional and passionate person, or does the control of emotions make a better person? Here there are two clear types. Passionate people without reason are neurotics, and neutral individuals without emotions are robots. An affective person regularly checks his passion with reason, and a more neutral person gives his controlled reason meaning by showing passion once in a while.

Analysis and synthesis. Is the competent person a detached, analytical person who is able to divide the big picture into ready-to-eat pieces, always selecting for shareholder value? Or is it somebody who puts issues in the big picture and gives priority to the rather vague statement "stakeholder value"? At Shell, Van Lennep's "helicopter view" was introduced as a significant characteristic of a modern leader—the capability to ascend and keep the overview, while being able to zoom in on certain aspects of the matter. This is another significant characteristic of the competent reconciler, namely the ability to know when and where to go in deep. Pure analysis leads to paralysis, and the overuse of synthesis leads to an infinite holism and a lack of action.

Doing and being. "Getting things done" is an important characteristic of a manager. However, shouldn't we keep the rather vulgar "doing" in balance with "being," as in our private lives? As a reconciler you have to be yourself as well. From our research it appears that successful reconcilers act the way they really are. They seem to be one with the business they are undertaking. One of the important causes of stress is that "doing" and "being" are not integrated. Excessive compulsion to perform, when not matching someone's true personality, leads to ineffective behavior.

Reconciling Aspects of Time

The sixth dimension of culture is related to time:

Sequential and parallel. Notably, effective reconcilers are able to plan in a rigorous, sequential way, but at the same time stimulate parallel processes. This reconciliation, which we know as "synchronize processes to increase the sequential speed"—or "just in time" management—seems also to be very effective in integrating the long and short term.

Reconciling the Inner and the Outer Worlds

The seventh dimension of culture is related to one's attitude toward the environment:

Push and pull. This final core competence for today's reconcilers is the ability to connect the voice of the market with the technology the company has developed and vice versa. This is not about technology push or market pull. The competent reconciler knows that the push of technology finally leads to the ultimate niche market, that part without any clients. If you only choose for the market, the client will be unsatisfied. I believe that leaders are not adding value, because only simple values add up.

Though the questions are asked in a linear fashion, by combining them we see when people have scored high on both, adding to the score on the reconciliation side of this competence. Next to the reconciliation score, it also allows us to see the preference for the seven dimensions, depending on which of the linear scales one scores highest.

Realization

After one has recognized, respected, and reconciled cultural differences, the next task is to develop a process in which the resolutions are implemented and rooted in the organization. This competence is well described by John Adair in his action-centred leadership model.[17] Competent managers and leaders should have full command of three main areas of the action-centred leadership model and should be able to use each of the elements according to the situation. Being able to do these things, while keeping the right balance, gets results, builds morale, improves quality, develops teams and productivity, and is the mark of a successful manager and leader.

The key to nurturing leaders is to make sure your company recognizes excellence at three levels: strategic, operational, and team. "It is a common fallacy that all an organization needs is a good strategic leader at the helm," writes Adair.[18]

The three parts are as follows.

Achieving the Task

A competent manager in achieving the task is a person who identifies aims and vision for the group connecting a variety of means. He or she identifies resources, people, processes, systems, and tools that help implementation and establish responsibilities, objectives, accountabilities, and measures. Competence is shown in setting standards, quality, time, and reporting parameters and one that monitors and maintains overall progress toward implementation

Managing the Team or Group

The competent implementer for the group establishes, agrees, and communicates standards of performance and behavior and establishes shared values for the group. He or she monitors and maintains discipline, ethics, integrity, and focus on objectives and resolves group conflict, struggles, or disagreements. This competent manager looks for complementarities in the composition of the group and develops the collective capability of the group. He or she motivates the group and provides a collective sense of purpose and identifies, develops, and agrees team and project leadership roles within group.

Managing Individuals

Competences of the manager for each individual must include an understanding of the team members as individuals, recognizing each person's personality, skills, strengths, needs, aims, and fears. This person evaluates and supports individuals for faster implementation and identifies and agrees appropriate individual responsibilities and objectives. As such he or she gives recognition and praise to individuals to acknowledge effort and good work and identifies, develops, and utilizes each individual's capabilities. He or she develops individual freedom and authority and is extending thinking beyond one's own field of knowledge.

Using the Intercultural Competence Profiler (ICP)

The ICP is normally completed online. On completion participants can download and save their own personal profile report as a PDF file for archiving and/or printing (Figure 11.4). Additional basic biographical data of the respondent provides more extensive benchmark comparisons across our rapidly evolving ICP database. Extensive feedback, extended interpretations, and theoretical background to the ICP are available in a series of interactive web pages in the web-based ICP support center. Participants can explore their own personal profile through online tutorials that offer further insights, "coaching" advice, and suggestions for competence development.

To accommodate different client/participant needs we have developed several versions of the ICP. For example, in the "360°" version, a participant's own self-assessment scores can be triangulated with peer feedback. This can even be based on additional input from clients, customers, or suppliers. The "Organization" version is oriented to an analysis of the competence of the business unit and/or wider organization rather than the individual. In the "Diversity" version, the focus is on diversity and ethnicity rather than country-derived cultures.

Data we have collected has already demonstrated that ICP profiles provide an objective measure for both the individual and the organization. Significantly it reveals identification of the maturity of the life-cycle phase: for example, does the person or organization need cross-cultural awareness or leadership development or to realize business benefits? Thus one can identify the relative need for cross-cultural awareness training, development of mindset changes and corresponding behavior for performance, through to achieving global business benefits by integrating cultural differences. And of course, "before" and "after" measurements provide evidence of the impact of any intervention that can be correlated with improved business performance.

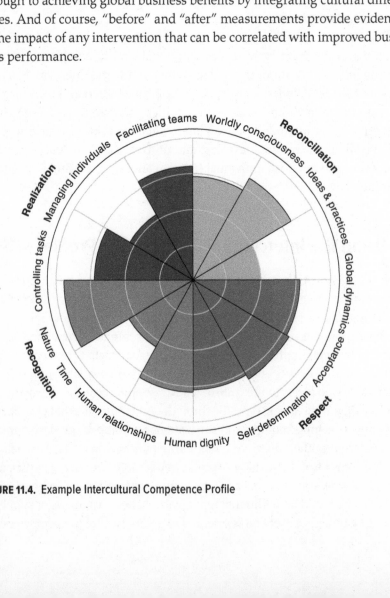

FIGURE 11.4. Example Intercultural Competence Profile

As explained, we recognized the limitations of our earlier cross-cultural instruments that positioned people on bipolar scales of mutually exclusive extremes of the seven dimensions and therefore extended these instruments. Along with the ICP model summarized above, we have also produced an extended version of Belbin's Team Roles model,[19] a version of the Myers–Briggs Type Indicator (MBTI) that we call the Integrated Type Indicator, and an Integrated Scorecard that extends Kaplan and Norton's Balanced Scorecard.

Intercultural Competence Profile (ICP) Reporting

The ICP provides an overall evaluation of a respondent's approach to dealing with cultural differences and links directly to the THT methodology, thus providing a road map as people progress through the total learning experience.

The personalized feedback participants receive is an attempt to describe certain modes of thought, sensitivities, intellectual skills, and explanatory capacities that, in some measure and contribute to the formation of intercultural competence. We distinguish four aspects of intercultural competence that relate to the four steps of Recognition, Respect, Reconciliation, and Realization. It also serves as a "training needs analysis" in that it highlights areas of strength and weaknesses and, therefore, priorities for personal development of skills and knowledge and subsequent effective behaviors. See: www.ridingthewavesofculture.com.

> "When you can measure what you are speaking about, you know something about it. But when you cannot measure it, your knowledge is of a meager and unsatisfactory kind."

12

Toward International and Transnational Management

Fons Trompenaars and Charles Hampden-Turner

THIS BOOK has elucidated national and corporate culture differences, of which we have found a great many. So wide and pervasive are these variations that they would seem to confirm the doubt expressed at the beginning as to whether universal or general principles of "how to manage" are feasible or useful.

Yet the implication of the research presented here is that universals exist at another level. While you cannot give universal *advice* that will work regardless of culture, and while general axioms of business administration turn out to be largely American cultural axioms, there are *universal dilemmas or problems of human existence.* Every country and every organization in that country faces dilemmas:

- In relationships with people
- In relationship to time
- In relations between people and the natural environment

While nations differ markedly in *how* they approach these dilemmas, they do not differ in needing to make some kind of response. People everywhere are as one in having to face up to the same challenges of existence.

In this chapter we look at some of the specific problems faced by international management, in terms of structure, strategy, communications, and human resources, and consider a common approach to their solution.

Our research method consists of stories, scenes, situations, and questions that put two moral and/or managerial principles in conflict. The researchers force the managers to choose one over the other. In reality the answers managers gave may be considered as their first and second "foundation stones" in building the *moral edifice* that we present. Some, for example, felt that you had to give priority to a universal rule (universalism) and behave in particular instances accordingly. Some felt that you had to give priority to your affection for particular people (particularism) and develop whatever universals you could out of such obligations. But few were actually rejecting the alternative solution out of hand, and as the figures show it is rare for any national result to be anywhere near 100 percent in favor of any priority. Almost all our problems, and their solutions, are recognizable all over the world.

There is another important respect in which all the world's managers are the same. Whichever principle they start with, the circumstances of business and of organizing experience require them to reconcile the dilemmas we have been discussing. You can prosper only if as many particulars as possible are covered by rules, yet exceptions are seen and noted. You can think effectively only if you consider both the specifics and the diffuse wholes; the segments are as important as the integrations. Whether you are at heart an individualist or a communitarian, your individuals must be capable of organizing themselves, and your communities are only as good as the health, wealth, and wisdom of each member.

It is crucial to give status to achievers, but equally crucial to back strategies, projects, and new initiatives from people who have not yet achieved anything—in other words, to ascribe status to them in hope of facilitating success. Everyone should be equal in their rights and opportunities, yet any contest will produce a hierarchy of relative standings. Respect for age and experience can both nurture and discourage the young and inexperienced. Hierarchy and equality are finely interwoven in every culture. It is true that time is both a passing sequence of events and a moment of truth, a "now" in which past, present, and future are given new meanings. We need to accept influences from the depth of our inner convictions and also from the world around us.

In the final analysis, *culture is the manner in which these dilemmas are reconciled, since every nation seeks a different and winding path to its own ideals of integrity.* It is our position that businesses will succeed to the extent that this reconciliation occurs, so we have everything to learn from discovering what paths others have taken.

Problems for the Cross-Cultural Manager

We are not the first to note these differences. Geert Hofstede did so in his international samples of IBM employees,[1] as did Inzerilli and Laurent[2] in their research comparing Italian and French managers to those in the USA, Japan, and Europe. As we tracked the experience of Mr. Johnson of MCC from chapter to chapter, we found what these researchers have also noted, that favorite American solutions do not always solve the dilemmas of other nations. Since the USA has been the principal source of management theory, this is crucial information for all students of business practice.

For example, the matrix organization is a very clever reconciliation of the need to be organized by discipline and function, and the need to respond to projects, products under development, and customer specifications. But while this solves American, British, Dutch, and Scandinavian dilemmas, it directly threatens and contradicts the Family model described in Chapter 13, so that some Italian, Spanish, French, and Asian companies will have to devise a different solution.

Similarly, Peter Drucker's management by objectives is a justly famous reconciliation of an American dilemma that has rightly been adopted by like-minded nations. The conflict between equality and hierarchy, and the individual and the community is reconciled by getting individuals to pledge themselves freely to fulfill the key objectives of the community and the hierarchy. Voluntarily negotiated contracts join the person to the group. That is good, but not so good for nations that regard the performance of individuals as part of the relationship with the boss and who attribute excellence to the whole Family or relationship.

Pay-for-performance is similarly an attempted solution to the achievement-ascription dilemma. Why not ascribe status and financial rewards to employees in proportion to their achievements? Again, this has great appeal to those who put achievement first but none to those who put ascription first and seek to be the emotional "authors" of a subordinate's success. We discussed this problem in detail in Chapter 8, but it is so central to the issue that it bears an additional anecdote here.

An American computer company introduced pay-for-performance in both the USA and the Middle East. It worked well in the USA and increased sales briefly in the Middle East before a serious slump occurred. Inquiries showed that indeed the winners among salesmen in the Middle East had done better, but the vast majority had done worse. The wish for their fellows to succeed had been seriously eroded by the contest. Overall morale and sales were down. Ill will was contagious. When the bosses discovered that certain salespeople were earning more than they did, high individual performances also ceased. But the principal reason for eventually abandoning the system was the discovery that customers were being loaded up with products they could not sell on. As A tried to beat B to the bonus, the care of customers began to slip, with serious, if delayed, results.

Centralization Versus Decentralization

The main dilemma those who manage across cultures confront is the extent to which they should *centralize*, thereby imposing on foreign cultures rules and procedures that might affront them, or *decentralize*, thereby letting each culture go its own way without having any centrally viable ideas about improvement since the "better way" is a local, not a global pathway. If you radically decentralize you have to ask whether HQ can add value at all, or whether companies acting in several nations are worthwhile.

Decentralization is easier under some corporate cultures than others. To decentralize you have to delegate. This can be done in the individualistic, specific, and achievement-oriented cultures, but not so easily in the Family-like model where the communitarian, diffuse, and ascriptive parent remains the parent. Stories are common of the difficulties that Japanese managers have in decentralizing and delegating to foreigners. The Family communicates by a kind of in-house osmosis of empathy and bowing rituals that foreigners cannot easily share. Policies are made on the telephone lines to Tokyo because the intimate understandings between Japanese insiders are very difficult to delegate.

As most of our case histories and anecdotes have shown, miscommunication is far more common than dialogue. Nevertheless, centralizing and decentralizing are, like all the other dimensions introduced in this book, potentially reconcilable processes. A biological organism grows to higher levels of order and complexity by being more differentiated and more integrated. The more departments, divisions, functions, and differentiated activities a corporation pursues, the greater the challenge, and also the greater the importance of *coordinating all this variety*. As Paul Lawrence and Jay Lorsch[3] showed in the late 1960s, both overcentralized (overintegrated) and over-decentralized (overdifferentiated) companies underperform to significant degrees; differentiating and integrating need to be synergized or reconciled. The corporation with the best integrated diversity is the one that excels.

Group management is often fooled by a foreign subsidiary doing as it is asked by HQ, but essentially performing a corporate rain dance. The local managers know it will make no difference to the rainfall, but if HQ wants a list of everyone's qualifications and salaries to compare the two, they will provide one. Never mind that the qualifications have probably been invented to fit the existing salaries. When these perfect scores arrive HQ feels it is "in control" worldwide, but of course this is an illusion. The policy handbook says "we pay no bribes," but in many countries paid they will be. Relationships without presents are impossible.

The centralizing–decentralizing dilemma is often experienced as consistency versus flexibility of corporate identity. Is it more important for Shell to relate successfully in the Philippines by helping peasants to raise pigs, or should the strategy of being an energy company be used to maintain continuity? In practice helping pig farming has played a role in preventing oil pipelines from being blown up by communist insurgents. If you are digging for oil in Nigeria anyway, why not find some water too and build some desperately needed wells?

Examples of this kind show that the relationship between centralization and decentralization is a subtle one. It is not true that every differentiated activity takes you further from your core business simply because it is different. Water wells and pig farms may make all the difference between gaining business in less developed countries or losing it. It is *because we are all different that we have so much to exchange with each other.* In matters of culture, as in the relationship of the sexes, the difference can be the chief source of attraction. Italian design and Dutch engineering can lead to conflicts, as we have seen; they could also lead to a product made in heaven.

The ideal, then, is to differentiate in such a way as to make integration more effective, or to decentralize activities in such a way that an ever-broader diversity gets coordinated by the "central nervous system" of your corporation. In matters of cultural diversity there is always a challenge, but where this challenge is met valuable connections result.

Quality Not Quantity in Decentralization

It is not a matter of *how much* to decentralize, but *what* to decentralize and what to keep at corporate HQ. A company that does not centralize information cannot cohere at all, but this does not mean that decisions cannot be made locally. Arguably technical specifications, for example the rules, standards, and procedures by which oil refineries are operated, can be decided centrally, but what mix of products to refine could be decided nationally, close to customers' changing demands. Pricing may also be a local decision, sensitive to the proximity of competitors and the degree of overcapacity.

Financing decisions are normally allocated centrally or locally according to their size. National companies often pay a standard overhead to headquarters and get "free" legal, financial, planning, and personnel services; this arrangement tends to protect the role of centralized functions. You have to pay, so you might as well use them. Alternatively, HQ staff may provide consultancy services to national companies on request. Under this system, unnecessary staff services at HQ will shrivel on the vine if no one wants them, an arrangement that tends to favor decentralization.

International and Transnational Companies

The issues of centralization and decentralization have been fully discussed by Christopher Bartlett and Sumantra Ghoshal in relation to their analysis of global versus multinational, and international versus transnational corporations.[4] As they define them, global and multinational companies are both essentially centralized, in that their subsidiaries relate to the head company or country, even if not necessarily very strongly, rather than to the other companies or nations in the group. For these companies there are unlikely to be many foreigners in the top management team, and the myth of the universal applicability of management techniques is likely to be strong. In contrast, in both international and transnational corporate structures there is a significant attempt to overcome the dilemma of centralization versus decentralization; each of these in its own way sets out to manage diversity and gain competitive advantage from being located in different countries with special capacities. This book is aimed at those who are already operating on international or transnational levels, or aspire to do so.

The two forms take different paths to the reconciliation of centralizing and decentralizing. The international corporation moves out influence from its center to regions and nations, retaining a coordinative role, while the transnational corporation loses its center in favor of polycentric influences from different parts of its network.

The *international* corporation, of which Shell, Google, Microsoft, and Amazon are examples, breaks with the notion that national organizations are spokes around a wheel. National organizations have legitimate relationships with each other based on what it is that the customer wants and the best source of supply within the international system. HQ's role becomes not so much to instruct or to evaluate as to *coordinate*, to make sure that if one nation has embarked in a promising direction, other nations also learn from this. HQ facilitates this and possibly helps other nations to emulate the initiative.

International corporations are likely to have top management teams that are a microcosm of the whole system, with Germans, Dutch, French, Italian, and Japanese executives at company HQ where considerable businesses are located in those countries. These are not "delegates" or "representatives" in a foreign country, but full-time contributors to multicultural management so that, say, the Italian subsidiary has its cultural traits not only within but at the coordinating center.

As corporations move from a multilocal to an international form, the HQ behaves *less like a policeman and more like a consultant*. Functional and geographical chiefs are called coordinators, their authority stemming from the fact that they know what several functions, regions, or nations are doing.

The *transnational* corporation has four major characteristics:

1. Polycentrism
2. Value and purpose driven
3. Combining best local practices to next practices
4. Servant leadership

Polycentric. The transnational organization is polycentric rather than coordinated from the center. It consists of several centers of specialized excellence that will exercise authority and influence whenever they are qualified to do so by the challenge confronting the organization. The Swedish professor Gunnar Hedlund found this increasingly typical of some Swedish organizations such as IKEA and Ericsson, for example. Bartlett and Ghoshal regarded transnationalism as an important direction, which in some cases such as Philips and Matsushita has become a reality. Jay Ogilvy, an American academic, has spoken of heterarchies replacing hierarchies.[5]

All these predictions of the future form of the successful transnational imply a flatter corporate structure drawing on a multiplicity of points of expertise. Hence if a company was designing a new international sports car, the electronics might come from Japan, the engine and suspension from Germany, the design from Italy, the fiberglass shell from the USA, the mahogany wood finish from Britain, and the assembly might be done in Spain. National marketing departments will adopt different tactics to sell it, while exchanging experience and drawing upon each other's brand of management expertise. Each element in the "value-added chain" or loop would exercise authority on the issue of its own cultural strength. Robert Reich, the American political scientist, has argued that it does not really matter anymore who owns the company,[6] be they American shareholders, Europeans, or Asians. What matters is where the greatest value is added in the transnational network. Countries will prosper or stagnate by the skills they inject into these "value chains." In the economy of the future, knowledge is king and influence flows from wherever that knowledge resides.

Value and purpose driven. Whenever you need to reconcile central and decentral processes, it is important to create a context within which this is nurtured. A shared framework of purpose (raison d'être) is paramount. An increasing number of transnational firms have introduced yin and yang values so the context facilitates reconciliation on the value level: "we strive for teams that consist of creative individuals," "we give people direct feedback diplomatically," "we are ambitious with prudence."

Combining best local practices. Transnational organizations have a keen interest to learn from the best local practices and combine them into next practices that are globalized. So the latest software development in Greece is combined with hardware from Taiwan and made a standard in HQ New York. We see for example that the best local foods at McDonalds (the veggie burger in India and the McFlurry in Canada) are first regionalized and further developed in order to become a standard on the global offering of McDonalds.

Servant leadership. As described in Chapter 8, most leadership models are culturally biased. In order to be able to move leaders around and have them lead multicultural teams effectively, a consistent transnational leadership model is very helpful. Successful transnational firms increasingly find out that servant leadership, leaders that gain their authority by serving their colleagues, is one of those models. So leaders operating in HQ feel the drive to serve local colleagues and clients. But at the same time local leaders feel the responsibility to contribute to the quality of the global offerings of the organization.

Figure 12.1 gives a good impression of the previous arguments and categorizations.

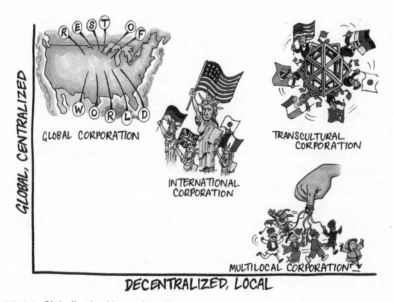

FIGURE 12.1. Globalization Versus Localism

In the transnational company influence can be exercised by any nation on others and can start at any point, accumulating value as it goes and "circling" to reconcile cultural strengths.

What is important about transnationalism is that it follows the circular reconciliations sketched at the ends of Chapters 3 through 10; it combines the qualities of various cultures. The methodology of reconciliation is discussed in detail in Section III.

You can join Italy's particularism to Germany's universalism, or join American individualism and inner-directed creativity to Japanese rapid communitarian exploitation of new products and other-directed skills of customer satisfaction. Where countries specialize in what they do best, the transnational circuits so formed could prove unbeatable. The remaining question is how the transnational organization is to survive the complete atrophy of its center.

Human-Resource Management in the Future

The main preoccupation of our analysis of cultural differences has been under the general heading of human resources. In the recruitment of the senior managers of the future, large companies seem at present to be at some disadvantage. The notion that it is desirable to gain "power" by climbing high in large organizations is currently somewhat out of fashion; autonomy is more sought after, and the attraction to recruits of internationalism is more likely to lie in the experience, knowledge, and investigation of multiple cultures. Recruits will want to plan their own careers in the international and transnational corporation of the future, and some career "ladders" may look more like "walkways." Companies that succeed in reconciling the centralization versus decentralization dilemma will have learned how to rotate their employees internationally (especially the highfliers), how to work in several languages, and how to make decisions at many points on the globe and to spread their effects.

Once the scarce commodity of intelligent managers has been attracted, the future transnational will set out to give them further training in cross-cultural awareness, starting with learning how to recognize a cultural problem, which, as we have seen, is often unidentified; it is often seen as not a problem but, for example, "the stubbornness of south Europeans about incentive schemes." People who resist American universals are seen as traditional, unbusinesslike, or even backward.

The Growth of Information

The Dutch author once gave a seminar in Thailand that saved a company $1.5 million. It was not, alas, the result of any insights he imparted. A French executive sitting next to a Thai executive of the same company discovered that the latter was about to build a pilot plant that would duplicate something the French had just completed. This is indicative of the frequent failure of internal corporate communications.

The development of information technology, however, presents new problems. IT has its own curious forms of absolutism. Given the high capacity, high speed, and high cost of digital solutions, the impulse following their installation is to generate a great deal of information as quickly as possible, thereby reducing the cost per byte.

At HQ to know everything statistical about your subsidiary before it has even discovered this itself is, therefore, much prized. We have heard of subsidiary companies called up during breakfast because of time zone differences with complaints that tin wastage rates in the canning plants are up 50 percent.

This approach can have disastrous consequences for intercultural communication, and it militates against the development of international or transnational structures. The head of a national subsidiary is paid in part to use his or her discretion, free of oversight. If you seek a genuine cultural contribution from a foreign subsidiary, you cannot check up on it daily. Information should go first and foremost to those whose operations it concerns, with a lag before HQ gets it. This gives time for local answers to be found and action to be taken.

A company will remain a centralized, directive, global organization so long as information is used for power and advantage. Because information depends on input, it is easily distorted. Subsidiaries punished for not meeting their forecasts will lower the forecast next time. IT can give an illusion of control that does not survive closer examination.

In the international and transnational structures, national operating companies communicate because they wish to and because the parallel activities of other companies in nearby markets are opportunities and resources. The IT philosophy in these structures states that every national company is free to take major initiatives without prior consultation but should keep the network informed of its actions. It has local autonomy but no right to secrecy about the exercise of that autonomy after the fact. All interested parties must know what has been done. A good software system for keeping networks informed is the highlight system. Any interested subsidiary or centralized function can tap into those activities that concern it. This allows for ad hoc project groups to take advantage of any number of converging lines of research or activity. The hallmark of the international or transnational structure is lateral connections between activities capable of being catalyzed to the advantage of the whole network. Recall that in this structure subsidiaries connect to subsidiaries. Like hounds hunting for a fox, anyone may pick up the scent, bay loudly, and have the others follow the new direction.

Software, moreover, may be more or less culturally compatible with how managers think. Diffuse ways of thinking and learning are often diagrammatic and configurative. Streams of words are more linear, specific, and sequential. "Windows" allow for selective viewing of information by those interested. The shape of software needs to be a microcosm of the larger structure and consistent with it. There is software for scenarios of alternative futures, for creative connections between ideas, for alternative applications of key technologies, and for spin-offs.

Implications for Business Strategy

Culture can all too easily put brakes on any movement to internationalize. Universalism tends to create global structures in which the values of the home country are celebrated worldwide. Individualism can produce multinational structures in deference to the individuality of each nation. Inner-directedness also contributes to global or multinational structures depending on whether the inner-direction is toward a parent company (a global structure) or a national group (a multinational structure).

Equality, other-directedness, and achievement orientations will encourage internationalization, and it is notable that both the Dutch and the Swedes, who display these attributes, are quite successful internationally. Family-style corporate cultures may work well in their countries of origin but be difficult to transfer overseas. Global cultures with standardization as a principle will be rejected in nations with Family-style traditions, especially if the "universals" are foreign. Task-oriented cultures with clearly defined short-term goals might also offend Family feeling with their on-again, off-again relationships and their "two fathers."

The principal implication for business strategy is a healthy respect for the "founding beliefs" of foreign cultures and the images they have chosen to create coherence. A "strange" culture usually has values neglected in ours, and to discover these is to find lost parts of our own cultural heritage. Hence Family-style cultures can remind us that work is not necessarily alienating, impersonal, and self-seeking. We can benefit from such insights without putting our relatives on the payroll or feeling like children when the boss walks in. International and transnational structures allow us to *synthesize the advantages of all cultures while avoiding their excesses.* Families are quite capable of nurturing independence and encouraging achievement. Managing across cultures gives you more possible pathways to your goal.

The only strategic system open to a genuinely international company will be the system described by Michael Goold[7] as *strategic control.* Here strategy is neither laid down by the center nor subject to strict financial parameters, but fed to the center by national companies. They propose and the center coordinates, criticizes, approves, and adds its own funds. What occurs is a multicultural negotiation.

An international or transnational structure greatly reduces its own powers unless it gives a free rein to certain national cultural proclivities. Strategies tend to vary with national culture; hence inner-directed, universalistic, specific, achievement-oriented cultures—typically, the English-speaking ones—talk as if they were engaged in military campaigns, saturating consumers with a withering hail of commercials and generally conquering and occupying markets. In contrast, outer-directed, particularistic, diffuse, and ascription-oriented cultures—typically, the Japanese—speak as if they were serenading customers before transacting business with them. They do not use the word "strategy" at all, although they clearly have a method of coevolving with customers. Individualist cultures with a sequential view of time, like the USA and Britain, are usually short-term in their business strategies. Communitarian cultures with a synchronic view of time, like Germany and Japan, are typically long-term strategically.

An international or transnational structure that does not allow those willing to postpone rewards for several years to do so could miss out on the secret of Asian and German economic strengths. Within the international or transnational structure a microcosm of international economic competition is going on. We would be foolish not to notice who is winning or why, and to fail to apply the lessons.

Local HR and Valuing Competences

One interesting way of combining the universal values generated by the head office with local flexibility and the impact of national cultures arises in assessment procedures. HQ or global HR makes a list of what is to be appraised but leaves their priority to the national operating company. Shell, for example, operated its HAIRL system of basic appraisal. This stands for Helicopter (the capacity to take a broad view from above), power of Analysis, Imagination, sense of Reality, and Leadership effectiveness. We were interested to discover if these were equally important to various Shell operating companies and asked participants in several seminars to prioritize HAIRL for themselves. The results were as follows.

NETHERLANDS	FRANCE	GERMANY	BRITAIN
Reality	Imagination	Leadership	Helicopter
Analysis	Analysis	Analysis	Imagination
Helicopter	Leadership	Reality	Reality
Leadership	Helicopter	Imagination	Analysis
Imagination	Reality	Helicopter	Leadership

There is no inherent reason, it seems to us, why all nations should place equal weight on all values. If the Dutch want to stress realism, so be it. They find most of the oil by drilling where it really is and not where they imagine it to be. Prioritizing the values of assessment can tell us a lot about how cultures vary. It is the theme of this book that all cultures need to be both universalist and particularist, both individual and communitarian, both ascriptive and achieving, both inner- and outer-directed. Their difference lies in their priorities, where they "start." We have argued the essential *complementarity* of values. To post an individualist to communitarian Singapore can help to make that communitarianism more responsive to individuals, and the reverse would be true of posting a Singaporean to the USA.

We should not forget that different priorities are not all equally successful. From studying different value priorities in different cultures comes vital clues as to how we can better manage our own affairs.

Local Freedom to Reward

It is similarly possible to have a universal rule that "success must be rewarded commensurate with its size," yet leave the form of that reward up to the national company. Our case study of MCC conveyed that message. That company was unable to accept that while it could have a central philosophy of pay-for-performance, it needed to decentralize its application. Managers around the world are in favor of the principle; the difficulty is that they all mean different things by pay and different things by performance. It is entirely reasonable that a person in a communitarian culture should seek to reward the team members for his or her own successful efforts. The team gets the money the individual helped generate; he or she gets the respect, affection, and gratitude, which is not such a bad bargain. That the high performer in an individualistic society might like to attract rewards away from colleagues is also entirely reasonable. The solution is for communitarian and individualist cultures to give group rewards and personal rewards in accordance with their own judgments and results. After all, no culture pays salaries entirely as bonus for individual effort; part is always fixed, so we are talking about relative emphasis. In a truly international or transnational corporation, *every nation would be charged with finding its optimal mix between personal and group rewards*, with more of that reward for successful operations. This application of co-opetition works to reward individuals for what they contribute to the team and to reward the team for what it does to make individuals excel.

If we do this we might be surprised. Do individuals in Western cultures create value because of extrinsic rewards like money, or because their peers encourage them? The answers could be instructive.

Hierarchical versus egalitarian pay structures could also be up to the national company. Relatively equal pay may improve cooperation. Relatively unequal pay may increase competition among employees. How much of each works best? The company should have a fixed ratio of its turnover to distribute as it sees fit. National companies might also be given the discretion to take lower salaries overall so as to reduce prices to customers, using a strategy of "increasing market share." The notion that everyone is motivated principally by money rewards needs to be challenged. Those willing to take long-term advantage of wage control strategies should be encouraged. Corporate cultures based on the image of the Family may not care so much about wage levels. Those who work principally for each other's affection can be fiercely competitive on costs, as the Japanese showed in the nineties. Pay-for-performance tends to be expensive.

Especially when people are poor, a group or communitarian orientation may be crucial for takeoff. A group bonus scheme used by Shell Nigeria, for example, consisted of a water well and irrigation scheme for the town the employees lived in, which materially benefited their homes and neighborhood besides raising their status in the community. Arguably such a scheme was far more valuable to individual employees than dividing the cost of the project between them and giving them the money instead.

The Error-Correcting Manager

Other cultures are strange, ambiguous, even shocking to us. It is unavoidable that we will make mistakes in dealing with them and feel muddled and confused. The real issue is how quickly we are prepared to learn from mistakes and how bravely we struggle to understand a game in which "perfect scores" are an illusion, and where reconciliation comes only after a difficult passage through alien territory.

We need a certain amount of humility and a sense of humor to discover cultures other than our own—a readiness to enter a room in the dark and stumble over unfamiliar furniture until the pain in our shins reminds us where things are. World culture is myriad of different ways of creating the integrity without which life and business cannot be conducted. There are no universal answers, but there are universal questions and dilemmas, and that is where we all need to start.

Globalization Index

The use of the web-enabled Globalization Index instrument enables respondents to consider and reflect on their organizations' readiness to be effective in international/global business. It uses the THT construct and model of reconciliation to analyze responses from multiple-choice questions on the way in which their organization and various functional disciplines operate across the world. Supplementary questions enable responses to be cross-referenced with the corporate culture and other aspects of global business performance and strategy. Respondents consider both the actual situation and ideal modes of operation for their organization.

For the organization, the Globalization Index is particularly suited to reviewing actual or intended strategic alliances, takeovers, and mergers with organizations of different national and corporate cultures. In addition, a range of options are presented to be considered by the organization in terms of possible changes in modes of working, systems, or structure to realize true globalization. Research by THT demonstrates clear linkages between modes of business operation and bottom-line business results. The index measures the organization on the grids shown in Figures 12.2 through 12.4.

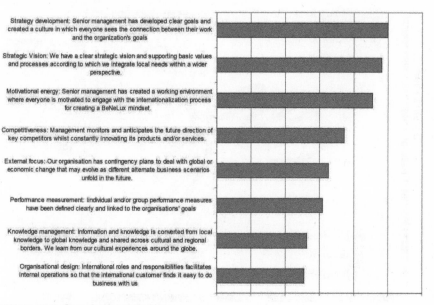

FIGURE 12.2. Organizational Readiness

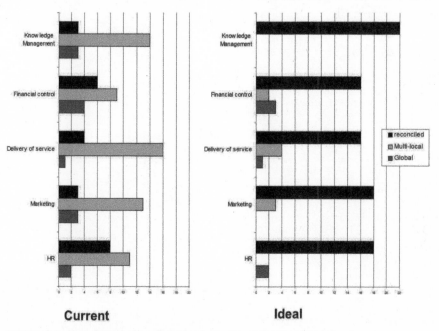

FIGURE 12.3. How Organization Operates in the World (by Functional Area)

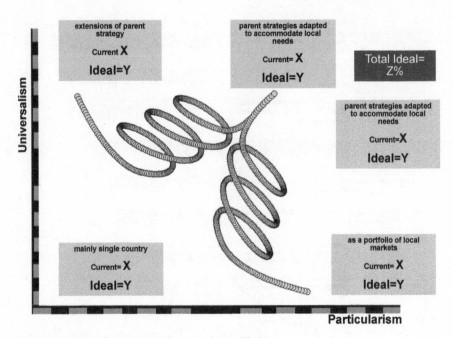

FIGURE 12.4. How Organization Operates in the World

Corporate Cultures and Change Management

13

National Cultures and Corporate Cultures

Fons Trompenaars and Charles Hampden-Turner

WHEN PEOPLE set up an organization, they will typically borrow from models or ideals that are familiar to them. The organization, as we explored in Chapter 2, is a subjective construct, and its employees will give meaning to their environment based on their own particular cultural programming. The organization is like something else they have experienced. It may be deemed to resemble a Family, or an impersonal system designed to achieve targets. It may be likened to a vessel that is traveling somewhere, or a missile homing in on customers and strategic objectives. Cultural preferences operating across the dimensions described in the previous chapters influence the models people give to organizations and the meanings they attribute to them.

This chapter explores four categorical types of corporate culture and shows how differences between national cultures help determine the type of corporate culture chosen. Employees have a shared perception of the organization, and what they believe has real consequences for the corporate culture that develops.

Organizational culture is shaped not only by technologies and markets, but by the cultural preferences of leaders and employees. Some international companies have European, Asian, American, or Middle Eastern subsidiaries that would be unrecognizable as the same company save for their logo and reporting procedures. Often these are fundamentally different in the logic of their structure and the meanings they bring to shared activity.

Three aspects of organizational structure are especially important in determining corporate culture.

1. The general relationship between employees and their organization
2. The vertical or hierarchical system of authority defining superiors and subordinates
3. The general views of employees about the organization's destiny, purpose, and goals and their places in this

Thus far we have distinguished cultures along single (linear) dimensions: universalism–particularism, for example, and individualism–communitarianism. In looking at organizations we need to think in two dimensions, generating four quadrants. The dimensions we use to distinguish different corporate cultures are *equality–hierarchy* and *orientation to the person–orientation to the task.*

This enables us to define four categorical types of corporate culture, which vary considerably in how they think and learn, how they change, and how they motivate, reward, and resolve conflicts. This is a valuable way to analyze organizations, but it does have the risk of caricaturization. We tend to believe or wish that all foreigners will fit the stereotypes we have of them. Hence in our very recognition of "types" there is a temptation to oversimplify what is really quite complex.

The four types can be described as follows:

1. The Family
2. The Eiffel Tower
3. The Guided Missile
4. The Incubator

These four metaphors illustrate the relationship of employees to their notion of the organization. Figure 13.1 summarizes the images these organizations project.

Each of these types of corporate culture is an "ideal type." In practice the types are mixed or overlaid with one culture dominating. In many organizations the same corporate culture permeates everywhere, while in others there may be considerable variety in different functional areas like the corporate culture of R&D compared to marketing and sales. Even so, this categorization into four extreme types is useful for exploring the basis of each type in terms of how employees learn, change, resolve conflicts, reward, motivate, and so on. Why, for example, do norms and procedures which seem to work so well in one culture lose their effectiveness in another?

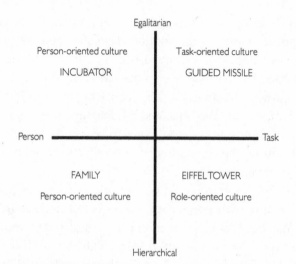

FIGURE 13.1. Four Types of Corporate Culture

The Family Culture

We use the metaphor of Family for the culture that is at the same time *personal*, with close face-to-face relationships, and *hierarchical*, in the sense that the "father" of a Family has experience and authority greatly exceeding those of his "children," especially where these are young. The result is a *power-oriented* corporate culture in which the leader is regarded as a caring father who knows better than his subordinates what should be done and what is good for them. Rather than being threatening, this type of power is essentially intimate and (hopefully) benign. The work of the corporation in this type of culture is usually carried forward in an atmosphere that in many respects mimics the home.

The Japanese recreate within the corporation aspects of the traditional Family. The major business virtue is *amae*, a kind of love between persons of differing rank, with indulgence shown to the younger and respect reciprocated to the elder. The idea is always to do *more* than a contract or agreement obliges you to. The idealized relationship is *senpai–kohai*, that between an older and younger brother. Promotion by age means that the older person will typically be in charge. The relationship to the corporation is long-term and devoted.

A large part of the reason for working, performing well, and resolving conflict in this corporate culture is the pleasure derived from such relationships. To please your superior (or elder brother) is a reward in itself. While this affection may or may not be visible to outsiders (the Japanese, for example, are often very restrained emotionally) it is nevertheless *there*, whether subdued Japanese-style or conveyed unmistakably by voice, face, and bodily gesture Italian-style. The leader of the Family-style culture weaves the pattern, sets the tone, and models the appropriate posture for the corporation and expects subordinates to be "on the same wavelength," knowing intuitively what is required; conversely, the leader may empathize with the subordinates.

At its best the power-oriented Family culture exercises power *through* its members acting with one accord. Power is not necessarily *over* them, although it may be. The main sanction is loss of affection and place in the Family. Pressure is moral and social rather than financial or legal. Many corporations with Family-style cultures are from nations that industrialized late: Greece, Italy, Japan, Singapore, South Korea, and Spain. Where the transition from feudalism to industrialism was rapid, many feudal traditions remain.

Family-style corporate cultures tend to be *high context* (see Chapter 7), a term that refers to the sheer amount of information and cultural content *taken for granted* by members. The more in-jokes, the more Family stories, traditions, customs, and associations there are the higher the context and the harder it is for outsiders to feel that they belong or to know how to behave appropriately. Such cultures exclude strangers without necessarily wishing to do so and communicate in codes that only members understand.

Relationships tend to be *diffuse* (see Chapter 7). The "father" or "elder brother" is influential in *all* situations, whether they have knowledge of the problem or not, whether an event occurs at work, in the canteen, or on the way home, and even if someone else present is better qualified. The general happiness and welfare of all employees is regarded as the concern of the Family-type corporation, which often provides housing and considers the size of their families and whether their wages are sufficient for them to live well.

Power and differential status are seen as "natural," a characteristic of the leaders themselves and not related to the tasks they succeed or fail in doing, any more than a parent ceases to be a parent by neglecting certain duties. Above the power of the leader may be that of the state, the political system, the society, or God. Power is *political* in the sense of being broadly ordained by authorities, rather than originating in roles to be filled or tasks to be performed. This does not mean that those in power are unskilled or cannot do their jobs; it means that for such an organization to perform well the requisite knowledge and skills must be brought *to* the power centers, thereby justifying the existing structure. Take the following testimony by a British manager:

> "In Italy I was introduced to my counterpart, the head of applications engineering. I asked him about his organization, his department, and the kind of work they were engaged in. Within minutes he had given me a dozen names and his personal estimate of their political influence, their proximity to power, and their tastes, preferences, and opinions. He said almost nothing about either their knowledge, their skills, or their performance. As far as I could tell, they had no specific functions, or if they had my informant was ignorant of them. I was amazed. There seemed to be no conception of the tasks that had to be done or their challenge and complexity."

It did not occur to the British manager that this Family model is capable of processing complexity without necessarily seeing itself as a functional instrument to this end. The authority in the Family model is unchallengeable in the sense that it is not seen to depend on tasks performed but on status ascribed. A major issue becomes that of getting the top people to notice, comprehend, and act. If older people have more authority, then they must be briefed thoroughly and supported loyally in order to fulfil the status attributed to them. *The culture works to justify its own initial suppositions.*

In our own research we tested to what extent managers from different cultures saw their leaders "as a kind of father" or to what extent they thought the leader "got the job done." In the family culture where the father figure is dominant amongst the leaders, subordinates are not left alone to get the job done. There is a continuous process of supervision. We see that the Asian cultures like Singapore, Hong Kong, Philippines, and Indonesia are toward the top of the chart. The results are shown in Figure 13.2, where we see one of the widest ranges of national variances of response. Another question asked of managers in the process of this research was to think of the company they work for in terms of a triangle, and to pick the one on the diagram (Figure 13.3) that best represents it. The steepest triangle scores five points and so on down to one.

The scores of nations where the leader is seen as a father (Figure 13.2) correlate closely with the steepness of the triangles in Figure 13.3. The

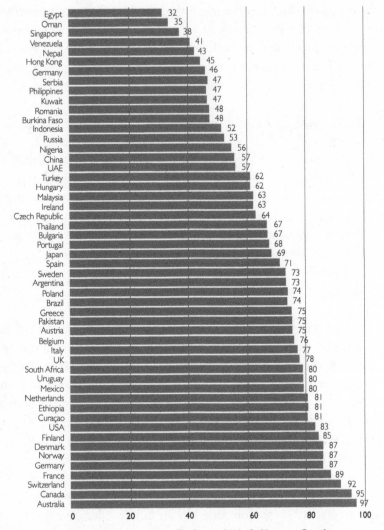

FIGURE 13.2. Percentage of Respondents Opting to Be Left Alone to Get the
        Job Done

familial cultures of Turkey, Venezuela, and several Asian countries have the
steepest hierarchies; the image combines attachment to subordination with
relative permanence of employment. Nearly all of these are also to be found
in the top third of Figure 13.2.

Family cultures at their least effective drain the energies and loyalties
of subordinates to buoy up the leader, who floats on seas of adoration.
Leaders get their sense of power and confidence *from* their followers, their

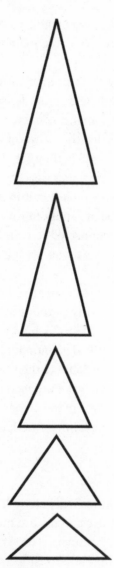

Turkey
Pakistan
Venezuela
China
Hong Kong
Singapore
India
Austria
Ethiopia
Malaysia
Mexico
Brazil
Nigeria
Spain
Bulgaria
Belgium
Thailand
France
Greece
Argentina
Indonesia
Philippines
Japan
Portugal
Italy
Finland
Ireland
UK
South Korea
Germany
Switzerland
Netherlands
Australia
Sweden
Norway
Denmark
Canada
USA

FIGURE 13.3. Company Triangles

charisma fueled by credulity and by seemingly childlike faith. Yet skill-ful leaders of such cultures can also catalyze and multiply energies and appeal to the deepest feelings and aspirations of their subordinates. They avoid the depersonalization of management by objectives; management by subjectives works better. They resemble the leaders of movements aim-ing to emancipate, reform, reclaim, and enlighten both their members and society, like the American civil rights movement; such movements also are essentially Family-type structures, resocializing members in new forms of conduct.

Family cultures have difficulty with project group organization or matrix-type authority structures, since here authority is divided. Your function has one boss and your project another, so how can you give undivided loyalty to either? Another problem is that the claims of *genuine* families may intrude. If someone is your brother or cousin they are *already* related to your Family back home and should therefore find it easier to relate closely to you at work. It follows that, where a role or project culture might see nepotism as corruption and a conflict of interest, a Family culture could see it as reinforcing its current norms. A person connected to your Family at home *and* at work has one more reason not to cheat you. Families tend to be strong where universalism is weak.

A Dutch delegation was shocked and surprised when the Brazilian owner of a large manufacturing company introduced his relatively junior accountant as the key coordinator of a $15 million joint venture. The Dutch were puzzled as to why a recently qualified accountant had been given such weighty responsibilities, including the receipt of their own money. The Brazilians pointed out that this young man was the best possible choice among 1,200 employees since he was the nephew of the owner. Who could be more trustworthy than that? Instead of complaining, the Dutch should consider themselves lucky that he was available.

The Eldest Child

Quite often employees in Family cultures will behave like "the eldest child" left in charge of the Family while their parents are out, but relinquishing that authority as soon as a "parent" returns. The American manager of a plant in Miami, Florida, found this relationship with his Venezuelan second-in-command. The plant processed and packaged PVC. The process required high standards of quality control. The product had to be mixed in exactly the correct proportions or it was dangerous. Irregularity in mixing and blending had to be reported immediately when it occurred and the line concerned closed down at once, or unsalable product would accumulate. A decision to shut down was an expert one requiring detailed knowledge. Even a delay of minutes was extremely costly. It was better on the whole to shut down prematurely than to shut down too late.

The Venezuelan deputy knew very well when the product was satisfactory and when it was not. When his manager was away from the plant and he was in charge, he brought any line whose quality was failing to an immediate halt. His judgment was both fast and accurate. When the manager was there, however, he would look for him, report what was happening, and get a decision. In the time it took to do that, considerable product was wasted. However many times he was told to act on his own, that his judgment was respected and that his decision would be upheld, he always reverted to his original practice.

This was a simple case of a clash between the task orientation assumed by the American and the Family orientation of the Venezuelan. The American had delegated the job of controlling the quality of PVC production. As he saw it this was now his deputy's responsibility, whether he himself was in his office or away. It was required by the necessity of the process. But for the deputy, his authority grew when he was left in charge and shrank the moment his "parent" returned. Decisions should be taken by the most authoritative person *present*. He would no more usurp the authority of his parents once they returned home than would any child left temporarily in charge.

Some well-known research by Inzerilli and Laurent,[1] an Italian and a French researcher, and confirmed by Denison[2] showed the much higher appeal among Italian, French, and Japanese managers of the "manager who knows everything." This was on the basis of posing the question "Is it important for a manager to have at hand precise answers to most of the questions raised by subordinates?" We all know that in the complexity of modern conditions it is becoming harder for managers to know even part of what their subordinates know as a group. Yet the supposition that your manager *does* know everything may require you to discuss everything with him, thus encouraging the upward movement of information to the apex of the organization, a process that contributes to learning. We must beware, therefore, of dismissing the Family metaphor as primitive, pretentious, or feudal. Its intimacies can process complex information effectively, and wanting your "father" to know a great deal may have more desirable results than neither expecting nor wanting your boss to know very much. A visionary leader who mobilizes his or her employees around superordinate goals needs their trust, their faith, and their knowledge. The Family model can often supply all three.

The results of the question posed in Chapter 7 on whether a company is responsible for providing housing (see Figure 7.6) also show those nations in which the Family is a natural model. In these cultures there is almost no boundary for the organization's responsibilities to the people in its employ. These even extend to where and how they are housed. Japanese employers make it their business as to whether you are married, how many children you have, and accordingly how much more you need to be paid. The company may help you find housing, help get your children into schools, offer you consumer products at reduced prices, make recreational facilities available, and even encourage you to take vacations with work colleagues. The belief is that *the more the company does for your Family, the more your Family will wish its breadwinner to do for the company.*

Thinking, Learning, and Change

The Family corporate culture is more interested in intuitive than in rational knowledge, more concerned with the development of people than with their deployment or utilization. Personal knowledge of another is rated above empirical knowledge about him or her. Knowing is less hypothetical and deductive, more by trial and error. Conversations are preferred to research questionnaires and insights to objective data. *Who* is doing something is more important than *what* is being done. If you invite the Japanese to a meeting, they will want to know who will be there before specific details about the agenda.

Change in the power-oriented Family model is essentially political, getting key actors to modify policies. Among favorite devices are new visions, charismatic appeals, inspiring goals and directions, and more authentic relationships with significant people. Bottom-up change is unlikely unless it is insurgent and seriously challenges the leaders, in which case major concessions may be made.

Training, mentoring, coaching, and apprenticeship are important sources of personal education, but these occur at the behest of the Family and do not in themselves challenge authority but rather perpetuate it. Family-style cultures can respond quickly to changing environments that affect their power. Their political antennae are often sharp.

A Dutch manager delegated to initiate change in the French subsidiary of a Dutch group described to us how impressed he was at the precision and intelligence of the French managers' response to his proposals. He returned three months later to find that nothing had happened. He had failed to realize that it was also necessary to change the management team; the strategic proposals had simply been a front behind which the Family continued to operate as before.

Motivating, Rewarding, and Resolving Conflict

Because Family members enjoy their relationships, they may be motivated more by praise and appreciation than by money. Pay-for-performance rarely sits well with them, or any motivation that threatens Family bonds. They tend to "socialize risk" among their members and can operate in uncertain environments quite well. Their major weakness occurs when intra-Family conflicts block necessary change.

Resolving conflict often depends on the skill of a leader. Criticisms are seldom voiced publicly; if they are the Family is in turmoil. Negative feedback is indirect and sometimes confined to special "licensed" occasions. (In Japan you can criticize your boss while drinking his booze.) Care is taken to avoid loss of face by prominent Family members since these are points of coherence for the whole group. The Family model gives low priority to *efficiency* (doing things right) but high priority to *effectiveness* (doing the right things).

The Eiffel Tower Culture

In the Western world a bureaucratic division of labor with various roles and functions is prescribed in advance. These allocations are coordinated at the top by a hierarchy. If each role is played as envisioned by the system, then tasks will be completed as planned. One supervisor can oversee the completion of several tasks; one manager can oversee the job of several supervisors; and so on up the hierarchy.

We have chosen the Eiffel Tower in Paris to symbolize this cultural type because it is steep, symmetrical, narrow at the top and broad at the base, stable, rigid, and robust. Like the formal bureaucracy for which it stands, it is very much a symbol of the machine age. Its structure, too, is more important than its function.

Its hierarchy is very different from that of the Family. Each higher level has a clear and demonstrable function of holding together the levels beneath it. You obey the boss because it is his or her *role* to instruct you. The rational purpose of the corporation is conveyed to you through him. He has legal authority to tell you what to do, and your contract of service, overtly or implicitly, obliges you to work according to his instructions. If you and other subordinates did not do so, the system could not function.

The boss in the Eiffel Tower is only incidentally a person. Essentially he or she is a role. Were the boss to drop dead tomorrow, someone else would replace him or her and it would make no difference to your duties or to the organization's reason for being. The successor might of course be more or less unpleasant, or interpret the role slightly differently, but that is marginal. Effectively the job is defined and the discharge of it evaluated according to that definition. Very little is left to chance or the idiosyncrasies of individuals.

It follows that authority stems from occupancy of the role. If you meet the boss on the golf course, you have no obligation to let him or her play through, and your boss probably would not expect it. Relationships are *specific* (see Chapter 7), and status is *ascribed* (see Chapter 8) and stays behind at the office. This is not, however, a personal ascription of status as we see it in the Family. Status in the Eiffel Tower is ascribed to the role. This makes it impossible to challenge. Thus bureaucracy in the Eiffel Tower is a depersonalized, rational-legal system in which everyone is subordinate to local rules and those rules prescribe a hierarchy to uphold and enforce them. The boss is powerful only because the rules sanction him or her to act.

Careers in Eiffel Tower companies are much assisted by professional qualifications. At the top of German and Austrian companies, which are typically Eiffel Tower models, the titles of professor or doctor are common on office doors. This is extremely rare in the USA.

Almost everything the Family culture accepts the Eiffel Tower rejects. Personal relationships are likely to warp judgments, create favoritism, multiply exceptions to the rules, and obscure clear boundaries between roles and responsibilities. You cannot evaluate your subordinate's performance in a role if you grow fond of that person or need his or her personal loyalty for yourself. The organization's purpose is logically separate from your personal need for power or affection. Such needs are distractions, biases, and intrusions by personal agendas upon public ones.

Each role at each level of the hierarchy is described, rated for its difficulty, complexity, and responsibility, and has a salary attached to it. There then follows a search for a person to fill it. In considering applicants for the role the personnel department will treat everyone equally and neutrally, will match the person's skills and aptitudes with the job requirements, and will award the job to the best fit between role and person. The same procedure is followed in evaluations and promotions.

We tested the influence of the *role* culture as opposed to the more *personal* culture by posing the following dilemma to managers (Figure 13.4).

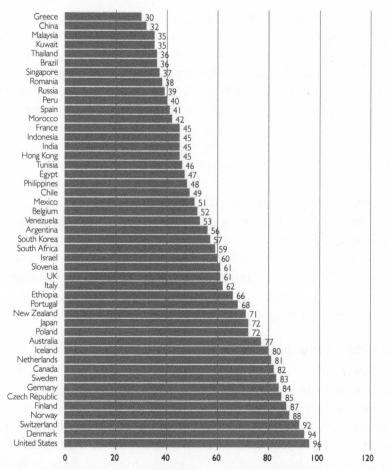

FIGURE 13.4. Percentage of Respondents Opting for Role Rather Than Personality

Two managers talk about their company's organizational structure.

A. One says: "The main reason for having an organizational structure is so that everyone knows who has authority over whom."

B. The other says: "The main reason for having an organizational structure is so that everyone knows how functions are allocated and coordinated."

Which one of these two ways usually best represents an organizational structure?

Those nations most attracted to putting roles before people, largely North American and northwest European, opt by large majorities for B. Here *the logic of subordination is clearly rational and coordinative*. In option A it is left unspecified. The organization legitimates existing power differences.

The Eiffel Tower points to the goals to be achieved by the edifice, which is relatively rigid and has difficulty pointing in different directions. If, for example, the Eiffel Tower company needs to achieve goals inconsistent with hierarchical coordinated roles, say inventing new products, then its structure tends to impede achievement. On the other hand, it is well designed to renew passports or check insurance claims, where the rules are devised in advance and consistent treatment is legally required.

In one of our workshops the head of strategic planning in a major German company gave a one-hour presentation on his company's strategic planning. He spent 45 minutes on how his firm was organized and the remaining 15 on strategic issues. Over lunch the Dutch author asked him why he had not wanted to give 60 minutes to strategic issues. "But I did," was his reply. For him, structure *was* strategy.

Thinking, Learning, and Change

The way in which people think, learn, and change in the role-oriented Eiffel Tower company is significantly different from similar processes in the Family. For employees in the Eiffel Tower, the Family culture is arbitrary, irrational, conspiratorial, cozy, and corrupt. Instead of following set procedures that everyone can understand and having objective benchmarks that employees agree to conform to, the Family is forever shifting goalposts or suspending competitive play altogether.

Learning in the Eiffel Tower means acquiring the skills necessary to fit a role and hopefully the additional skills to qualify for higher positions. In Eiffel Tower companies, people or "human resources" are conceived of as similar to capital and cash resources. People of known qualifications can be planned, scheduled, deployed, and reshuffled by skill sets like any other physical entity. Manpower planning, assessment centers, appraisal systems, training schemes, and job rotation all have the function of helping to classify and produce resources to fit known roles.

Change in the Eiffel Tower is effected through *changing rules*. With any alteration in the company's purpose must come changes in what employees are formally required to do. For this reason, the culture does not adapt well to turbulent environments. In theory, constant rule-change would be necessary, but this would in practice bewilder employees, lower morale, and obscure the distinction between rules and deviations. Change in an Eiffel Tower culture is immensely complex and time-consuming. Manuals must be rewritten, procedures changed, job descriptions altered, promotions reconsidered, qualifications reassessed. "Restructuring" or "rationalization" tend to be dreaded words in Eiffel Tower cultures. They usually mean wholesale firings and redundancies. Such companies resist change and when it becomes inevitable suffer major dislocation as a consequence.

An American manager responsible for initiating change in a German company described the difficulties he had had in making progress, although the German managers had discussed the new strategy in depth and made significant contributions to its formulation. Through informal channels he had eventually discovered that his mistake was not having formalized the changes to structure or job descriptions. In the absence of a new organogram, this Eiffel Tower company was unable to change. Like the Dutch manager, above, who had similar problems in dealing with a French Family company, his assumption was that once an intellectual decision had been agreed upon, instant action would follow. Both of these managers came from task-oriented Guided Missile cultures themselves (see below).

Motivating, Rewarding, and Resolving Conflict

Employees of the Eiffel Tower are ideally precise and meticulous. They are nervous when order and predictability is lacking. Duty is an important concept for the role-oriented employee. It is an obligation people feel within themselves rather than an obligation they feel toward a specific individual.

Conflicts are seen as irrational, pathologies of orderly procedure, offenses against efficiency. Criticisms and complaints are typically channeled and dealt with through even more rules and fact-finding procedures.

The Family and the Eiffel Tower in Conflict

MCC, the company employing Mr. Johnson, whose problems we have been following throughout this book, is broadly speaking a task-oriented company, and many of Mr. Johnson's difficulties have arisen through clashes with colleagues whose expectation of companies are much closer to the Family model. (The final installment of Mr. Johnson's story will be found at the end of this chapter.) Another example of what happens when these two models find themselves side by side is the story of Heinz, a manager from a large German multinational, experienced and outstandingly successful, who was selected to help a Colombian packaging material company get out of the red. All stakeholders, the Colombian government included, acknowledged that modernization and more professional management were needed. Heinz wanted to make the factory profitable and more efficient by introducing new production and quality standards.

The most important person in the company next to Heinz was Antonio, a Colombian, designated to take over Heinz's job after the German had completed his mission. After almost a year of working in Colombia, Heinz concluded that the activities in the factory had not improved significantly despite his best efforts.

The following are excerpts from a consultant's report (rewritten by Leonel Brug) in which Heinz and Antonio were interviewed separately.

ANTONIO'S STORY

Antonio is very positive about Heinz's technical and organizational capabilities. The need to increase efficiency is undeniable, and the production processes still need much work. Heinz is quite right on this score.

Antonio is, however, shocked by the way Heinz is trying to impose his methods and ideas on the Colombians. He describes this as turning them into robots; he is dehumanizing the whole organization.

He says Heinz seems obsessed with time and money. People hardly count at all. He yells at workers for taking longer breaks than they should, forgetting that the previous week they worked overtime without extra pay, without complaint, and, of course, without thanks. He does not seem to realize that punctuality is not possible. We have people reporting for work who walked when the bus broke down, and he shouts at them as they limp in at the gate. Antonio is amazed that they come to work at all.

There are two men who waded a river to get to work when the floods washed the bridge away, and yet Heinz still wanted to dock their pay. Antonio refused to do this. He told Heinz, "Look, they have to *want* to come to work, to be appreciated here, or absenteeism will become far higher than it already is."

HEINZ'S STORY

Heinz explains that the factory was a real mess when he arrived. There was no order, no procedure, no discipline, and no responsibility.

He complains that Antonio is always making excuses. Everything is a special case or an exceptional circumstance. He runs around like a wet-nurse trying to discover why the employees are unhappy or disturbed. He is forever telling Antonio to let them stand on their own two feet.

Employees think they can turn up to work when it is convenient for them, despite the fact that they know production cannot start until nearly all of them arrive. They wait for things to go wrong and then act as if they are making heroic gestures of self-sacrifice. He has told them repeatedly that he does not need them to stay late, he just needs them to get to work on time.

> "They have more colorful excuses than a tale of the Wild West. To hear them tell it they only come to work at all because they love us. And that they were late because their brothers missed an appointment or some bridge fell down or who knows what. We get 'scenes of village life' here every day."

Heinz explains that he has told Antonio that he does not want to bully or harass employees, he just wants to keep to agreements, deadlines, and schedules. He does not believe that is too much to ask.

In this rather extreme example, it should be noted that Heinz represents a very sophisticated Eiffel Tower culture and Antonio quite an unsophisticated Family one. In the hands of a sophisticated Family culture, like many Japanese companies, the consequences could be different. Nor are cultures necessarily exclusive. Families can "take on" the exacting rules of Eiffel Towers and become formidable competitors. The finest combinations lie beyond stereotypes and simple contrasts.

The Guided Missile Culture

The Guided Missile culture differs from both the Family and the Eiffel Tower by being *egalitarian*, but differs also from the Family and resembles the Eiffel Tower in being impersonal and task-oriented. Indeed the Guided Missile culture is rather like the Eiffel Tower in flight. But while the rationale of the Eiffel Tower culture is means, the Guided Missile has a rationale of ends. Everything must be done to persevere in your strategic intent and reach your target.

The Guided Missile culture is oriented to tasks, typically undertaken by teams or project groups. It differs from the role culture in that the jobs members do are not fixed in advance. They must do "whatever it takes" to complete a task, and what is needed is often unclear and may have to be discovered.

The National Aeronautics and Space Administration (NASA) pioneered the use of project groups working on space probes that resembled Guided Missiles in the sense that task completion was the end goal. It takes roughly 140 different kinds of engineers to build a lunar landing module, and whose contribution is crucial at exactly what time cannot be known in advance. Because every variety of engineering must work harmoniously with every other, the best form of synthesis needs to be discovered in the course of working. Nor can there be any hierarchy that claims that "A's expertise is greater than B's expertise." Each knows most about his or her part. How the whole will function needs to be worked out with everyone's participation. All are *equals*, or at least potentially equal, since their relative contributions are not yet known.

Such groups will have leaders or coordinators who are responsible for sub- and final assemblies, but these generalists may know less than specialists in each discipline and must treat all experts with great respect. The group is egalitarian because it might need the help of any one expert in changing direction toward its target. The end is known but the possible trajectories are uncertain. Missile cultures frequently draw on professionals and are cross-disciplinary. In an advertising agency, for example, one copywriter, one visualizer/artist, one media buyer, one commercial film buyer, and one account representative may work on a campaign yet to be agreed upon by the client. All will play a part, but what part depends on the final campaign the client prefers.

Guided Missile cultures are expensive because professionals are expensive. Groups tend to be temporary, and relationships as fleeting as the project and largely instrumental in bringing the project to a conclusion. Employees will join other groups, for other purposes, within days or weeks and may have multiple memberships. This culture is *not* affectionate or mutually committed, but typifies the *neutral* cultures discussed in Chapter 6.

The ultimate criteria of human value in the Guided Missile culture are how you perform and to what extent you contribute to the jointly desired outcome. In effect, each member shares in problem-solving. The relative contribution of any one person may not be as clear as in the Eiffel Tower culture where each role is described and outputs can be quantified.

In practice, the Guided Missile culture is *superimposed* upon the Eiffel Tower organization to give it permanence and stability. This is known as the matrix organization. You have one (Eiffel Tower) line reporting to your functional boss—say, electrical engineering—and another (Guided Missile) line óf responsibility to your project head. This makes you jointly responsible to your engineering boss for quality engineering and to your project leader for a viable, low-cost means of, say, auto emissions control. The project has to succeed, and your electronics must be excellent. Two authorities pull you in different, although reconcilable, directions.

Thinking, Learning, and Change

The Guided Missile culture is *cybernetic*, in the sense that it homes in on its target using feedback signals and is therefore circular rather than linear. Yet the "missile" rarely, if ever, changes its mind about its target. Steering is therefore corrective and conservative, not as open to new *ends* as to new *means*.

Learning includes "getting on" with people, breaking the ice quickly, playing the part in a team that is currently lacking, being practical rather than theoretical, and being problem-centered rather than discipline-centered. Appraisal is often by peers or subordinates rather than by someone further up the hierarchy.

Change comes quickly to the Guided Missile culture. The target moves. More targets appear, new groups are formed, old ones dissolve. People who hop from group to group will often hop from job to job, so that turnover tends to be high, and *loyalties to professions and projects are greater than loyalties to the company.* The Guided Missile culture is in many respects the antithesis of the Family culture, in which bonds are close and ties are of long duration and deep affection.

Motivating, Rewarding, and Resolving Conflict

Motivations tend to be *intrinsic* in this culture. That is, team members get enthusiastic about, identify with, and struggle toward the final product. In the case of Apple the enthusiasm is about creating an "insanely great device." The product under development is the superordinate goal for which the conflicts and animosities of team members may be set aside. Unless there is high participation there will not be widespread commitment. The final consensus must be broad enough to pull in all those who work on it.

This culture tends to be individualistic since it allows for a wide variety of differently specialized people to work with each other on a temporary basis. The scenery of faces keeps changing. Only the pursuit of chosen lines of personal development is constant. The team is a vehicle for the shared enthusiasm of its members, but is itself disposable and will be discarded when the project ends. Members are garrulous, idiosyncratic, and intelligent, but their mutuality is a means, not an end. It is a way of enjoying the journey. They do not need to know each other intimately and may avoid doing so. Management by objectives is the language spoken, and people are paid by performance.

The Incubator Culture

The Incubator culture is based on the existential idea that organizations are secondary to the fulfillment of individuals. Just as "existence precedes essence" was the motto of existential philosophers, so "existence precedes organization" is the notion of Incubator cultures. If organizations are to be tolerated at all, they should be there to serve as *Incubators for self-expression and self-fulfillment*. The metaphor here should not be confused with "business incubators." These are organizations that provide routine maintenance and services, plant equipment, insurance, office space, and so on for embryo businesses so that they can lower their overhead costs during the crucial start-up phase.

However, the logic of business and cultural incubators is quite similar. In both cases the purpose is to free individuals from routine to more creative activities and to minimize time spent on self-maintenance. The Incubator is *both* personal and egalitarian. Indeed it has almost no structure at all and what structure it does provide is merely for personal convenience: heat, light, word processing, coffee, and so on.

The roles of other people in the Incubator, however, are crucial. They are there to confirm, criticize, develop, find resources for, and help to complete the innovative product or service. The culture acts as a sounding board for innovative ideas and tries to respond intelligently to new initiatives. Typical examples were the start-up firms in Silicon Valley, California, in Silicon Glen in Scotland, and on Route 128 around Boston. The companies are usually entrepreneurial or founded by a creative team that quit a larger employer just before the payoff. Being individualist, they are not constrained by organizational loyalties and may deliberately take a "free ride" until their eggs are close to hatching. In this way larger organizations find themselves successively undermined.

Cultural Incubators are not only small innovative companies. They can be doctors in group practice, legal partners, some consultants, chartered surveyors, or any group of professionals who work mostly alone but like to share resources while comparing experiences. Some writers see the Incubator as the organizational wave of the future. Others see any decline of Silicon Valley as evidence that this culture cannot survive maturity and is but a temporary phase in starting up an organization from an ad hoc basis. Others point to the rarity of Incubator cultures outside the "enclaves of individualism" in the USA, the UK, and the English-speaking world.

Just as Incubators have minimal structure, so they also have minimal hierarchy. Such authority as individuals do command is strictly personal, the exciting nature of their ideas and the inspiration of their vision leading others to work with them.

Incubators often, if not always, operate in an environment of intense *emotional* commitment. However, this commitment is less toward people per se than to the world-changing, society-redeeming nature of the work being undertaken. The personal computer gave "power to the person"; gene-splicing could save crops, save lives, and rescue the economy and represents an odyssey into the unknown, wherein "the journey is the reward."

Incubator cultures enjoy the process of creating and innovating. Because of emotional commitment, shared enthusiasms, and superordinate goals, the Incubator at its best can be ruthlessly honest, effective, nurturing, therapeutic, and exciting, depending as it does on face-to-face relationships and working intimacies. Because the association is voluntary, often underfunded, and fueled largely by hope and idealism, it can be the most significant and intense experience of a lifetime. But this is very hard to repeat or sustain, since the project no sooner succeeds than strangers must be hired and the founders' special relationships are lost. Incubators are typically limited in size by the leaders' "span of control," since it becomes hard to communicate spontaneously and informally with more than 75 to 100 people.

Thinking, Learning, and Change

Change in the Incubator can be fast and spontaneous where the members are attuned to each other. Roger Harrison[3] has likened the process to an improvising jazz band, in which a self-elected leader tries something new and the band follows if it likes the theme and ignores the theme if it does not. All participants are on the same wavelength, empathically searching together for a solution to the shared problem. But because a customer has not defined any target, the *problem itself is open to redefinition* and the solution being searched for is typically generic, aimed at a universe of applications.

American start-up companies with Incubator cultures rarely survive the maturing of their products and their markets. This culture learns to create but not to survive altered patterns of demand. The "great designers" of the novel products continue to be the heroes of the company long after the focus has shifted to customer service and to marketing.

Motivating, Rewarding, and Resolving Conflict

Motivation is often wholehearted, intrinsic, and intense, with individuals working "70 hours a week and loving it" as the T-shirts at Apple Computer used to read in its earlier days. There is competition to contribute to the emerging shape of something new. Everyone wants to get his or her "hands on." There is scant concern for personal security, and few wish to profit or have power apart from the unfolding creative process. If the whole succeeds, there will be plenty for everyone. If it does not, the Incubator itself will be gone. In contrast to the Family culture, leadership in the Incubator is *achieved*, not ascribed. You follow those whose progress most impresses you and whose ideas work. Power plays that impede group achievement will be reviled. Conflict is resolved either by splitting up or by trying the proposed alternatives to see which works best.

Which Countries Prefer Which Corporate Cultures?

As we have already said, these "pure types" seldom exist. In practice the types are mixed or overlaid with one culture dominating. Nevertheless, in different national cultures one or more of these types clearly dominate the corporate scene and, if we list the main characteristics of the four types, it becomes easy to refer back to the national cultural dimensions discussed in the preceding chapters. In the four models employees relate differently, have different views of authority, think, learn, and change in different ways, and are motivated by different rewards, while criticism and conflict resolution are variously handled.

The reader, however, should interpret this cautiously. Smaller companies *wherever* located are more likely to take the Family and Incubator forms. Large companies needing structure to cohere are likely to choose Eiffel Tower or Guided Missile forms. In France, for example, smaller companies tend to be Family and larger companies Eiffel Tower. In the USA Guided Missile companies may dominate among large corporations, but the archetypal Incubators are to be found in the Silicon Valley paradigm.

Measurement Through the Corporate Culture Profiles (CCP)

We have developed a 14-item questionnaire to measure the current and ideal organizational value orientations. The Corporate Culture Profiler is a multifunctional instrument that enables participants to review and examine the interpretations employees give to relationships with each other and with the organization as a whole. Specifically, the CCP looks at the perceived current and idealized perceptions of issues such as Corporate Effectiveness (toward mission/goals), Efficiency, Loyalty, Learning, and Values, as well as possible other areas as per the request of the individual client. This tool can be used within a group or organization internally, or with two groups involved in an integration process, allowing the leaders and/or teams to address key identified tensions and prioritize distribution of time and resources Like other corporate culture diagnostic tools, the CCP offers a simple diagnosis of the dominant culture in your organization using four typologies: Incubator, Family, Guided Missile, and Eiffel Tower.

This is helpful in mergers and acquisitions, strategic change, diversity, globalization, or other related issues.

Benefits of the CCP
- Provides a rigorous assessment of key issues rather than assumed needs
- Offers a road map for future action
- Benchmarking against THT's cultural, industry, or sector databases
- Secures engagement with organization/conference/workshop participants as they feel their key issues are being addressed

Limitations of the CCP
- Looks at preferences only
- Zero-sum calculations

Figure 13.5 and 13.6 give examples of a Corporate Culture Profile.

Feedback on your Corporate Culture:

Explanation underlying the Trompenaar's model of Corporate Culture:

Culture is to the organization what personality is to the individual - a hidden yet unifying theme that provides meaning, direction and mobilization that can exert a decisive influence on the overall ability of the organization to deal with the challenges it faces. Our interest here is in examining the interpretations employees give to their relationships with each other and with the organization as a whole. Thus we are all concerned with issues such as:

- How does one learn, change and resolve conflicts?

- How do we motivate and reward people in the different corporate images?

- How can we facilitate different functional areas with differing cultures work together effectively ~ such as research staff with marketing?

A corporate culture has a profound effect on organization effectiveness, because it influences how decisions are made, human resources are used and how the organization responds to the environment.

Trompenaars' 4 Corporate Cultures:

Our model identifies four competing organizational cultures which are derived from two related dimensions: • Task or Person (high formalization versus low formalization) • Hierarchical or Egalitarian (high versus low centralization) Combining these dimensions gives us four possible culture types. Note that any single (real) organization (such as your own) is likely to show characteristics of more than one stereotype ~ but often with one that is dominant.

Corporate Culture Tensions:

Many established models for corporate change tend to develop change strategies based on transforming the organization from the current to ideal culture. These models can be criticized for two principal and recurring reasons: 1. they tend to underestimate the difficulty involved in achieving or sustaining the change, and 2. they tend to discard the current situation in favor of a new future and thus throwing out the best of the what already exists.

Corporate Culture Dilemmas:

In contrast, our approach is to consider the tensions between these extremes. All organizations need stability and change, tradition and innovation, public and private interest, planning and laissez-faire, order and freedom, growth and decay. The change problem from the 'current' to 'ideal' situation cannot be "solved" in the sense of simply being eliminated. These differences that generate tensions are the source of a series of dilemmas.

Managing change in our framework is about reconciling these dilemmas. In this way we can overcome the limitations of current change models because we are neither simply throwing away the past, nor seeking to change a well embedded resistant self-preserving corporate culture.

FIGURE 13.5. Corporate Culture Profile (CC) Explanation

Summary of Corporate Cultures

We have defined four broad types of corporate culture, which are closely related to the national differences described in earlier chapters. Just as national cultures conflict, leading to mutual incomprehension and mistrust, so corporate cultures collide. Attempts to "dice" the Family with a matrix can cause rage and consternation. Getting cozy with subordinates in the Eiffel Tower could be seen as a potentially improper advance. Asking to be put in a group with a special friend is a subversive act in the Guided Missile culture. Calling your boss "buddy" and slapping him or her on the back will get you thrown from the Eiffel Tower, while suggesting in an Incubator that everyone fill out time sheets will be greeted with catcalls. (If you really want to discover norms, *break them*; reading this chapter is intended as a less painful alternative.)

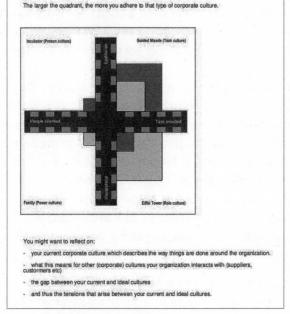

Corporate Culture Profile (CC):

Reading your Corporate Culture Profile:

The four quadrants represent the four different extreme types of corporate culture we distinguish.

The coloured regions in each quadrant indicate the relative degree to which you have rated:

☐ the current situation in your organization (grey) and

■ the ideal corporate culture you would prefer to work in (blue).

The larger the quadrant, the more you adhere to that type of corporate culture.

You might want to reflect on:

- your current corporate culture which describes the way things are done around the organization.

- what this means for other (corporate) cultures your organization interacts with (suppliers, customers etc)

- the gap between your current and ideal cultures

- and thus the tensions that arise between your current and ideal cultures.

FIGURE 13.6. Corporate Culture Profile (CC) Results

Yet the types exist and must be respected. Really successful businesses borrow from all types and ceaselessly struggle to reconcile them. We turn to this process in the next chapter. First, however, we should say goodbye to Mr. Johnson.

Back in St. Louis at the MCC management meeting, Mr. Johnson reported on the introduction of pay-for-performance. It had been resisted widely, and where it had been tried, in parts of southern Europe, the Middle East, and Asia, early results showed it had failed. The meeting listened in silence. The atmosphere was distinctly cool. "Well," said the CEO, "how do you plan to cope with these problems, Bill? I'm sure we don't need the HR function to tell us that there are a lot of different people and opinions in the world."

Johnson had by now decided that he had nothing to lose, so he voiced a concern he had felt for many months. "I realize we make machines, but I sometimes ask myself if we are letting the metaphor run away with the organization. These are people, not microprocessors or integrated circuits, which can be replaced if they don't work."

"I wish we *could* operate more like a computer," interrupted the finance manager. "We hire quality people to do as we tell them, and function in ways they are trained. Either they do this or we get somebody else. What's wrong with that?"

The CEO was trying to calm things down. "I have to disagree there," he said. "I see this company as more of an *organism*. If you go to Barcelona and chop off heads, don't be surprised if the body dies. If we take out some subsidiary's right hand we can't expect it to work well in the future. What I can't understand is why Bill can't get them to see that we're all one organism and that the hands and feet can't go off in all directions."

Suddenly all the exasperations of the last few months came to the surface. For a moment Johnson had thought that the CEO was supporting him, but it was the same old message: get the whole world to march in step with us.

"What *I've* been through in the last eight months is about as far from a smoothly running computer or a living organism as you could get. I'll tell you what it's really like, because I was reading the story to my kids. It's like that crazy croquet game in Alice in Wonderland where she has to play with a flamingo as a mallet, waiters bending over as hoops, and hedgehogs as balls. The flamingo twists its head round to look at Alice, the hoops wander off, and the balls crawl away. The result is chaos.

"Other cultures aren't part of a machine, or the organs of a supranational body. They're different animals, all with logic of their own. If we asked them what game *they* are playing, and got them to explain the rules, we might discover when we aren't holding a mallet at all, or even get the hedgehog to go in the right direction."

Was Mr. Johnson promoted, or given the job of overseeing the welfare of MCC pensioners? My guess is that he is running a small but fast-growing consultancy somewhere, specializing in cross-cultural management.

Enhanced Measurement:
Our Organization Value Profiler (OVP)

Culture is to the organization what personality is to the individual—a hidden yet unifying theme that provides meaning, direction, and mobilization that can exert a decisive influence on the overall ability of the organization to deal with the organizational challenges and thus the dilemmas it faces. A corporate culture has a profound effect on an organization's effectiveness, because it influences how decisions are made, how human resources are used, and how the organization responds to the environment.

In order to elicit the values of organizations that will challenge and influence their performance, we have developed the Organization Value Profiler (OVP) model. This 48-item instrument enables us to identify the possible similarities and differences of the organizational cultures involved. The OVP is a multifunctional instrument that enables participants to review and examine the interpretations employees give to relationships with each other and with the organization as a whole. How is it different from the CCP? The CCP measures your preference and is therefore based on a zero-sum proposition. You have to choose one out of four options 14 times. The OVP offers you more or less the same options, but you can score high on all. So where the CCP looks at the dominance of your hand, the OVP looks at how you clap.

Unlike other corporate culture diagnostic tools, the OVP goes beyond simple diagnosis and serves as the basis for the reconciliation of the key tensions that owe their origin to mergers and acquisitions, strategic change, diversity, globalization, or other factors. It is also intended to be "culture-free"—that is, applicable to a diverse range of organization cultures across the world. We have seen too many other models that display an Anglo-Saxon or US signature and have only been validated in the national cultures where they were developed.

The OVP is able to diagnose the different corporate cultures of the parties engaged in the integration process and will clearly show the value dilemmas that the new group is facing. It is an organizational culture scan based on the degree of formalization and flexibility and on the degree of hierarchy and openness to the environment.

It still has our underlying four quadrant model of corporate culture, as described below, but further subdivides each quadrant leading to a full 12-segment model (Figure 13.7).

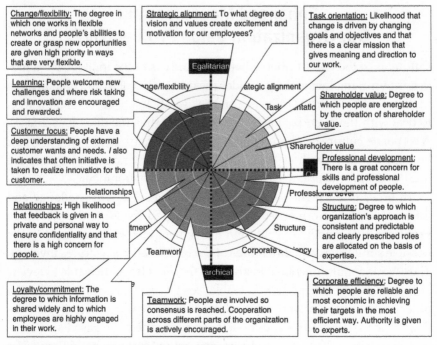

Change/flexibility: The degree in which one works in flexible networks and people's abilities to create or grasp new opportunities are given high priority in ways that are very flexible.

Learning: People welcome new challenges and where risk taking and innovation are encouraged and rewarded.

Customer focus: People have a deep understanding of external customer wants and needs. *I* also indicates that often initiative is taken to realize innovation for the customer.

Relationships: High likelihood that feedback is given in a private and personal way to ensure confidentiality and that there is a high concern for people.

Loyalty/commitment: The degree to which information is shared widely and to which employees are highly engaged in their work.

Strategic alignment: To what degree do vision and values create excitement and motivation for our employees?

Teamwork: People are involved so consensus is reached. Cooperation across different parts of the organization is actively encouraged.

Task orientation: Likelihood that change is driven by changing goals and objectives and that there is a clear mission that gives meaning and direction to our work.

Shareholder value: Degree to which people are energized by the creation of shareholder value.

Professional development: There is a great concern for skills and professional development of people.

Structure: Degree to which organization's approach is consistent and predictable and clearly prescribed roles are allocated on the basis of expertise.

Corporate efficiency: Degree to which people are reliable and most economic in achieving their targets in the most efficient way. Authority is given to experts.

FIGURE 13.7. Organization Value Profiler (OVP) Model

The four segments represent how the organization orientates itself to four basic processes in terms of task/strategy/mission, role/efficiency/consistency, power/human relations/involvement, and person/learning/adaptability. Within each of the subsegments we explore specific aspects that together determine the major orientations.

In great contrast with the normal cookie-cutter graphical models, including the CCP, our questionnaire has been designed to reflect our underlying philosophy that bipolar scales (where more of one alternative means less of the other alternative) are fundamentally inappropriate for the type of assessment we are seeking.

We undertook extensive formal research and field testing to finalize the questions, including Cronbach's alpha reliability analysis and triangulation with face-to-face and online semi-structured interviews.

Respondents can score any subcomponent high or low, and the subcomponents collectively combine to form the constructs being assessed. In this way, one can score high on all 4 quadrants and all 12 segments. No longer is an organization of only one stereotype. This reflects our conceptual framework where an integrated organization harnesses the strengths of all extremes and is not restricted to choosing between extreme options.

By using cross-validating questions, we have verified whether opposites and contradictions within one corporate culture have been reconciled. So for example we ask respondents to rate statements such as "There is a clear and overt strategy for the future"(Guided Missile) and "Through our short-term thinking we are quick on our feet" (Incubator). They are validated by a combination reconciling question such as "We are able to meet short-term demands without compromising our long-term vision."

In our older version of these types of model questionnaire (and those of other authors), we would have to show a scale between short- and long-term orientations. In this new reconciling framework we can score high or low on both! And a high score on both indicates a more powerful and higher performance culture.

Another example is the tension between task (Guided Missile) and people (Family) orientation that we explore with the contrasting questions "There is a lot of teamwork" and "People strive for self-realization" and the validating question "We have teams that consist of creative individuals."

In this way, the OVP shows how healthy an organizational culture can be by covering all 12 segments *and* the reconciliation between those segments.

External validation (against departmental or functional performance indictors) shows that the higher the scores on *all* segments, the higher the score on the validating questions, which correlates directly with higher long-term performance of the organization.

Figure 13.8 shows some sample scores. Low-performing organizations score low on all segments. Industry "followers" have an average score, and "market leaders" score high on all segments, showing that they have an integral culture reconciling all contradictions in their business.

We can also explore "current" and "ideal" cultures by asking respondents to indicate two sets of ratings for their own organization. Alternatively, we can compare the value orientation profiles of both parties in a merger.

A cultural values assessment that compares the organizations that want to integrate will identify opportunities and obstacles to cultural change. It will help define the necessary guidance in the development of personal alignment, group cohesion, and structural alignment processes. This provides the foundation for identifying key performance indicators that will be used in the final step of values management.

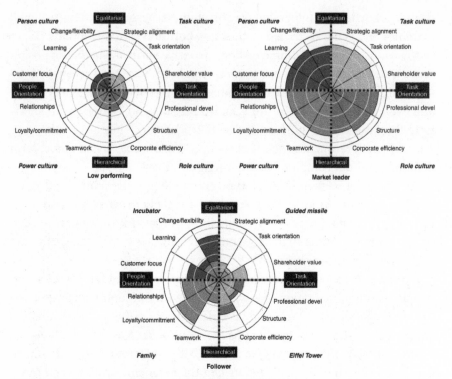

FIGURE 13.8. Sample Organization Value Profiler (OVP) Scores

The value dilemmas that were selected from the interview and web-based processes are triangulated with the dilemmas raised from the OVP.

Measurement for Key Players:
The Personal Values Profiler

For assessing the personal values of key players we use our Personal Values Profiler (PVP) that offers important insights into the relationships employees have with their organization.

The PVP enables participants to review and examine their personal values in the context of their professional work.

There are no right or wrong answers, and no orientation to any particular values is better or worse. People from different cultures or professions will necessarily have different perspectives and will wish to pursue and prioritize their interests that are not necessarily the same as those of others.

Exploring how individuals personally give priorities to different values and how these differ from other employees across an organization offers important insights into the relationships employees have with their organization.

This provides understanding of matters concerning resistance or support for change, and the capacity for stability, sustainability, and innovation. These can exert a decisive influence on the overall ability of the organization to deal with the challenges and dilemmas it faces.

This PVP (Personal Values Profiler) is usually cross-linked to our OVP (Organization Values Profiler) to provide further important comparisons to corporate culture.

The PVP has been developed by combining and extending our earlier frameworks based on our intellectual property. Each component has been subject to rigorous research and testing with extensive application in many client situations across the world and is also linked to our main corporate culture database of over 140,000 responses. This PVP/CCP combination is usually cross-linked to our OVP (Organization Values Profiler) to provide further important comparisons to corporate culture. In our arena of mergers and acquisitions, for example, we need to be alert for mismatch between the values that will support the key purpose of the newly formed company and the PVPs of key players.

See examples at www.ridingthewavesofculture.com.

14

A New Framework for Managing Change Across Cultures

Fons Trompenaars and Peter Woolliams

THIS CHAPTER is dedicated to give you a new way of looking at managing cultural change. The main message is focused around how to enrich the existing organizational culture by its opposite. So if the preference is short-term results, how can one contextualize that within the context of a long-term vision? And if you push your products and services, how can you do it in a way that involves the customer? A new paradigm for the management of change is proposed. Most existing frameworks tend to want to discard the current situation in favor of a new corporate culture, thus discarding the best of what already exists. The authors argue that changing an organization's culture is a contradiction in terms. This is because cultures act to preserve themselves and to protect their own living existence. So rather than seeing change as a "thing" opposing continuity, it is considered as a difference. The authors believe organizations seek change to preserve the company, profitability, market share, and core competence. The reason for changing certain aspects is to avoid changing in other respects. In short, organizations must reconcile change with continuity in order to preserve an evolving identity. The new methodology is centered on diagnosing the tensions between the current and ideal corporate culture. These tensions manifest themselves as a series of dilemmas. The new approach for the management of change is to reconcile these dilemmas. Compromise alone is insufficient. The authors demonstrate with examples and offer a new conceptual framework on how seemingly opposing values deriving from change imperatives can be integrated to achieve a "win-win" outcome.

247

Many researchers have suggested models for change that seek to embrace culture change within organizations (corporate culture), while others have alluded to issues of change across national cultural boundaries. Most models, however, can be criticized for two principal and recurring reasons: (1) they tend to underestimate the difficulty involved in achieving or sustaining the change, and (2) they tend to want to discard the current situation in favor of a new future, thus throwing out the best of what already exists.

After an extended period of research over many years and developing dilemma theory with Hampden-Turner,[1] the authors have come to a different view based on extensive evidence collected across the world from a large number of diverse organizations. The authors believe that changing an organization's culture is a contradiction in terms. This is because cultures act to preserve themselves and to protect their own living existence. So rather than seeing change as a "thing" opposing continuity, the authors see it as a difference. The authors believe organizations seek change to preserve the company, profitability, market share, and core competence. The reason for changing certain aspects is to avoid changing in other respects. In short, organizations must reconcile change with continuity in order to preserve an evolving identity.

Thus the authors offer a new approach to change. The overall core framework requires an assessment of the differences between the current corporate culture and some envisaged "ideal" future corporate culture. But established models for change then develop a change strategy based on transforming the organization from the current to an ideal culture. In contrast, this approach considers the contrast between these extremes. All organizations need stability and change, tradition and innovation, public and private interest, planning and laissez-faire, order and freedom, growth and decay. These are the opposites leaders wrestle that put tensions into their world, sharpen their sensitivities, and increase their self-awareness. The problem of changing from the "current" to the "ideal" situation cannot be "solved" in the sense of being eliminated but can be wisely transcended. Successful leaders get surges of energy from the fusing of these opposites.

Thus these differences that generate tensions are the source of a series of dilemmas. Managing change in this methodology is therefore about reconciling these dilemmas. In this way, the limitations of current change models can be overcome because this methodology is neither simply throwing away the past nor seeking to change a well-embedded, resistant, self-preserving corporate culture.

Context and Background

As Peter Senge noted,[2] the word "change" means several, often contradictory, things. Sometimes it refers to the external world of technology, customers, competitors, and such like. Sometimes it refers to internal changes such as practices, styles, and strategies. The authors will refer to change as the changes in shared assumptions, values, and practices of organizational actors as they are stimulated by changes in the environment. Although executives often intervene because the pace of internal change is not keeping up with that of the external world, it will not be assumed that all change needs to be led from the top down. The authors strongly believe that change processes where leaders are not involved are like uphill skiing: it is possible, but one needs to be a very good athlete.

Because the focus is on cultural change, the role of the leader is crucial because he or she symbolizes the culture and is the main creator of culture. The authors believe, however, like Senge, that cultural change is not simply the responsibility of the "Hero-CEO." It is striking how the Anglo-Saxon model of change has dominated the world of change management. It is based too often on a task-oriented culture and the idea that traditions need to be forgotten as soon as possible. What is the alternative? The approach needs to be amended from a "what" and a "why" process into a "through" process that takes the existing culture to be reconciled with the new culture.

A New Unified Model for Managing Change as a "Through" Process

Conventional approaches frame the change problem in terms of "what," "why," and/or "how." To focus solely on "why" may not translate effectively to "what" and/or "how." "How" questions place the effort on means where diagnosis is assumed or not even undertaken at all and therefore the ends sought are not considered. To focus on ends requires the posing of "what" questions. What is one trying to accomplish? What needs to be changed? What are the critical success factors? What measure of performance is one trying to achieve? Ends and means are relative, however, and whether something is an end or a means can only be considered in relation to something else. Thus often, the "true" ends of a change effort may be different from those intended. In this regard, the "why" questions may be useful.

According to Lewin's force-field theory,[3] organizations are in dynamic tension between forces pushing for change and forces resistant to change. Established change management practice has interpreted this on the basis that it is management's task to reduce the resistance to change and increase the forces for change. But under the dilemma theory approach, this is only a compromise solution. It ignores the fact that increasing the force for change may increase people's resistance, for example. We therefore offer a new approach that requires a whole new logic. By applying an inductive analysis to the evidence and research data, they offer a "through" question approach.

Cultural Change as a Through–Through Process

Basic to understanding cultural change is the understanding that culture is a series of rules and methods that a society or organization has evolved to deal with the regular problems that face it.

Countries and organizations face dilemmas in dealing with the tension between the existing set of values and the desired ones. While cultures differ markedly in how they approach these dilemmas, they do not differ in needing to make some kind of response. They share the destiny to face up to different challenges of existence. Once the change leaders have become aware of the problem-solving process, they will reconcile dilemmas more effectively and therefore will be more successful.

All change processes have in common the need for a diagnosis of the values in use (the existing values system) and mapping the espoused and desired values (the ideal value system). The change process is energized by the tension between the two. Note again that it is not simply the replacement of the existing with the desired.

The Place of Corporate Culture in Implementing a New Design

It is becoming more frequently recognized that change initiatives have failed because aspects of corporate culture have been ignored. Simply "adding" the culture component, however, does not suffice.

This explains perhaps why culture is very often ignored. Values are not artifacts that can be added. They are continuously created by interactions between human actors and not "just out there" as solid rocks. As such, culture is only meaningful in the context in which the change process unfolds.

This approach therefore seeks to integrate culture in all the steps that need to be taken in the change process. Even the sequence of steps is affected by the dominant culture at hand.

Much of our inductive thinking has its origin firstly in our portfolio of effective diagnostic and analytical tools and models, and secondly in the large and reliable database that has been established based on data collected from these. This enables us either to facilitate or let organizations themselves make a diagnosis of the tensions they are facing.

Structure is a concept that is frequently used in the analysis of organizations, and many definitions and approaches exist. The interest here is in examining the interpretations employees give to their relationships with each other and with the organization as a whole. Culture is to the organization what personality is to the individual—a hidden yet unifying theme that provides meaning, direction, and mobilization that can exert a decisive influence on the overall ability of the organization to deal with the challenges it faces.

Just as individuals in a culture can have different personalities while sharing much in common, so too can groups and organizations. It is this pattern that is recognized as "corporate culture" as described in the previous chapter.

While we could have categorized these orientations using Cameron and Quinn's competing values framework,[4] or Charles Handy's early ideas on corporate culture,[5] we found our adapted model more discriminating. In our diagnostic phase, we sought to compare the current corporate culture, as perceived by an organization's members, contrasted with what we each would consider to be the ideal corporate culture. Exhaustive data mining and correspondence analysis of 140,000 cases on corporate culture models reveals tensions derived from the following scenarios. (In Table 14.1, the top six are ranked from the most frequent to least frequent.) In fact, all combinations are found in the extensive database, but these are the most significant.

TABLE 14.1. Scenarios Resulting from Changes from Current to Ideal Cultures

CURRENT	IDEAL	OUTCOME SCENARIO
Guided Missile	Incubator	Scenario 1
Eiffel Tower	Guided Missile	Scenario 2
Family	Guided Missile	Scenario 3
Eiffel Tower	Incubator	Scenario 4
Family	Incubator	Scenario 5
Incubator	Guided Missile	Scenario 6

Following the proposed methodology, the management of change therefore involves answering two questions:

1. What are the dilemmas that will be faced when seeking to change from the "current" to the "ideal" organization?
2. How can these dilemmas be reconciled?

For each of the scenarios, different dilemmas can be expected. Using web-based "interview" techniques (WebCue), we have also invited members of a large number of client organizations to elicit and delineate their dilemmas. Over 50,000 such responses have been collected, which can be clustered into a number of recurring dilemmas. We are therefore able to review these aspects of the change process based on what we have found with actual clients. Each of the model change scenarios discussed is an attempt to generalize from real change processes from these clients while avoiding issues of confidence and ethics.

In each of the separate descriptions, particular steps are highlighted to provide a good sense of how this works in consulting practice. Figure 14.1 is a representation of the process, but the entry point one chooses is culturally dependent.

In some respects, the pervasive nature of implicit culture can make it difficult to change. Even at the explicit level, traditional practices become enshrined as "sacred cows" that cannot easily be challenged. In an ideal world, the authors would go back and challenge the implicit values behind each of these explicit constructs in order to check whether they were still the best way of delivering and reinforcing those values. When the products of culture become "sacred cows," they can inhibit change. This is especially important when importing sacred cows to new cultures. As the culture of an organization is often "owned" and lived at the highest level, managers can feel they have little ability to influence or change the

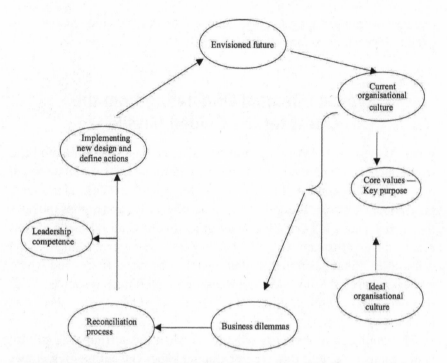

FIGURE 14.1. A New Framework for Managing Change Across Cultures

real culture of the organization in a material way without some top-down action.

These extremes might be summarized by saying:

> "On the one hand, we need to change the corporate culture to be convergent with our new business mission. Or, on the other hand, to develop a new business mission that is compatible with our existing corporate culture."

In our research and work with clients, we have found that the change process of an organization is the essence of a leader's raison d'être.[6] In the change process, a leader faces dilemmas he or she needs to reconcile in the areas of people, time, and nature. Successful leaders do not change from one horn of the dilemma to its opposite horn. They are not trying to compromise between extremes of value orientations, from extreme individualism to teamwork, from universal rules to learning exceptions, from performance expectations to the respect for seniority. The leader with success tries to integrate seemingly opposing orientations into a process that changes the qualities of each of the orientations.

Typical Dilemma Originating from the Quest for the Guided Missile

It is striking how the Anglo-Saxon model of change has dominated the world of change management. A company formulates a set of new goals, preferably in the context of a clear vision, hires some managers for a marginal $300,000 a year (excluding the bonus, obviously), and dumps the ones that do not believe in its clearly defined goals. In this Guided Missile–driven model, the organization is interpreted as a task-oriented instrument at the disposal of shareholders (remember, people who never share) and where managers have an MBA and employees are called human resources. With that name brainwashing, it hurts less when one is kicked out: "Gee, I was just a resource."

The challenge is obviously what to do when the surrounding culture is not compatible with this type of change logic. The authors remember an American manager of a global technology company who had launched a very successful change program in Rochester, New York, and after launching the formula in Europe, he cried on their shoulders. In great despair, he described how unbelievably inflexible the French and Germans tend to be. He had done a whole round in Europe and within each of the countries many seemed very much supporting our vision. Initially, the Germans had some problems with the process: they wanted to know all details of the procedures and how they were connected to the envisioned change. The French, in turn, were worried about the unions and how to keep their people motivated. But nonetheless, the internal consultants and management left these conversations with the sense that they had all agreed to a shared approach. Yet, when the manager came back some three months later to check how the implementation was going, he was surprised and disappointed to find that in France and Germany nothing had started yet. Anyone with a little sensitivity for cross-cultural affairs would have predicted this.

We have collected and analyzed some 4,000 examples of such critical incidents. The principal findings are summarized in Table 14.2 in terms of the frequently repeating dilemmas for differing scenarios.

The New Methodology in Practice

Irrespective of where one chooses to start, the authors distinguish the following steps for a change intervention:

1. Developing an envisioned future in order to develop a sense of what to go for
2. Diagnosing the current corporate culture with the cross-cultural profiler (CCP)
3. Defining core values and key purpose to develop a sense of what one stands for
4. Defining the ideal corporate culture with CCP embedding core values and key purpose
5. Defining major business dilemmas caused by the tensions between envisioned future and key purpose and between current and ideal corporate cultures
6. Reconciling four or five major business dilemmas
7. Diagnosing the current leadership competence to reconcile major value dilemmas
8. Implementing new design and defining concrete action points to be taken as defined by the change agents

TABLE 14.2. Repeating Dilemmas Found for the Different Scenarios

CURRENT: GUIDED MISSILE	IDEAL: INCUBATOR
Typical dilemmas	
Leadership	Depersonalized authority versus development of creative individuals
Reconciliation	Attribute the highest authority to those managers who have innovation and learning as prime criteria in their goals
Management	Consistent goal-orientation around task versus the power of learning
Reconciliation	Make learning and innovation part of the task description
Rewards	Extrinsic reward job done versus intrinsic reward self-development
Reconciliation	Describe task in terms of clearly stated innovation outputs

CURRENT: GUIDED MISSILE	IDEAL: FAMILY
Typical dilemmas	
Leadership	Depersonalized authority versus authority is personally ascribed to the leader
Reconciliation	Attribute the highest authority to those managers who have made internalization of subtle processes a prime criterion in their goals
Management	Consistent goal-orientation around task versus the power of politics and know-who
Reconciliation	Make political sensitivity part of the task description
Rewards	Extrinsic reward job done versus reward long-term loyalty
Reconciliation	Describe task in terms of loosely stated long-term outputs

CURRENT: GUIDED MISSILE	IDEAL: EIFFEL TOWER
Typical dilemmas	
Leadership	Depersonalized authority versus authority ascribed to the role
Reconciliation	Attribute the highest authority to those managers who have made reliable application of expertise a prime criterion in their goals
Management	Consistent goal-orientation around task versus expertise and reliability
Reconciliation	Make reliable expertise and long-term commitment part of the task description
Rewards	Contribution to the bottom line versus increasing their expertise in doing a reliable job
Reconciliation	Describe task in terms of expertise and reliability in its application

CURRENT: INCUBATOR	IDEAL: GUIDED MISSILE
Typical dilemmas	
Leadership	Development of creative individuals versus depersonalized authority
Reconciliation	Attribute the highest authority to those managers who have innovation and learning as prime criteria in their goals
Management	Versus consistent goal-orientation around task
Reconciliation	Make learning and innovation part of the task description
Rewards	Intrinsic reward self-development versus extrinsic reward job done
Reconciliation	Describe task in terms of clearly stated innovation outputs

(continued)

TABLE 14.2. Repeating Dilemmas Found for the Different Scenarios, *continued*

CURRENT: INCUBATOR	IDEAL: FAMILY
Typical dilemmas	
Leadership	Negation of authority versus authority is personally ascribed to the leader
Reconciliation	Get the support of the leaders so they underline the importance of learning and creativity; they become servant leaders of learning
Management	The power of learning around innovation versus the power of politics and know-who
Reconciliation	Celebrate the achievements of the present learning environment, to take the best practices from them, personalize them and make them historical events
Rewards	Intrinsic reward self-development versus reward long-term loyalty
Reconciliation	Members are personally held accountable for the long-term commitment to the company

CURRENT: INCUBATOR	IDEAL: EIFFEL TOWER
Typical dilemmas	
Leadership	Negation of authority versus authority is ascribed to the role
Reconciliation	To hold the innovators responsible for the reliability of their output
Management	The power of learning around innovation versus power of expertise and reliability
Reconciliation	Decentralize the organization into more learning centers where roles are described in a very sharp way and aimed at learning and innovation
Rewards	Intrinsic reward self-development versus increasing their expertise in doing a reliable job
Reconciliation	Use creativity and knowledge to build reliable systems and procedures enabling them to become even better in their creations

CURRENT: FAMILY	IDEAL: INCUBATOR
Typical dilemmas	
Leadership	Authority is personally ascribed to leader versus development of creative individuals
Reconciliation	To get the support of the leaders so they underline themselves the importance of learning and creativity; they become servant leaders of learning
Management	The power of politics and know-who versus the power of learning
Reconciliation	Take the best practices from the past, codify them, and apply them to the present learning environment
Rewards	Long-term loyalty versus intrinsic reward self-development
Reconciliation	Members are personally held accountable to motivate creative individuals and create learning environments

CURRENT: FAMILY	IDEAL: GUIDED MISSILE
Typical dilemmas	
Leadership	Authority is personally ascribed to the leader versus depersonalized authority
Reconciliation	Attribute the highest authority to those managers who have made internalization of subtle processes a prime criterion in their goals
Management	The power of politics and know-who versus consistent goal-orientation around task
Reconciliation	Makes political sensitivity part of the task description
Rewards	Reward long-term loyalty versus extrinsic reward job done
Reconciliation	Describe task in terms of loosely stated long-term outputs

(continued)

TABLE 14.2. Repeating Dilemmas Found for the Different Scenarios, *continued*

CURRENT: FAMILY	IDEAL: EIFFEL TOWER
Typical dilemmas	
Leadership	Authority is personally ascribed to the leader versus authority ascribed to the role
Reconciliation	Management needs to understand the technical aspects of the activities they manage; they become servant leaders of experts
Management	The power of politics and know-who versus expertise and reliability
Reconciliation	Get the support of management for the implementation of crucial systems and procedures
Rewards	Reward long-term loyalty versus increasing expertise in doing a reliable job
Reconciliation	Members apply their power to the advantage of increasing the expertise of their colleagues

The fifth step is crucial because it integrates business and cultural challenges. The authors do not believe that a change process can be genuine if strategic business issues and cultural values are disconnected. Unfortunately, this is often the case in change practice. But the key proposition is that, from the inputs of the envisioned future, core values, and key purpose, and between current and ideal corporate cultures, all the ingredients are available to stimulate management to think about what basic dilemmas they need to resolve from their actual business to the desired one.

The dilemmas are best phrased as "on the one hand . . . on the other . . ." Participants are often invited to phrase the tensions they feel in actual business life and then relate them to the tensions they feel between current and ideal cultures. So, for example, as an actual business tension, "I feel that our organization is so much focused on next quarter results, we don't have enough time to be creative and come up with our next generation of innovations." This would be consistent with the scenario in which the current corporate culture is a Guided Missile and the dominant espoused profile is an Incubator.

It is often found that a certain organizational culture has developed because the context best suits the main dilemmas leader(s) are facing in business. So an Incubator culture is often the result of a leader who strives for a core value of entrepreneurship and innovation while having an envisioned future of becoming the most path-breaking organization in the field of cross-cultural management thinking and consulting. A Guided Missile culture is a much better-suited context for leaders who want to help clients gain the highest return on their investments in the financial service sector while holding a core value of integrity and transparency.

But business environments and challenges are changing continuously. Once an organizational culture has established itself, it creates new dilemmas (or its changing environment will) on a higher level. For example, a dominant Incubator culture can create a business environment where many innovative ideas are born but where the management and commercialization of these fails on aspects of a more market-sensitive Guided Missile culture. Conversely, a dominant Guided Missile culture can lead to an environment where employees are so much guided by their market price that it needs a Family culture to create a necessary longer-term vision and commitment.

By asking leaders of organizations to phrase the major tensions they feel as "on the one hand . . . on the other . . . ," the authors linguistically program them to see both sides of the equation. In order to facilitate this balance in the approach, as well as the link to business, a number of pro formas are used to elicit the basic description of their current and ideal organizational culture profiles, components they want to retain and discard, as in the basic framework shown in Table 14.3.

TABLE 14.3. Basic Pro Forma Framework

On the one hand, we want to keep the following values and behavior of our current organization:	On the other hand, we need to develop the following values and behavior for supporting our envisioned future and core values:
1.	1.
2.	2.
3.	3.
4.	4.
5.	5.

It is ensured that the various lists comprise those that are most crucial to reconcile in view of the envisioned future. It is ensured that the formulation of the horns of the dilemma are both desirable and are linked to business issues. Examples are: "On the one hand we need to focus on reliable technology (typical for a dominant Eiffel Tower culture), while on the other we need to be constantly informed by our main customers (typical for dominant Guided Missile)," or "On the one hand we need to constantly mentor and coach our young graduates for constant learning (Incubator), while on the other hand we need to focus on the income of this quarter (Guided Missile)," or "On the one hand we need to develop and sustain a loyal workforce and thrive on rapport (Family), while on the other hand we need to be able to judge their performance based on report (Guided Missile)."

Reconciling the Change Tensions

The introductory and overview nature of this chapter does not allow all the detailed steps of the reconciliation process to be covered, but Figure 14.2 shows the basic template used to represent the dilemma graphically.

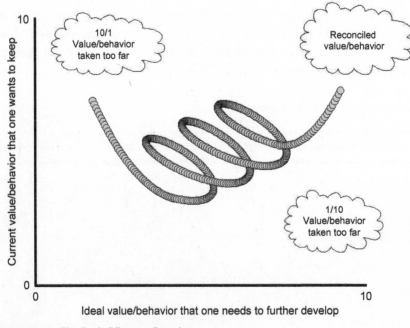

FIGURE 14.2. The Basic Dilemma Template

Essentially, this template uses a dual axis in order to invite participants to have the current values and behavior dialogue with the ideal ones. This dialogue is essentially stimulated by asking the question "How can we, through the current value or behavior that we want to keep, get more of the ideal value or behavior we want to strive for?" To stick to the previous examples, the essence of reconciliation is achieved when one can answer the question "How can we, through focusing on our reliable technology, get better informed by our customers?" or "How can we, through coaching our young graduates, increase the income of this quarter?" Note that one needs to change the "natural" mindset quite fundamentally. The traditional change processes often inquire about how one can change from one (current) value or behavior to another desired set of values or behavior. The creative juices that are flowing from the integration of seemingly opposing values is astonishing. But also from a process standpoint, resistance to change is often broken (at least conceptually) because of the need to keep and further develop the values that are positively graded about the existing state of the organization. It is a process of enriching values through change rather than replacing one value or behavior with another. Be aware that the spiral starts at the side of the current value/behavior axis and goes through the aspired value to an end somewhere at 10/10, where both values are integrated on a higher reconciled state. Once this position has been achieved conceptually, it is time for the final stages.

Once the leader or groups of relevant leaders are in agreement on the dilemmas that need to be reconciled, the action points to be taken evolve naturally. Very often, it is crucial to know the typical levers that need to be pulled in an organization to increase the effective actions that need to be taken. This is very often dependent on the type of organizational culture that the organization currently holds. In Family-oriented cultures, the function of HR often plays a crucial role, while marketing and finance dominate in the Guided Missile cultures. The best levers to be pulled in the Incubator are often related to learning systems and intrinsic rewards, while, in the Eiffel Tower systems, procedures and manufacturing often play a crucial role. The template in Table 14.4 has been used to give some guidance for looking at the action points to be taken.

TABLE 14.4. Guidance Template for Action to Be Taken

The Market (Think about what you could do in areas of customers, time-to-market response, flow of information from and to customers.)	Structure and Design (Consider what could be done in areas of the design of your organization, both formally and informally, basic flows of materials and information.)
Human Resources (Consider areas such as management development, staff planning, appraisal, and rewards.)	Strategy and Envisioned Future (Review vision of leaders, mission statements, goals, objectives, business plans, and the like.)
Business Systems (What can you do in areas of IT systems, knowledge management, manufacturing information, quality systems?)	Core Values (Think about action points that could enhance the clarity of values, how to better translate them into behavior and action.)
Who is taking action and carries responsibility? (Consider for each of the possible action points who is responsible for the outcome.)	How will we monitor the change process? (Consider milestones and qualitative and quantitative measures of genuine change.)
1.	1.
2.	2.
3.	3.
4.	4.
5.	5.

Conclusions

Using the framework introduced in this chapter, the authors have helped many client organizations to reconcile such dilemmas. Of course, as soon as one is removed, another pops up. But in today's rapidly changing, ever oligopolistic world, this is the very essence of organizations. Our aim has been to raise the debate for a new logic for the management of change.

15

Your Values for the Next Transformation

Fons Trompenaars and Charles Hampden-Turner

"HI, SIR, can you please help us to give life to our values again? We had such a great set that worked initially, but the energy is lost a bit. We need to revamp them now we are getting into another transformation process. And honestly we don't know what to do to inspire our people another time."

Do you recognize this set of questions?

In the beginning of this century the introduction and implementation of values into behaviors was at its peak. But it has lost a little of its popularity. Not that corporate leaders aren't convinced that the creation of a high-performing and thus a value-based culture is essential to the achievement of their goals. Neither is there a lack of awareness that values are just stale expressions if they are not translated into actual behaviors. But people need to be also aware that some of the values and behaviors need continuous reminders to be implemented. And the drastic change in organizational challenges require a drastic change in the behaviors demanded by the organizational business environment. How can we deal with this meta dilemma of endurance and change?

Here are some ways to bring about culture change that sticks.

Match Strategy with Culture

We see culture as supportive to reconcile business dilemmas, rather than cultural change as a side dish, and we believe in a blended approach of digital and face-to-face (asset-based) consulting.

Culture has always been seen as functional in solving the problems and dilemmas of mankind. So the Dutch needed consensus because it helped them fight water effectively. And the Americans seem to be so legalistic because they are highly mobile and don't have the circumstances to build a relationship they can trust. And why do the Japanese love micro- and nanotechnology Obviously, because there is little space.

Culture is the way we solve problems and reconcile dilemmas. It starts with certain behaviors that seem to work. When a behavior works, we call it a value, and when the value helps in surviving, it becomes a norm. When the value becomes a norm, we develop beliefs.

We therefore conclude that *the value of a value is the degree to which it helps groups of people to reconcile dilemmas.*

This means that in our consulting work we start by capturing the main business dilemmas. This needs to be done by triangulation—the combination of interviews, linguistic analysis, and questionnaires in all forms and shapes. For this purpose we have developed a variety of apps that can be found on www.ridingthewavesofculture.com with details of how to access.

So for example we have developed apps that capture the dilemmas between two companies engaged in an merger or acquisition* and the dilemmas of innovation.† We have a high-performing team app that measures the dilemmas a team experiences in areas of leadership, communication, and decision-making.‡ And we have an app that measures the dilemmas between current and desired corporate culture.§

The outcomes are validated by interviews and desk research (linguistic analysis) with a series of key strategic dilemmas as an outcome.

From there we engage key players (often top leaders) in a Dilemma Reconciliation Workshop. A dilemma can be defined as two propositions that are in apparent tension. A dilemma describes a situation where one has to choose between two good or desirable options. For example, on the one hand we need to centralize globally, while on the other hand we also need to decentralize locally. Most organizational issues and business and leadership challenges can be framed as a tension between two or more desirable value propositions in apparent conflict. We define these competing demands as dilemmas. Organizations in any culture need to deal

---

* http://www.ridingthewavesofculture.com/manda
† http://www.ridingthewavesofculture.com/innovation
‡ http://www.ridingthewavesofculture.com/itp
§ http://www.ridingthewavesofculture.com/change

with the competing demands of different stakeholders, including clients/customers, shareholders, employees, business processes, and the external environment more generally. The relative priority given to these dilemmas, how they are initially manifested, and the approaches to resolving them are culturally determined.

Dilemma reconciliation is a way of thinking that moves beyond either-or thinking, and even and-and thinking. By using through-through thinking the aim is to synthesize seemingly opposing viewpoints, giving value, respect, and appreciation to different sides of a value proposition. This unique methodology teaches people and organizations to address competing demands. By bringing together competing demands, objectives, and values, innovative solutions are discovered.

And the seven-step process ends with steps 6 (action and monitoring progress) and 7: What are the values and behaviors we need to develop in order to support the dilemma to be reconciled? In this way we make it very apparent that values are there to be matched with strategic dilemmas.

Focus on a Few Critical Shifts in Behavior

"We have these excellent values on all our posters, and our staff seems to like them. But how can we make them work at work?" The implementation of values in actual behavior seems to be a big challenge. And what behavior should we prioritize?

The success of an organization is dependent on its ability to build a culture that supports the organization's goals. In our experience building such a culture requires answering the following three questions:

What binds and connects people that can energize them into inspiring and winning performance: what do we stand and go for? This area is about establishing the values, translating these, and making it work in the day-to-day business context (concrete behavior, business results, communication, etc.). For this purpose we have designed the V2B workshops to build on the inherent energy that comes from values that are genuinely shared within the organization, but they need to be interpreted or "translated" to become relevant in people's daily work. The V2B process builds on the powerful, centuries-old adage "Don't do upon others what you don't want to be done upon yourself." Participants in a V2B workshop explore in depth the behavior they mutually expect from each other in intact teams. From this they then jointly create an internal Charter of Behavior capturing a limited number of observable desirable and undesirable behaviors for further embedding and "living."

What separates people and keeps them divided: what are the issues and dilemmas that confront people? This concerns the identification and reconciliation of business dilemmas and the implementation of win-win solutions. We use values and dilemmas as the basis for strategic decision-making. Values should be defined according to their position within a dimension of seemingly opposing value orientations such as consistency and flexibility. Honoring each of these opposites is equally important for successful business performance and requires their integration into a reconciled strategy. Our Dilemma Reconciliation Process (DRP) facilitates this integration.

How should the leadership act to benefit and build on what binds, deal with what divides, and create leadership throughout the organization? In this area we focus on developing the competences of a leader to Recognize, Respect, Reconcile, and Realize (4R's) through reconciling the shared business dilemmas. In particular, *reconciling dilemmas is what distinguishes leaders*, as they more than others require the capability to deal with dilemmas. Now more than ever, a leader's capacity to both direct the organization and its people and work in their service is being recognized as vital for creating a sustainable organization. We challenge leaders to reflect on their own leadership style and behavior, to identify areas for growth, and to practice new behaviors and techniques to bring out the best in their employees and organization. Leaders will enhance their competence to define and frame the major business issues and learn how to address and resolve the tensions between seemingly opposing values in a measurable and creative way.

Once the V2B process has been installed the Charter of Behavior will be taken as a framework for the desired behavior of the members that teams are held accountable for. This very often is done by a checking in and a checking out process before and after meetings, a buddy system, and an integration into the appraisal process. The focus on one or two behaviors at a time works most effectively.

Honor the Strengths of Your Existing Culture

"We have tried defining our values and even their implementation but it seems very often to lead to pathologies that hurt the organization" is another quote we often hear.

Let us start with a statement: *Any value disconnected from its opposite leads to a pathology.*

We have seen that organizations develop preferences like individuals do as many psychological indicators show. Successful organizations, however, combine opposites. So if we take our seven meta opposites, they encompass possibly seven dualities that are reconciled as follows: We standardize our best customization (universalism versus particularism). We strive for teams that consists of creative individuals. We passionately control our emotions (neutral versus affective). We give people direct feedback with diplomacy (specific versus diffuse). We act as servant leaders (achievement versus ascription). We speed up sequences by synchrony (sequential versus synchronic). And we push our technology through the pull of the market (internal versus external control).

How can we embed these dual or yin and yang values and the desired behaviors and competences within the organization, for which the responsibility lies with the leaders of the organization?

CDPQ or La Caisse, one of the largest pension funds of Quebec, recently introduced three dualities of values reflecting their overarching belief in ambition, innovation, and collaboration. This led to a very harsh environment in the beginning of the financial crisis. They were so innovatively ambitious that no collaboration could lead them out of the swamp. The values became pathologies because they were not counterbalanced by their opposites. Now they are trying to help their leaders to integrate the specific with the diffuse by ambition and prudence, innovation and rigor, and finally accountability and collaboration (Figure 15.1). Leaders are now asking, How can prudence help me to frame my ambition? How can being rigorous help me with innovation? And how can I be held accountable for being collaborative?

At CDPQ they have chosen to adapt a Charter of Behavior and ask questions such as, how can I see when you have used rigor to become more innovative, and how has prudence helped you to get more ambitious?

This is very much in line with the dual values of Pepsico International and Applied Materials: We strive for teams that consist of creative individuals, and we give people direct feedback with diplomacy.

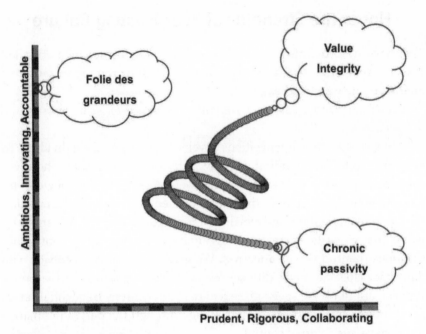

FIGURE 15.1. Connecting Opposites

Jeff Bezos of Amazon has had to grasp the dilemma of selling to a special group with whom deep relationships were developed in the area of music and books or to a broad array becoming the largest retailer in the world. His Internet selling model has the advantage of being *simultaneously* very broad and at the same time deep, personal, and customized, creating communities of people giving feedback on the products. And Amazon's values and behaviors reflect that. Isn't it interesting that Amazon is opening analogue stores and that Google is opening pickup stores when they were so digital from the outset?

And what do we find in sports environments as good examples? A coach like Louis van Gaal could sharply analyze the situation into the deepest and most specific details and combine those into the larger whole by inviting partners of players to celebrate the latest win. It is the total personality that needs to be involved to make analyses worthwhile.

Finally, after an analysis of the current and desired organizational culture we often find dilemmas in values, too. For example, we found a family-owned organization that naturally believed in collaboration and engagement but wanted to have more initiative and pushback to the customer as well.

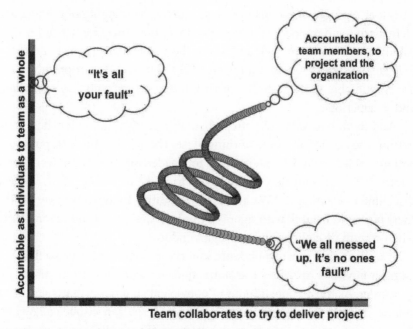

FIGURE 15.2. Holding Individuals Accountable for Team Results

Generally speaking, collaboration should not reduce accountability (Figure 15.2). What was missing from the existing equation is the potential power of teams. A team should not be confused with a committee. Committees delegate. Teams make promises to fellow members that each person will take particular actions and at the next team meeting each must show those promises were kept. Everyone is responsible to each other, to the team, to the joint project, to the customer, and to the organization. The advantage of teams is that they become jointly accountable for the success of their project. The very existence of this duality suggests teams are not being deployed strategically to good effect. Collaboration in teams should strengthen not weaken accountability. Unlike committees, teams are temporary, lasting only as long as the project lasts. This entails being accountable for the success of collaboration. We illustrate what can go right or wrong in this. To have the team hold members accountable can misfire if they gang up on him or her and say, "It's all your fault! We were just helping you." Similarly, collaborating can sometimes lead to "everyone" being at fault and hence no one in particular, and so all excuse each other and agree to hide what actually happened. You can get collaboration without accountability and accountability without collaboration.

But at top right of the diagram you achieve the integrity of both values. Here, each team member is responsible to all the others for her or his contribution to the joint project; and where there is a mess-up it is not difficult to locate its source. One or more person(s) did not keep their promises and are accountable to them, to the project, to the organization, to customers, and to superiors.

And then their value of entrepreneurship seemed to hinder them from getting the discipline to make things last. The hard thing is to put foundations under them. We interviewed top leadership, and these were some quotes: "If you innovate you are going to make mistakes. Have you the discipline to clean up?" "We are more innovative than we believe. I think there is a slight overkill with rigor." "I think we are actually more innovative when certain disciplines and principles endure."

It is clear that our respondents saw these dualities as reconcilable. If being innovative dissolves the status quo, someone must reinstitute the new order. As the demonstrations of nonviolent civil rights marchers attest, you need an iron discipline not to lose control. You can disobey a law only if a new law can be made from the manner of your disobedience. Scientific innovation obeys laws of science or discovers new laws and rigorously

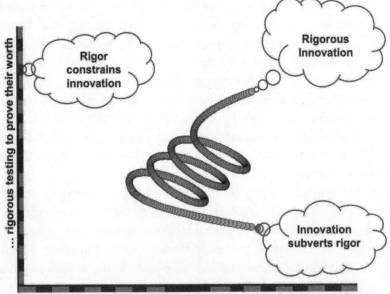

FIGURE 15.3A. Reconciling Both Values

obeys these. The most eloquent speech or original prose still obeys the rules of grammar and would not be understood if it failed to do so. The most brilliantly inventive enterprise still needs to meet all its legal obligations, pay those who helped it, and fulfil its contracts.

In order to be fair to both current and ideal values, we actually need two solutions, one that puts innovation ahead of discipline and another that puts discipline ahead of innovation (Figure 15.3A and B). The English language insists on subject-verb-object, and we must obey this. Hence, we could say:

> "Innovative concepts being new require rigorous testing to prove their worth."

Or we could say:

> "Only by the rigorous mastery of your discipline can you innovate through it."

Note the epithets at top left and bottom right in Figure 15.3B. When rigor is taken too far, you get the restraint of innovation and an irrelevant discipline imposed. When innovation is taken too far, discipline is subverted and

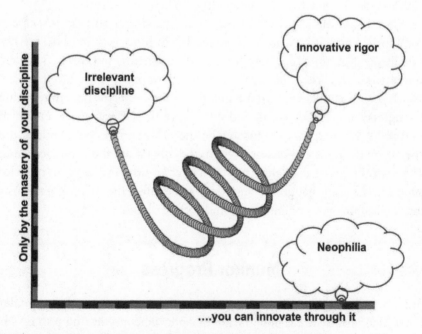

FIGURE 15.3B. Reconciling from the Opposite Direction to Figure 15.3A

innovation lauded regardless (neophilia). The two values must be reconciled at top right in each case. We achieve innovation through discipline and find new rigor through innovation.

The example above shows the importance of respecting the current culture, but in the transformation process it needs to enrich itself by connecting to apparent opposite values. Dualities are an expression of that reconciliation.

Integrate Formal and Informal Interventions Through Leadership

In any culture change process it is crucial that top leaders practice what they preach and walk the talk. The essence of leadership is to distinguish a problem from a dilemma by asking the question, "Can we solve it by more money or time?" If the answer is yes, it is a problem, if no you might have a dilemma in house. The essence of leadership is to be a reconciler in chief. You listen well to get the opposites on the table, and when they both make sense you ask the question "How can orientation A help me to get more of orientation B?" So Steve Jobs asked, "How can I make aesthetics functional, and how can I make high-tech beautiful?" The rest is history.

Effective leaders also make sure that hard and soft processes are combined. The hard stuff, often embedded in processes and HR, are the frameworks within which soft processes can nurture and thrive. The best combination to elicit its power is the What-How matrix introduced by Jack Welch at GE. Staff is measured regularly on their effectiveness in reaching the agreed-upon tasks (what) and if they live the GE values (how). Welch said the easy category were those who did or did not do both ends of the spectrum: they got a bonus or were fired. Difficult are the combined ones. The staff that lived the values but didn't achieve the tasks got an offer for support. The staff that got the task done but against the values got a warning. That's how you combine hard and soft processes!

Monitor Progress

Since we strongly believe in the value-based organization, in particular those that stimulate the integration of opposites, monitoring progress is

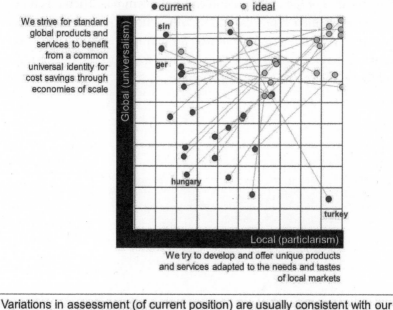

We strive for standard global products and services to benefit from a common universal identity for cost savings through economies of scale

Global (universalism)

● current   ○ ideal

sin

ger

hungary

turkey

Local (particlarism)

We try to develop and offer unique products and services adapted to the needs and tastes of local markets

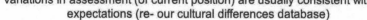

Variations in assessment (of current position) are usually consistent with our expectations (re- our cultural differences database)

FIGURE 15.4. Dilemma Grid

essential. And the way to do it is quite simple. At the beginning of each process we ask participants where they are on the dilemma grid (Figure 15.4). After a while we ask what progress they have observed, and what evidence-based incidents (if any) they can describe the progress with. Finally we ask whether the dilemmas chosen to work on are still valid and worth the investment. This data is accumulated and processed by leadership and appropriate actions taken.

Conclusion

In order to make cultural change stick we argue that first of all culture needs to be instrumental to serve the achievement of strategic goals and to reconcile the major strategic and cultural dilemmas. The process of change is an enrichment process (by integrating opposite orientations) rather than a replacement one. And the role of the leader is crucial in the success of the implementation. For the interventions that means that you start with the diagnostics of the business and cultural dilemmas. Then it is time for a dilemma reconciliation process ending with action points and recommended values. It is crucial that this is followed by an implementation process called Values to Behavior. And finally a process that monitors progress is required. In all stages the role of the leader is crucial.

Reconciling Cultural Dilemmas

16

Reconciling Cultural Dilemmas

Fons Trompenaars and Charles Hampden-Turner

A s we have explained throughout the book, every country and organization faces certain universal dilemmas. A nation's culture is expressed in the way people within it approach these dilemmas. Once we have learned to recognize differences and respect that cultures have the right to self-determination, we need to consider how we can both overcome problems of misunderstanding that can easily arise and leverage the business benefits of the different viewpoints by connecting them and securing the benefits of both.

Recognizing Cultural Differences

An American CEO had exchanged customary, polite greetings with his Japanese opposite number; a ritual the American felt had gone on far too long. They had at last come to the root of the problem, and the Japanese president was being evasive, ducking all the straight questions and repeating that "with goodwill and sincerity" all such questions could be satisfactorily answered.

As part of the initial greeting ceremony the parties had exchanged *meishi* (business cards), and the American CEO, conscious of Japanese custom, had laid the cards on the table in front of him in the same pattern as the seating arrangement for the Japanese delegation. In this way he could call everyone by name, having a convenient reminder in front of him.

As the meeting grew more stressful and his impatience with evasive answers grew, he picked up one of the cards, absentmindedly rolled it into a cylinder, unrolled it again, and crossly cleaned his nails. Suddenly he felt the horrified eyes of the entire Japanese delegation on him! There was a long pause, and then the Japanese president stood up and withdrew from the room. "We would like to call an intermission," the Japanese interpreter said. The American looked at the battered *meishi* in his hand. It was the one the Japanese president had given him.

This example aptly demonstrates the devastating effects that insufficient awareness of cultural differences may have. If the CEO had merely been following a long list of tips, or dos and don'ts, it is somehow unlikely that "don't abuse the *meishi*" would have been on the list. After all, there are thousands of possible mistakes.

But a *systematic* understanding of cultural differences would have enabled the CEO to have foreseen this pitfall and others. Had he remembered that the Japanese rarely answer directly, like to build a relationship before coming to the point, give their presidents very general duties, many of them ceremonial, so that they do not know the details, and regard *meishi* as symbolizing the status of the person referred to as well as the quality of the relationship being created, then he would never have dreamed of mangling someone's *meishi* while that person was watching!

Cultural awareness, then, is understanding *states of mind*, your own and those of the people you meet. You can never be fully informed, since there is an infinite range of potential errors, but our seven dimensions of culture provide us with a frame of reference for analyzing ways in which people attribute meaning to the world around them.

One of the goals of cross-cultural training must therefore be to alert people to the fact that they are constantly involved in a process of assigning meaning to the actions and objects they observe. For cross-cultural training to be successful, it must not be limited to delivering more or less detailed information about other countries and cultures. If it is, even the most sophisticated model of cross-cultural differences will only enhance the particular stereotypes the participants have about another culture. So if we are approached by participants after a training course with comments like, "Thank you, Dr. Trompenaars, I already knew that I had difficulties working with the French. They are strange beings, and you have proved it empirically. The information you just gave me proves that I am right," we know that something has gone wrong.

Increasingly, professionals in cross-cultural management who seek to develop cultural competence sense the need to go beyond the defense of their own model. It is legitimate to have a mental model. We are all creatures of our culture. The problem is to learn to go beyond our own model without being afraid that our long-held certainties will collapse. The need to win over others to our point of view, to prove the inferiority of their way of thinking, reveals our own insecurities and doubts about the strength of our identity. Genuine self-awareness accepts that we follow a particular mental cultural program and that members of other cultures have different programs. We may find out more about ourselves by exploring those differences.

The seven dimensions all indicate ways in which another culture may start from seemingly "opposite" premises. But this does not invalidate our own frameworks. It is simply a different approach from which we can learn. Milton Bennett, a cross-cultural researcher, has found that people encountering foreign cultures may *isolate* themselves and *separate* their norms and values from those of the foreign culture.[1] But this only impedes self-awareness. Both sameness and difference tell us who we are: "I am like A, but *not* like B."

Respecting Cultural Differences

An initial step toward developing respect for cultural differences is to look for situations in our own life in which we would behave like a person from another culture. This is what helped a member of the purchasing department of a big European oil company who was negotiating an order with a Korean supplier. At the first meeting, the Korean partner offered a silver pen to the European manager. The latter, however, politely refused the present for fear of being bribed (even though he knew about the Korean custom of giving presents). Much to our manager's surprise, the second meeting began with the offer of a stereo system. Again the manager refused, his fear of being bribed probably heightened.

When he gazed at a piece of Korean china on the third meeting, he finally realized what was going on. His refusal had not been taken to mean "Let's get on with business right away," but rather "If you want to get into business with me, you had better come up with something bigger." How embarrassing his refusal must have been for the Korean partner became clear to him when he remembered a similar situation in his own life. On one of his first dates with his wife, he had bought her a small present. But from the expression on her face, he could easily tell that it was not quite what she had expected. Remembering this made him accept the fact that the Korean partner was simply trying to establish a relationship and had no intention of bribing him. To avoid similar misunderstandings in future encounters with Korean partners, the manager decided to try to communicate that he, too, was interested in good relationships but that he felt no need to exchange expensive presents. (One alternative he might have come up with could have been to offer presents that were of little material value, but nevertheless signaled appreciation and interest.)

This story illustrates how we can learn to appreciate and respect behaviors and values different from our own. Thinking about situations in your own life might help you understand that behaviors that seemingly differ are often different only in terms of the type of situation in which you observe them, not in terms of their function. This will prevent you from prematurely valuing a behavior as negative and, more important, help you understand what the other person is actually trying to do. In understanding the other's intentions, and in possibly signaling that you do understand those intentions, you take the first step toward developing a shared meaning with your partner.

Generally speaking, what is strong in another culture will also be present in some form in our own culture. We speak of "guilt cultures" and "shame cultures," for example: those which try to make us feel guilty for breaking rules, and those which demand public apologies and subject the miscreant to the hostile stares of their group, or "loss of face." This is a significant difference between West and East, but who has never wished the ground would open up because of an excruciatingly embarrassing lapse?

Respect is most effectively developed once we realize that most cultural differences are in ourselves, even if we have not yet recognized them. For example, we often think that the Japanese are mysterious, even unreliable. You never know what they are feeling or thinking, and they always say yes, even when they are negative about something. But don't we have situations in which the same happens to us? If your own child has given a rather nervous and halting performance in her first solo in a school concert but must go on again after the interval, you might well say "Wonderful, darling" to give her confidence, even though you don't actually believe her performance was good.

Or suppose a minority employee who has been subject to discrimination in your company comes to see you in despair. You are worried that he might injure himself, sue the company, or attack his supervisor. It is likely that you would work on reestablishing your relationship with this employee, gaining his confidence, *before* suggesting that he might consider alternative forms of behavior. You would obviously be tactful and indirect in making these suggestions. You would be behaving in a "Japanese" manner because the circumstances warrant it. But perhaps circumstances in Japan make the sense of self so vulnerable that one usually tiptoes around another person's sensibilities. If we assume that most Japanese have a frail sense of self, their behavior makes very good sense! We would be wise to do the same when in Japan.

Consider another case encountered by a German engineer in South Africa. We all work for money, and most of us have a sense of pride and duty in our work, but the money–duty continuum may be radically different in different cultures. The engineer gave his maid a Christmas bonus, and she promptly disappeared for two months, since as she saw it she had no need to work. He was appalled. Of course we don't know her motives: she may have felt no obligation to an employer she disliked, but a sense of duty to an employer she did like. Or perhaps being a maid is only something she did in desperate circumstances. The engineer's wife concluded that she was "lazy," but such a judgment came from her own frame of reference.

To sum up, both awareness and respect are necessary steps toward developing intercultural competence. But even their combined power may not always suffice. In workshops, people often ask questions such as: "Why should we respect and adapt only to the other culture? Why don't they respect and adapt to ours?" We will come back to this question when we discuss reconciliation.

Another, perhaps more interesting problem is that of mutual empathy, a term employed by Milton Bennett.[2] What happens when one person attempts to shift to another culture's perspective when at the same time the other person is trying to do the same thing?

Motorola University once prepared carefully for a presentation in China. After considerable thought, the presenters entitled it "Relationships Do Not Retire." The gist of the presentation was that Motorola had come to China in order to stay and help the economy to create wealth. Relationships with Chinese suppliers, subcontractors and employees would constitute a permanent commitment to building Chinese economic infrastructure and earning hard currency through exports.

The Chinese audience listened politely to this presentation but was quiet when invited to ask questions. Finally one manager put up his hand and said, "Can you tell us about pay-for-performance?"

What was happening here is very common. Even as we move toward other people's perspective, they have started to move toward ours, and we pass each other invisibly like ships in the night. Remember that those Chinese who come to a presentation by a Western company may already be pro-Western and see Western views as potentially liberating. This dynamic is especially strong when a country is small and poor. When a drug salesperson from a US company meets with the minister of health from Costa Rica, the former's salary may be 10 times the latter's. This kind of encounter only hardens our prejudices: "See, they all want to be like us."

But foreign cultures have an integrity that only some of their members will abandon. In the Vietnam War the USA found that the genuine nationalists among the Vietnamese were very much tougher than their own opportunist allies. People who abandon their culture become weakened and corrupt. We need foreigners to be themselves if partnerships are to work. It is this very difference that makes relationships valuable.

This is why we need to *reconcile* differences—be ourselves yet see and understand how the other's perspectives can help our own.

Reconciling Cultural Differences

Once we are aware of our own mental models and cultural predispositions, and can respect and understand that those of another culture are legitimately different, then it becomes possible to reconcile differences. Why do this? We are in the business of creating wealth and value, not just for ourselves, but for those who live in different cultural worlds. We need to share the values of buying, selling, of joint venturing, of working in partnership.

Take two companies, one in the Netherlands and one in Belgium. The first was innovation-oriented. The second relied on its strong traditional reputation and the prestige ascribed to it by Belgian culture. The status of the two companies was derived from achievement and ascription respectively. They could have quarreled endlessly about their comparative worth, but they did not. Rather they jointly strove to establish a reputation for both innovation and quality that they then achieved.

We have found nine processes to be useful in achieving reconciliation, plus a model that represents them all:

1. Perceiving complementarity
2. Using humor
3. Mapping out a cultural space
4. Expressing dilemmas as processes using present participles

5. Dovetailing object language and meta-language
6. Applying frames and contexts
7. Sequencing values
8. Visualizing values as waveforms
9. Synergizing virtual circles
10. Summarizing the processes: the double helix

Perceiving Complementarity

The Danish scientist Niels Bohr proposed a theory of complementarity. The ultimate nature of matter is manifested both as specific particles and as diffuse waves. Nature reveals itself to us as a response to our measuring instruments. There is no one form "out there," but forms depend on how we perceive them and how we measure them.

Throughout this book, all our seven dimensions have represented continua with two extremes. Universalism and particularism are not separate but different, on a continuum between rules and exceptions. Things are more or less similar to the rule, or more or less dissimilar and hence exceptional. You could not even define rules without also knowing what exceptions were. The terms are therefore complementary.

It is the same for all seven dimensions. The individual is more or less separate from the group. "Being by yourself" requires a group if the difference is to register. There can be no specific part without a concept of the diffuse whole. Directing yourself from inside outward is necessarily in contrast to being directed from the outside inwards. To say that we seek to integrate our values and that all cultures look for integrity and reconciliation implies recognition that values are holistic to begin with.

Using Humor

We often become aware of dilemmas through humor, which can signal an unexpected clash between two different perspectives.

Values taken to extremes often suggest that the opposite value is really present, rather than the proclaimed one: "The more he talked of his honor, the faster we counted our spoons." "Why does the ascent of the preacher's rhetoric in TV evangelism so often accompany the descent of his pants?" the *New York Times* once asked.

Corporations who announce that they "trust their people" may end up breaking into their offices at night and rifling their desks, because they cannot be seen distrusting them publicly but are secretly concerned about a spate of thefts. For the "lowdown" on what really happens in the corporation, look at the cartoons stuck on the walls of employees' offices. They are often incisive satires of the official line and reveal what the dilemmas really are.

Humor is so important because it is the ultimate proof of a dilemma being reconciled. The work of comedy writers such as John Cleese, (*Monty Python* and *Fawlty Towers*), John Sullivan (*Only Fools and Horses*), and Matt Groening (*The Simpsons*) are quite different from our professional work, but are complementary. We have in common the functional use of humor. Like Arthur Koestler, they all believe that humor is very much linked with creativity. Why? Because humor is the process of discovering that two apparently opposite logics turn out both to be logical. That is what makes you laugh. As Koestler has shown, humour is built on *bisociation,** the ability mentally and emotionally to traverse both paths of a bifurcating line of thought, the recognition of which provokes laughter. Bisociation through humor allows managers a more complex view of their organization: it offers an and . . . and rather than an either/or orientation to the contradictions of managing and organizing.

Mapping Out a Cultural Space

Another effective process for exploring dilemmas is to turn their "two horns" into axes to create a cultural space. We can map some or all of the seven dimensions on this cultural space. The map is constructed through either interviews or questionnaires. Issues we have mapped recently include the following:

---

* Arthur Koestler, *The Act of Creation*, Penguin, 1990. Koestler has coined the term *bisociation* in order to make a distinction between the routine skills of thinking on a single plane, as it were, and the creative act, which, as he tries to show, always operates on more than one plane.

A. Given the pluralism of local initiatives in Europe, is it possible to exercise any strategic leadership from US HQ which is applicable to all the units concerned? (Universalism-particularism dilemma)

B. Given the obvious desirability of getting our best products on to the market according to the value of their achievements, is it possible to attain this while giving the autonomous R&D for high-potential products the space they need to mature? (Achievement-ascription dilemma)

C. Given the need for a quick response to very swiftly changing markets in the USA, is it possible to keep ourselves committed to a long-term vision developed at our center in South Korea? (Short-term/long-term dilemma)

Respondents drew attention to the first three dilemmas in words paraphrased below:

Universalism–Particularism Dilemma

- The markets in Europe could be served much better if our American HQ could only understand the particular needs we have over here.
- If the Europeans could only understand what it takes to become a truly global company.
- We know here in the USA very well what different markets need, but we need to co-educate them in order not to fall into the trap of having very happy clients but no margins for us. Economies of scale force us to limit our offerings.

Achievement–Ascription Dilemma

- If we in R&D could get some more time to work out our very promising products without continuously being pushed by marketing, our products would be much better in the long run.
- You can't be innovative unless you are given some time to work things out. Customers need to leave you alone for a while.
- R&D people tend to deliver too-late products which the market frequently doesn't need. In marketing we should be more responsible and give R&D strict guidelines and deadlines.

- In our company we should have more trust in what we are developing. It is good stuff. Let's go for it wholeheartedly.

The Short-Term/Long-Term Dilemma
- The Americans hinder our long-term achievements because of their drive for quarterly results. Our vision is often jeopardized by a quest for the quick buck!
- It seems like in the Far East and in Europe there are no shareholders. The ease with which they accept quarterly losses would be unacceptable in the USA.

Most of these remarks clearly show basic dilemmas that are inherent in cross-cultural debates. In intercultural encounters people frequently complain of excessive rivalry and an inability to harmonize the efforts of different units representing different cultures.

Dilemma A can be mapped between the pluralism of local initiatives on the horizontal axis (particularism) and the universal truth of HQ on the vertical axis (Figure 16.1).

Dilemma B is between achievement and ascription (Figure 16.2). On one hand is identification with customers' viewpoints on the horizontal axis, because it is the customer who buys the achievements of the product. On the other hand, R&D wants to be committed to the product by ascribing status to it, which allows its development without being hindered by clients' needs too early or too frequently.

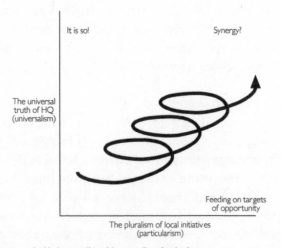

FIGURE 16.1. Dilemma A: Universalism Versus Particularism

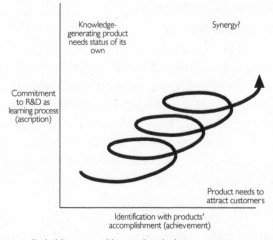

Knowledge-
generating product
needs status of its
own

Synergy?

Commitment
to R&D as
learning process
(ascription)

Product needs to
attract customers

Identification with products'
accomplishment (achievement)

FIGURE 16.2. Dilemma B: Achievement Versus Ascription

Dilemma C is between short- and long-termism (Figure 16.3). On the one axis the market demands a quick response and US shareholders look for good returns every quarter. On the other axis we find the long-term need to be framed by a vision that allows the short term to have meaning.

A dilemma must be mapped before it can be reconciled, so that we and clients have a clear definition of what has to be reconciled. The remaining steps in the process show how genuine reconciliation can be attained.

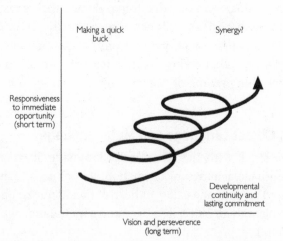

Making a quick
buck

Synergy?

Responsiveness
to immediate
opportunity
(short term)

Developmental
continuity and
lasting commitment

Vision and perseverence
(long term)

FIGURE 16.3. Dilemma C: Short-Term Responsiveness Versus Long-Term Vision

Expressing Dilemmas as Processes Using Present Participles

A noun can be defined as "a person, place, or thing." But a value is none of these, and we get into difficulty when we use nouns like universalism or particularism, loyalty or dissent to describe the horns of a dilemma. We have done so in this book because it is the convention of the social sciences to make phenomena look and sound physical, but it is still misleading. So, as a step on the road to reconciliation, we shall turn all nouns into present participles, ending in -*ing*, which transforms them into processes. Thus the dilemmas can be expressed as the following processes:

Universalizing versus particularizing

Individualizing versus communing

Specifying/analyzing versus diffusing/synthesizing

Communicating neutrality versus communicating emotion

Achieving versus ascribing (status)

Sequencing time versus synchronizing time

Directing oneself from inside versus going with the flow of the environment

Not all nouns can be made into present participles, but if we know what we want—to get rid of the "hard edges" and render the value as a process requiring the participation of people—then suitable words can be found. Since processes mingle in a way that things do not, we are now much closer to understanding that all seven dimensions are really continua, with a preponderance of one process at one end (yin) and a preponderance of the other process at the other end (yang). We have also softened the adversary structure of clashing nouns or "isms." This is what De Bono calls "water logic."[3]

Dovetailing Object Language and Meta-language

Since we are stuck with the structure of language, it is as well to consider how language achieves reconciliation. It does so by using a ladder of abstraction and putting one value (or horn of the dilemma) above the other, that is, by using both an object language and a meta-language and allowing them to dovetail.

Consider this famous quotation from F. Scott Fitzgerald:

> "The test of a first rate intelligence is to hold two ideas in your mind
> at the same time and still retain the capacity to function. You must,
> for example, be able to see that things are hopeless, yet be deter-
> mined to make them otherwise."

This might appear at first glance to be a contradiction, but it is not. Contradictions cancel each other out: they are meaningless. What the author has done here is to dovetail the two statements at different levels of language.

Meta-level	"be determined to make them otherwise"
Object level	"see that things are hopeless"

The object level is about things being hopeless. The meta-level is about the determination of the person who sees. The two statements are not contradictory because they do not apply to the same "things." The second is about the person seeing, not about the things seen.

This applies equally to our seven dimensions. We could say:

> "The test of a first-rate manager is to hold two ideas in your mind at
> the same time and still retain the capacity to function."

You must, for example, be able to see that a *particular* customer request is outside the *universal* rules your company has set up, yet be determined to qualify the existing rule or create a new rule based on this case.

Meta-level	Determined to qualify a rule or create a new one
Object level	Particular request breaks an existing rule

We could do the same for any of the seven dimensions. Take a small business unit that has enjoyed extraordinary success:

Meta-level	Ascribe importance to this strategy company-wide
Object level	Admire and reward this form of achieving

Top management has encouraged achievement in a particular unit and has ascribed universal importance to the strategy employed, so that other business units can benefit by emulating the particular achievement. Here both particularizing and universalizing, and achieving and ascribing have been reconciled.

Applying Frames and Contexts

In the previous example of language levels, you could say that the meta-level frames the object level:

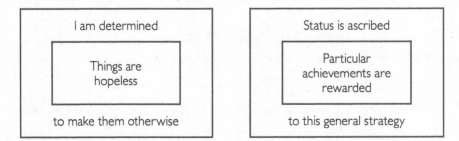

The usefulness of thinking in frame and contexts is that the latter contain and constrain the "picture" or the "text" within them. There is always a danger of people's value extremes "running away." "To see that things are hopeless" can lead to despair, unless framed by "a determination to make them otherwise." We might have concluded from the outstanding achievement of the business unit that top management should simply keep out of their way, but that would have prevented the organization learning from a local success.

The important thing to grasp is that text and context are reversible, as are the picture and the frame. We could focus on a very intelligent person and say: or we could say:

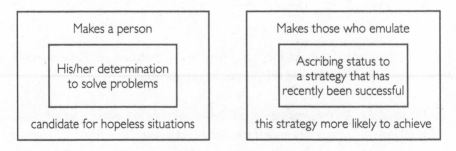

Sequencing Values

Values appear to clash and conflict when we assume that both must be expressed simultaneously. It isn't possible to be right and wrong, to universalize and particularize, to be steered from inside and from outside at the same time. One obviously precludes the other.

But it is possible to go wrong and then correct, to particularize and then generalize, to observe outer trends and dynamics and then direct yourself at your objective. So a major element in reconciling values is to sequence processes over time.

Visualizing Values as Waveforms

Have you ever stopped to wonder what would happen to our values if, instead of assuming they are things (such as colliding billiard balls), we assume that they are waveforms? Common sense assumes values to be like coins, jewels, or rocks. We could alternatively take the view that they are like water waves, electromagnetic waves, sound waves, or light waves. This makes a great deal of difference.

Consider the cycle of sleeping and waking, which looks like Figure 16.4.

the more awake I am   the more awake I am

... the better I sleep   ... the better I sleep

FIGURE 16.4. Cycle of Sleeping and Waking

Or consider music on various frequencies (Figure 16.5).

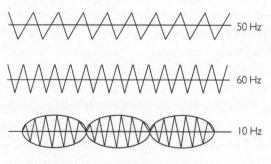

50 Hz

60 Hz

10 Hz

High-frequency sound + high-frequency sound
= low-frequency sound

FIGURE 16.5. Harmonizing Sound Frequencies

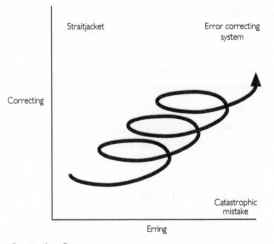

Straitjacket

Error correcting
system

Correcting

Catastrophic
mistake

Erring

FIGURE 16.6. Error Correcting System

If we have two different frequencies, 50Hz and 60Hz, these combine to form a beat frequency of only 10Hz, because a low-frequency wave has been created by harmonizing the two waves. The high-frequency sound is now "within" the low-frequency beat. If values are like sound waves, no wonder their harmony (what southeast Asians call *wa*) can be more beautiful still.

If the waveform is a legitimate expression of values and if the values alternate like sleeping and waking, relaxing and exciting, erring and correcting, then we can draw the waveform between the axes as in Figure 16.6.

Here we first err, then correct, then err again, then correct again, and so on. The entire process is called an *error correcting system*. We avoid both catastrophic mistakes (perhaps by using simulation) and the straitjacket of never making a mistake and thus missing the opportunity to learn and improve. Arguably if we want to learn fast, allowing many small errors that are quickly corrected might be the best way. "Error," of course, is relative. If we call the bottom 35 percent of our performance "errors," we will go on improving. If we call only 5 percent "errors" we may come to ignore them or hush them up.

The notion of learning by error correction is so important that we include this idea in all our dilemmas, especially the seven dimensions. Suppose that we were to create a waveform between universalizing and particularizing. It might look like Figure 16.7.

This is a diagram of how particular exceptions are encountered and noted before encompassing them within changed or reformed rules. No

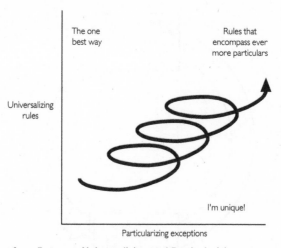

The one
best way

Rules that
encompass ever
more particulars

Universalizing
rules

I'm unique!

Particularizing exceptions

FIGURE 16.7. Waveform Between Universalizing and Particularizing

scientific law can ignore mounting anomalies. No legal statute can survive massive opposition. No corporate procedures can fail to account for a growing number of exceptions. In all such crises the old rules must be reformed or new ones created. The point is that if we want to improve the rules we must be able to refute them. Nor can we properly appreciate what is unique and outstanding unless we know what the common standards are.

We have retained the idea of error correction by rendering our waveform as a cycle. This assumes that we will periodically get things wrong and have to make a second "try" or circuit before improving on both axes.

Synergizing Virtuous Circles

An important test of optimal reconciliation that includes both ends of the values continuum, in even greater harmony, is the criterion of *synergy*. The word comes from the Greek *sunergos*, meaning "to work with." When two values work with one another they are mutually facilitating and enhancing. Thus ascribing importance to a major project makes it more likely that your working group will be inspired to achieve that project. That your company has recently been seen to be achieving the project makes it far more likely that senior management will ascribe great importance to it in next year's strategy deliberation. The virtuous circle looks like Figure 16.8.

Synergy is also present in nature. Steel alloys for jet engines are immensely stronger than the strength of all their components combined. The molecular chain in the alloy is simply a stronger structure.

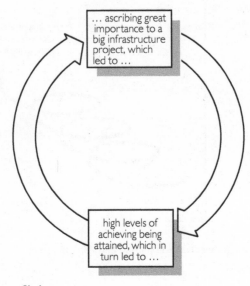

... ascribing great importance to a big infrastructure project, which led to ...

high levels of achieving being attained, which in turn led to ...

FIGURE 16.8. Virtuous Circle

Summarizing the Processes: The Double Helix

Finally we come to our model of models: DNA, the double helix molecular structure (Figure 16.9), borrowed from biological science. The double helix model helps to summarize the processes for reconciliation. The ladder of protein synthesis has four rungs. We have a ladder of values synthesis with a series of rungs (recognition, respect, reconciliation, and realization). The twisted ladder is full of *complementarities.* When the "pairs" come together unexpectedly it can be *funny.* We can use the uprights on each side of the ladder as cultural space for *mapping.* The twisted elements of the ladder constitute a growth *process.* Each twist of the spiral speaks the *language* of growth and contains coded instructions. Each turn of the helix is framed

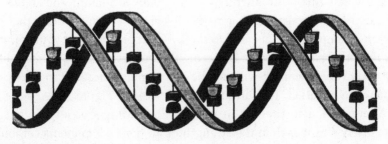

FIGURE 16.9. Double Helix

and *contextualized* by the helix within and around it, containing and constraining. The process is *sequential*. It constitutes *waveforms*, with synthesis producing growth and *synergy*.

In short, the double helix helps summarize all nine processes by which values are reconciled. It is a continuous process that repeatedly asks the question, "How can we get more of one extreme through connecting and combining it with more of the other?"

17

When Two Worlds Collide

The Integration of Cultures in a
Merger or Acquisition

Fons Trompenaars and Peter Woolliams

M ERGERS, ACQUISITIONS, and strategic alliances are increasingly pursued, not only to implement globalization strategies, but as a consequence of political, monetary, and regulatory convergence. Realizing the business benefits and creating wealth in an integration process is not easy since it demands joining values that are not easily joined; two out of three deals still do not achieve anywhere near the benefits that were originally anticipated.[1] It is assumed too often that delivering benefits simply requires the alignment of technical, operational, and financial systems and market approaches.

While any integration program should include fundamental operational matters, much more attention and effort need to be given to managing the cultural differences between the new partner businesses. Relational aspects like cultural differences and lack of trust have frequently been reported as being responsible for 70 percent of integration failures as described in the business press.[2]

Ultimately success derives from enabling people with different cultural perspectives to engage in meaningful discussions around the newly created business. The methodology that we have developed and that is one of the cornerstones of this book includes "dilemma thinking," which is central to bringing people together to discover what they share and where they differ. Of course, some steps need to be selected and adapted to the specific needs of an organization to develop a program for integration to deliver positive outcomes. It is crucial that the knowledge embedded in this process is transferred to the organization so that the ongoing and future operations continue to deliver growth goals through enhanced corporate success under the new leadership and management.

Different Types of Integration

One important consideration for an integration process is whether one takes over or is being taken over. Some argue that mergers do not exist; in the long run it is always an acquisition. Recall what Confucius said: "There is always one that offers the cheek and one that purses the lips!" But let us consider the meta-dilemma that summarizes these two extreme paradigms of acquiring or being acquired (Figure 17.1).

The extensive research evidence we have collected, and triangulated with real world application through our consulting, reveals that the 10,10 paradigm in the top right corner of Figure 17.1 is where a sustainable future that delivers the business benefits of the intended merger or alliance can be realized, if we apply a systematic methodology to reconcile the cultural differences.

FIGURE 17.1. Strategy of Managing Cultural Integration

Reconciling Business Dilemmas in Mergers

In a merger, many business dilemmas are inherent in the impending marriage between different ways of working in the legacy organizations. You should worry when there are no dilemmas to be found!

You might wonder why the organizations are merging in the first place. So with an organization we observed the dilemma between:

ON THE ONE HAND	ON THE OTHER HAND
"We need to supply (global or standardized) products/services."	"We need to supply products/services that respond to local tastes and needs."
"We need to develop our people."	"We need to keep people focused on delivering results."

The reconciliation of these dilemmas, in particular the first one, becomes crucial to the success of the new joint company. Of course these type of generic dilemmas manifest in specific ways in the particular circumstances and context of the merger.

The process of reconciling the business dilemmas is essentially the core of the strategy of new organizations striving to integrate. Although we are discussing business dilemmas here, it should be remembered that all cultures share these dilemmas. As explained throughout this book, how dilemmas are perceived, what meaning is given to aspects of these dilemmas, which side may be favored, and how they are initially approached is culturally determined.

If there is a conscious effort to synergize the strengths of the two legacy organizations, the combined organization has the highest chance of success. We guide our clients through our highly structured Dilemma Reconciliation Process (DRP).

The beauty of the DRP discussion framework is that the positives and negatives of both approaches are openly discussed without excessive value judgment. The reconciliation in "being more selective in their investment strategy" for one client, for example, was highly appreciated by all participants.

Selecting the investment decisions on how they could harness short-term results while also realizing the longer-term vision was an invitation to combine the best of both worlds and a great opportunity to avoid the stereotypes about the negatives of both legacy approaches.

Integrating Opposites as a Continuous and Creative Dialogue

Any integration process will be scattered with similar dilemmas in many areas, be it HR, loyalty programs, IT, or finance, as we considered earlier. The process we have been describing generates a "creative space," where the ultimate solution can be significantly better than any initial one-dimensional solution. We would call this the area where synergies are realized.

Here we find a very intense and rewarding process of dialogue between the different organization units—both operating companies and holdings. Given the likelihood of future integration processes, recognition of the value of this dialogue offers a significant contribution.

We have found that people succeed in achieving these types of synergy not because they are good at choosing one side over the other but because they are able to reconcile seemingly opposing values. Integrating two desirable aims that were in tension creates a new, enriched reality. So the issue is not choosing whether a sales or a service culture would make a better company. The challenge is discovering how we can use a more sophisticated service culture so we can sell more and vice versa.

Organizations that are able to reconcile their differences will create competitive advantage. If not, they will be amongst the 70 percent of mergers that fail. But more important, the DRP process invites the parties involved to engage in a creative dialogue rather than just complaining about each other in the corridor.

The Corporate Culture Profiler (CCP) for Cultural Dilemmas

We discussed in Chapter 13 how a corporate culture has a profound effect on an organization's effectiveness because it influences how decisions are made, how human resources are used, and how the organization responds to the environment.

To elicit the values of the existing organizations that will challenge and influence the merger or acquisition, we use our CCP (Corporate Culture Profiler) model and related app. This 14-item instrument enables us to identify the similarities and differences of the organizational cultures involved. The CCP is a multifunctional instrument that enables respondents to review and examine the interpretations they give to relationships with each other and with the organization as a whole.

The four underlying quadrants represent how the organization orientates itself to four basic processes in terms of task/strategy/mission, role/efficiency/consistency, power/human relations/involvement, and person/learning/adaptability. Within each of the subsegments we explore specific aspects that together determine the major orientations.

A cultural values assessment that compares the organizations that want to integrate will identify opportunities for and obstacles to cultural change. It will help define the guidance needed in the development of personal alignment, group cohesion, and structural alignment processes. This provides the foundation for identifying key performance indicators that will be used in the final step of values management. Values management is the process of reconciling cultural dilemmas arising between the combined organizations. The value dilemmas that are selected from interview and web-based processes are triangulated with the dilemmas raised from the CCP and its app (see Figure 17.2).

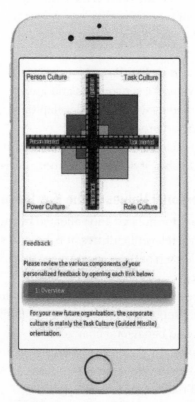

FIGURE 17.2. Results from CCP App

A good example in a merger of two organizations is the tension between task (Guided Missile), role (Eiffel Tower), and people (Family) orientations, which we explore with contrasting questions. The key dilemmas that evolved from the CCP were:

Guided Missile versus Family:

1. We need to cut costs wherever we can for the sake of our shareholder's return versus we need to invest for long-term sustainability.
2. We need to supply (global or standardized) products/services versus we need to supply products/services that respond to local tastes and needs.
3. We need to develop our people versus we need to keep people focused on delivering results.

Eiffel Tower versus Family:

4. We need to focus on the human element and take advantage of the experience of managing diversity versus we need to enhance a culture of leading-edge engineering autonomy.

Guided Missile versus Family:

5. We need to develop looser controls and greater management empowerment versus we need to develop tight top-down controls and more restricted procedures.
6. Our leadership style should be more participative and empowering versus our leadership style should be more decisive and directive.

What About the Personal Values of the Key Players?

Once the dilemmas are formulated and validated by the difference in corporate and possibly other relevant cultures, it is time to see how the personal values of the top leadership of the respective organizations help to reconcile the dilemmas at stake.

This process begins by profiling the personal values of the leadership group and their direct reports, and getting the commitment of the leadership group to values and behavioral change.

To assess the personal values of key players we use our Personal Values Profiler (PVP),* which offers important insights into the relationships employees have with their organization.

---

* See www.ridingthewavesofculture.com for further details.

In the new workplace of the coming decade, what matters for the individual and what matters for the organization need increasingly to be congruent. Differences between the PVP and CCP may reveal changes in the industry or functional discipline over time. Imagine a young woman electing to choose nursing as her chosen career because she perceives working as a nurse will be congruent with her personal values (PVP profile). However, after many years, she finds the reality of working in a city center publicly funded hospital to be to more about being verbally and physically abused by drunks and drug addicts and being concerned not to be sued for any practice that does not accord with strict (Eiffel Tower) guidelines. The need for efficiency and conforming to procedure would be reflected in the CCP and quite different from her PVP. Her response might be low motivation and performance or to leave and work for a private health clinic or cosmetic surgeon that would be a close match to her PVP.

The PVP provides understanding of matters concerning resistance or support for change and the capacity for stability, sustainability, and innovation. These can exert a decisive influence on the overall ability of the organization to deal with the challenges and dilemmas it faces.[3]

Final Selection of Values

Finally, a definitive decision on the core values must be taken in the context of the envisioned future and key purpose of the organization. The chosen values need to be instrumental to the achievement of the goals set for the organization, and they need to fit the purpose.

There are some alternative approaches to selecting the core values for an organization that can include:

- Values as helping key business dilemmas to be reconciled
- Values as helping key cultural dilemmas to be reconciled
- Values as giving life to purpose
- Values as extensions of personal values

Values arise from functionality and are fed by success. *The quality of a core value can be best demonstrated by its relevance to help solve the key dilemmas business leaders face.* They need to support the dilemma reconciliation process.

Therefore, the most preferred method of deriving the core values (because of its elegance) is to end the process of reconciliation of business dilemmas with the question *What values and behaviors do we need to develop to reconcile this dilemma?*

Values as constructs to aid the reconciliation of key cultural dilemmas. Next to vibrant discussions about functionality, it is also satisfying to see all parties engaging around a shared reality they want to create together rather than focusing only on differences. Obviously there are also some opposites possible when we look at the cultural side of the integration. These value clashes could lead to potential problems if not dealt with appropriately. A similar approach can be unfolded as used for the business dilemmas.[4]

Values as extensions of personal values. In some cases the original organizations have such different histories and so many vested interests that values to drive the future of the organization can best be defined starting from a clean sheet. Rather than brainstorming about what existing values would best fit the new company, we often advise the joint leadership to respond to the PVP. This will elicit the personal values of the leadership and compare them to an initial set of values they individually believe are appropriate for the organization. Ideally, there should be a match between the two, of course—and there usually is. Presumably that is why they are with the organization in the first place! In some cases it is very effective to start with the leaders' own values and reason from there.[5]

Continuous Reevaluation: Monitoring Change Toward the High Performance Culture

The progress and speed of the integration process depends largely on the specific situation. Each situation will require tailored plans, interventions and monitoring systems. Once you move into full-fledged preparation and beyond, there are checklists available to monitor the progress of implementation at the individual, company, and unit level. These checklists can be integrated into ongoing employee or engagement surveys.

Together with the online check on progress on the reconciliation of main dilemmas and Organization Values Profiler (OVP) and the instruments measuring the key reconciling indicators in HR systems, it will be possible to check regularly on implementation and, where necessary, interventions can be made on the spot.

M&A App for Self-Assessment

We have developed an app that helps individuals to assess the major cultural dilemmas as a result of a merger or acquisition.

What is the app? It provides users with a better understanding of and detailed information on the differences across organizational cultures. It provides users a new way of dealing with the tensions raised by different corporate cultures.

What is the purpose? This app is intended to develop users' understanding of the importance of corporate culture by providing example stereotypes from different types of organization. In spite of well-developed processes for due diligence, many mergers and acquisitions are still failing to deliver the expected business benefits due to clashes in corporate culture.

Use this app to explore our approach based on extensive research and consulting practice that integrates different cultures and harnesses the best of both.

What next? Go to www.ridingthewavesofculture.com/manda and try it out. This app enables you to quickly assess your organization's corporate culture and compare with your new business partner organization.

Conclusion

Today's world of business is complex, and simplistic approaches to integration do not work, which is why too many mergers fail to realize the expected benefits.

We have described our range of comprehensive solutions to help organizations truly reach their high performance culture and thus realize and sustain the business benefits of their mergers, acquisitions, and alliances.*

Finally, we emphasize that we have sought to demonstrate that it is not just a matter of avoiding conflict, misunderstanding, and embarrassment because of differences, but of using these differences to the new company's advantage and thereby delivering the business benefits of the integration through connecting these different viewpoints.

---

* For further information and for our complete discourse on this important topic we would like to refer the reader to *The Global Tango: Reconciling Cultural Differences in Mergers and Acquisitions* by F. Trompenaars and M. Nijhoff Asser, published by Infideas, Oxford, UK, 2010.

Culture in Practice

18

Creating a Culture of Innovation

Fons Trompenaars and Peter Woolliams

I N AN increasingly oligopolistic world, in which old ideas can be copied and replicated at ever lower costs, it is the constant renewal of creative solutions that is the ultimate differentiator of survival. Building a culture of innovation is today's number one management imperative in which HR must play a crucial role.

Much has been written previously about the recruitment, selection, and retention of creative talent and separately about product and process innovation. And even more about corporate culture and mechanistic and structural approaches to innovation in organizations. What is severely lacking is an overall framework that integrates these components and informs the HR professional to help the organization create a culture of innovation.

On the one hand we all observe an increasing standardization of the world, and on the other, an ever-growing diversity. Our core proposition is that when we can connect these extremes, we have the essence of what a culture of innovation is all about. The joining of what we share and where we differ is the new challenge for leadership.

But Western education and consumerism haven't helped because they have forced us to think in terms of linear models and forced choices. "Do you want tea *or* coffee?" The result is that most thinking emulates profiling instruments used by HR professionals that owe their origin to an American or Anglo-Saxon philosophy that is still dominated by its cultural signature with linear scales. Thus Kirton's KAI model (at least at the basic level) directs us to think in terms of profiling staff as *either* an Adaptor *or* an Innovator[1] and not how these attributes can be combined. Measurement of creativity is usually about the linear level (how much) rather than the nature and form of creativity and how it can be harnessed and linked to adaptation. Similarly, received wisdom prescribes that all team roles must be present in a group to make an effective team. But there is less guidance about how these contrasting roles can be combined to work together. How do we connect the contributions of innovative, idea-generating Plants by combining them with the adaptive Implementers who want to halt yet more innovations, freeze design, and deliver the current idea? And managing a *multicultural* innovative team adds even more tensions from contrasting orientations to resolve.

The evidence from our research and consulting shows that innovation requires us to combine differences. In turn, this requires identification of the dilemmas that derive from the tensions caused by personality differences, team role preferences, and value or cultural differences—whether from national, ethnic, or corporate cultures. In our findings, all people from all cultures and corporations share similar dilemmas, but their initial approach to them is culturally determined. For example, on the one hand should we be directing and "hands-on" in our management of staff or on the other hand empowering staff to be self-controlling and innovative? Realizing innovative potential will depend on both the autonomy of an organization's people and on how well the ideas arising from this autonomy can been connected, centralized, and coordinated.

What Does This Mean for Creating Innovative Teams?

Getting everyone to think the same way is a tempting strategy, but it is when opposites are integrated to work with each other that we realize the potential of an innovative team.

If members of a team play different roles and have different cultural orientations, then the team is full of potential conflict and misunderstanding. Within many organizations we asked members of their senior team what tensions they face in working with other members of their team that had "opposite" team roles to themselves. Note that the focus was on the dilemmas they faced when working with other team members by virtue of the team roles, and not aspects of personality or interpersonal relationships. Simply posing these questions instantly generated new insights into how they were working with others, and they were all well able to be creative about how they could reconcile their own ream role with opposite team roles. Consider a team member who was a Shaper, in Belbin's categorization.[2] What dilemma did she identify in working with the Finisher role in a team, and how could she work better in the future by reconciling this dilemma?

RESPONDENT		OTHER TEAM MEMBER
Shaper		**Finisher**
Challenging, dynamic, thrives on pressure. The drive and courage to overcome obstacles. But prone to provocation. Offends people's feelings.	Working with a contrasting team role	Painstaking, conscientious, anxious. Searches out errors and omissions. Delivers on time. But inclined to worry unduly. Reluctant to delegate.
This is what she said about herself: "It's difficult for me to take on and develop ideas I have not had an original input to."		And about her colleague: "May not appear interested in alternative viewpoints as focus is on detail and delivery."

This is what she proposed as a reconciliation

Request the finisher to structure meeting time to evaluate my new ideas and then to identify and discuss his or her concerns and how they could be overcome if my idea might be implemented.

Creative individuals and inventive teams are necessary, but they are not sufficient to generate conditions for the organization to be innovative.

How Can HR Directors Help Guide Their Organization?

It is too simplistic to expect a straight journey down a single path. It is becoming clear that any single corporate culture has its strengths and weaknesses. At any given time, most organizations have a single dominant corporate culture that struggles with less dominant orientations. The organization life cycle follows a series of transitions from one corporate culture to the next where each transition is prompted by a crisis. Each crisis arises when the organization outgrows the current culture. Here we find frequently occurring dilemmas that must be reconciled in order to progress from one culture to the next. Each dilemma requires an innovative solution, and a truly innovative organization copes successfully with each.

When people set up an organization, they will typically borrow from models or ideals that are familiar to them. The organization is a subjective construct, and its employees will give meaning to their environment based on their own particular cultural programming. The organization is like something else they have experienced. It may be deemed to resemble a family, or an impersonal system designed to achieve targets. It may be likened to a vessel that is traveling somewhere, or a missile homing in on customers and strategic objectives. Cultural preferences operating across the dimensions influence the models people give to organizations and the meanings they attribute to them.

We will explore four categorical types of corporate culture and how differences between national cultures help determine the type of corporate culture "chosen." Employees have a shared perception of the organization, and what they believe has real consequences for the corporate culture that develops.

We need to think in two dimensions, generating four quadrants. The dimensions we use to distinguish different corporate cultures are *equality versus hierarchy* and *orientation to the person versus orientation to the task*.

These four metaphors illustrate the relationship of employees to their notion of the organization. Figure 18.1 summarizes the images these organizations project.

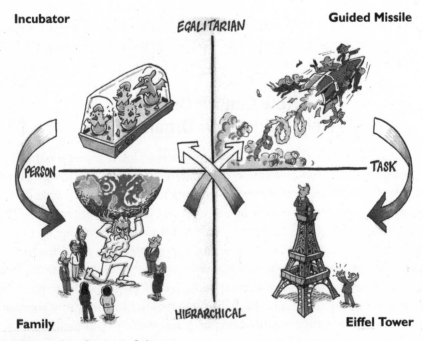

FIGURE 18.1. Four Corporate Cultures

So the prerequisite for an innovative organization is the reconciliation of a variety of cultures in order to face the changing dynamic world in which the organization operates. Cultures can learn to reconcile differences in values at ever higher levels—for example, so that better rules are created from a variety of exceptions that come with growth. But let's follow the typical life cycle of cultures.

Typical Life Cycle of Corporate Cultures

Organizational culture is the result of the way the fight between competing values manifests. If one value dominates its opposite, you run a risk, as you are not addressing the value that is subjugated—for example, Do people prefer to meet deadlines for short-term results or give priority for a visionary long-term future? Do people take individual responsibility or rather share in teams? Once reconciled, we create a culture of innovation, since innovation essentially is to combine values that are not easily joined, and therefore scarce and profitable. So Apple has combined esthetics with functionality, and Formula I racing has combined safety with speed (better known as aerodynamics).

Creative Entrepreneurship: Founders Know Everyone Personally

Typically organizations begin by the founders creating both a product (or service) and a market. As the organization grows, it exceeds the capacity of the founder to know everyone personally resulting in a *crisis of leadership* because management problems cannot be handled through informal processes.

From Invention to Intention: Growth Through Direction

The solution is to appoint a strong paternalistic manager who can pull the organization together in a kind of Family. Often a trusted relative of the founder is chosen who has to reconcile the original incubator culture with the developing family culture. Dilemmas manifest as team sprit versus individual creativity, and leading participative employees versus respect for authority. But later, people find themselves restricted by the cumbersome and restricted centralized authority. Their dilemma is now between following orders and taking initiative, so creating a *crisis of autonomy*.

From Intention to Invasion: Growth Through Delegation

It is difficult for leaders who had been successful at being directive to relinquish control and delegate, and the lower-level managers are not used to making decisions. The need to develop a task-oriented culture (which we caricature as a Guided Missile) becomes evident. But this gives rise to dilemmas of lord, servant, or servant leader and tensions from asking how we centralize lessons from decentralized locations and finally social learning versus technological learning. Innovative approaches are again required in which leaders need to lead by giving service to others. And concerns for people have to be connected with concerns for productivity resulting in a reconciling sociotechnical philosophy. In this way, the reconciliation of the Family with Guided Missile cultures means the inventions have gained intention through the directive infusion of long-term commitment with the support of loyal people. Furthermore, the intended inventions have obtained focus to the outside world and are ready for invasion.

From Invasion to Implementation: Growth Through Coordination

Just when we thought all was well, top management senses that it is losing control over a highly diversified operation. So the *crisis of control* arises. Now we need more formal reporting systems and committees, which results in a return to centralization. We caricature this as the rise of the role-oriented Eiffel Tower culture. Dilemmas now appear between meeting financial criteria versus developing people, focusing on customers versus internal processes, and whether we should meet benchmarks or transcend them. Standards and benchmarks become obsolete when we realize they are linear one-dimensional measures. So the question is not simply if people have lived up to the standards, but have the standards lived up to the people! Reconciling internal orientations with customer focus can be achieved by involving customers in improving internal processes!

From Implementation to Inquiring: Growth Through Collaboration

Most coordinating systems eventually gain a momentum of their own resulting in *a crisis of* "red-tape." Now the organization has become too large and complex to be managed through rigid, well-prescribed systems. Procedures take preference over problem-solving.

How do we sustain the innovation spirit of the organization now? We've given "intention to invention," invaded the market, and implemented the right processes while fighting the crises of leadership, autonomy, control, and red tape. New dilemmas involve striving to be right the first time or correcting errors quickly, learning explicitly or tacitly, and connecting the authority of sponsors with empowered teams.

From Inquiring to Innovation: Growth Through External Connections

By reconciling the dilemmas characteristic of this phase, the infinity loop is finally closed, and at the same time there is a need to go outside the organization.

The organization may now have exhausted what it can achieve from within itself, so growth now may depend on the design of extra-organizational solutions—such as buying a new small pioneering incubator that brings a fresh input of innovative ideas. This networking and alliance phase has more emphasis on the market than internal hierarchical concerns. The locus of innovation now shifts to networks and away from the individual firm.

The Culture of Innovation Profiler

In order to quantify organizational risk culture across 12 metrics in four quadrants (role, power, task, and person paradigms of corporate culture) we have developed a profiler out of our more generic Organizational Value Profiler that consists of 36 questions (see Chapter 13). The assumption here is that one can score high on each segment. It not only quantifies the starting position and preference of the organizational cultural orientations, benchmarks are possible on every individual question (12 questions), one for every segment (12 segments), and three for every quadrant (4 quadrants)

An asymmetrical current profile gives indications of where the organization is not dealing effectively with competing demands. Gaps between current and ideal profile elicit areas where performance needs to be improved. An alternative interpretation is that it also measures levels of ambition to build on current success to perform even better in the future. To move from current to ideal culture will create tensions between competing demands, and these can best be explored as dilemmas. Effective management of innovation results from embedding the reconciliations of the key dilemmas across the organization.

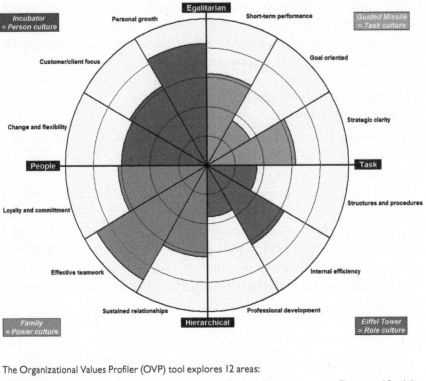

The Organizational Values Profiler (OVP) tool explores 12 areas:

- Short-term performance
- Goal orientation
- Strategic Clarity
- Structures and Procedures
- Internal Efficiency
- Professional Development
- Sustained Relationships
- Effective Teamwork
- Loyalty and Commitment
- Change and flexibility
- Customer Focus
- Personal Growth

FIGURE 18.2. Measuring Culture: Organizational Values Profiler (OVP)

Combining your responses on the individual dilemmas gives rise to the profile shown in Figure 18.2. The *ideal profile*, that is, innovation is managed in all areas, would be a completely filled-in large circle profile.

Corporate Culture: Why Some Areas of the Profile May Be Larger Than Others

How things are done around the organization provides meaning and direction that can exert a decisive influence on the overall ability of the organization to deal with the challenges it faces in supporting innovation.

The horizontal axis in the profile relates to concern for people (on the left) to concern for results (right). The vertical axis from hierarchical leadership (bottom) through to participative (top).

The net result of the way any one organization has developed its corporate culture over time, depending on its mission, founding entrepreneur, leadership style, environment, and so on, often will have led to more emphasis on some values than others. In the extremes the dominant competing values give rise to four organization stereotypes:

- **Role culture** (bottom right)—with a high degree of formal rules and procedures, and thus inflexible.
- **Power culture** (bottom left)—with power centralized around an autocratic leader, and thus manipulative and where status differentiates.
- **Person culture** (top left)—less formal rules and exists to serve the needs of its individual employees. Control is through persuasion and mutual concern.
- **Task culture** (top right)—flexible and dynamic in order to deliver results but is thus difficult to manage as it is designed to respond to rapid changes.

How We Score Your Ratings

We combine your responses to the individual rating questions to show the underlying competing demands on an X-Y grid. Your average is shown (Figure 18.3).

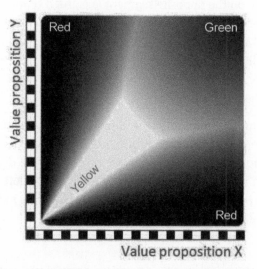

FIGURE 18.3. Spectrum of How Well Competing Demands Are Combined

- If you are positioned in a *red* region, you are at risk by giving too much emphasis on Value Y rather than its opposite Value X (or emphasizing X rather than Y).
- If you are positioned in a *yellow* region, you are at some risk because you have chosen a compromise by alluding only to some aspects of both values.
- If you are positioned in a *green* region, you are managing the complementarity of the tensions between these competing values, which supports innovation.

Ideally your organization should be managing the risk between all competing demands.

This new approach to innovation management seeks to overcome the limitations of a more traditional view of innovation that is purely based on the creativity of individuals and teams.

Innovation Index

At THT, we like to benchmark in context. For example the client wants to know how their organizational culture is an *Innovation factor* in the larger Innovation landscape.

In this case we will look at three individual benchmarks:

1. The number of segments that are scoring significantly surpassing industry/sector average
2. The score on the opposite segment (e.g., high score on procedures combined with high score on change/flexibility is supporting innovation)
3. The qualitative measure of the dilemmas that are retrieved by interviews and WebCue (e.g., the need for standards and compliance versus the need for flexibility)

By triangulating the quantitative and qualitative measures, we can truly benchmark the organizational performance on innovation.

Organizations are at risk when these competing demands are not addressed. We rate how you described your organization with an overall Innovation Rate Measure (IRM) as XX percent. A higher index is better and reflects how well innovation is being managed.

Feedback on Your Ratings

Below is a meta-level view of the way you described how your organization is coping with the dilemmas derived from the competing values. You can also scroll down to explore the individual dilemmas.

Now explore how you responded to each of the six key innovation dilemmas above:

1. **Time horizon.** Risk arises where short-term bottom-line results are pursued at the cost of human relationships that take a long time to develop (Figure 18.4).

In Figure 18.4 you see that the battle between competing demands of short term results and long term relationships is clearly won by the drive for short term performance. This particular score is not supportive of a culture of innovation.

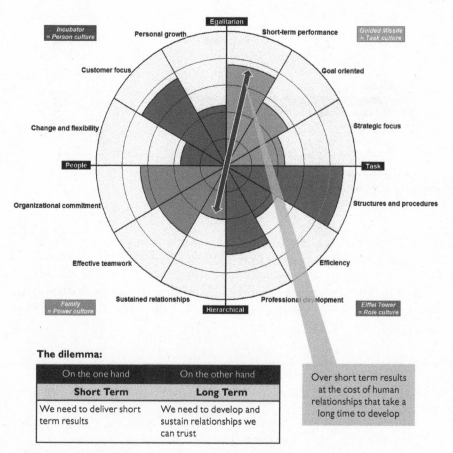

The dilemma:

On the one hand	On the other hand
Short Term	**Long Term**
We need to deliver short term results	We need to develop and sustain relationships we can trust

Over short term results at the cost of human relationships that take a long time to develop

FIGURE 18.4. OVP Definition: Short Term Versus Long Term

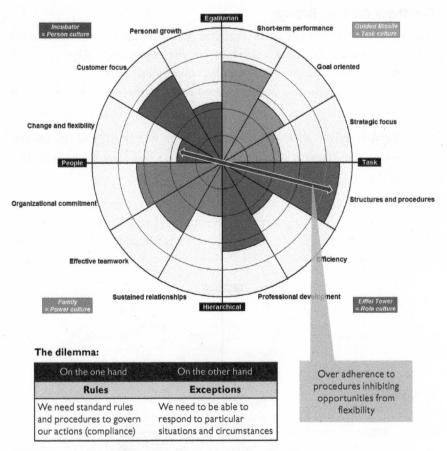

The dilemma:

On the one hand	On the other hand
Rules	**Exceptions**
We need standard rules and procedures to govern our actions (compliance)	We need to be able to respond to particular situations and circumstances

Over adherence to procedures inhibiting opportunities from flexibility

FIGURE 18.5. OVP Definition: Rules Versus Exceptions

2. **Change.** Risk arises where there is over adherence to procedures, inhibiting opportunities from flexibility (Figure 18.5).

The figure clearly shows that this organizational culture is dominated by procedures at the cost of change and flexibility. This is not nurturing innovation.

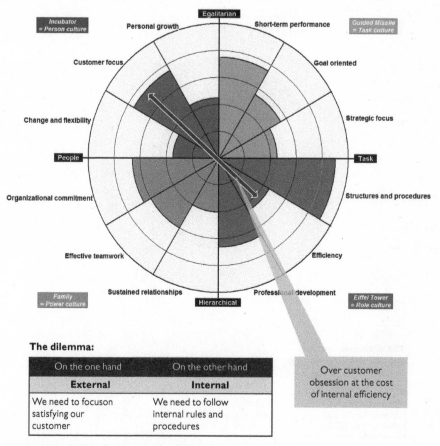

FIGURE 18.6. OVP Definition: External Versus Internal

3. Inside-out. Risk arises where there is over obsession with satisfying customers at the cost of internal efficiency (Figure 18.6).

Innovation is thriving on the combination of internal and external stimuli. The figure shows that this organization is having a preference to be driven by the outside world at the cost of following internal guidelines. This might hinder their innovative power.

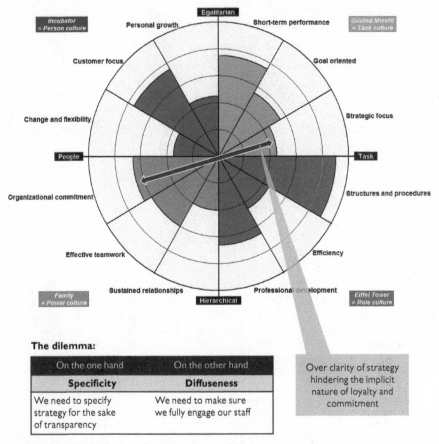

The dilemma:

On the one hand	On the other hand
Specificity	**Diffuseness**
We need to specify strategy for the sake of transparency	We need to make sure we fully engage our staff

Over clarity of strategy hindering the implicit nature of loyalty and commitment

FIGURE 18.7. OVP Definition: Specificity Versus Diffuseness

4. Focus. Risk arises where there is over focus on achieving goals at the cost of involving people for consensus (Figure 18.7).

This organization has a culture whereby organizational commitment and engagement is seen as much more important than strategic focus. Again not supporting a culture of innovation.

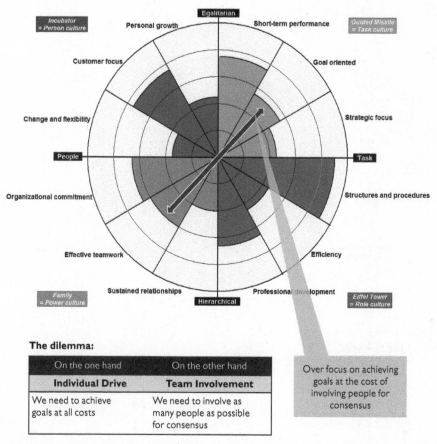

The dilemma:		
On the one hand	On the other hand	
Individual Drive	**Team Involvement**	
We need to achieve goals at all costs	We need to involve as many people as possible for consensus	

Over focus on achieving goals at the cost of involving people for consensus

FIGURE 18.8. OVP Definition: Individual Versus Team

5. **Co-opetition.** Risk arises where over clarity of strategy hinders the implicit nature of loyalty and commitment (Figure 18.8).

The figure seems to indicate a compromise (average score on both sides) between effective teamwork and goal orientation. This is not ideal for creating an environment where innovation thrives.

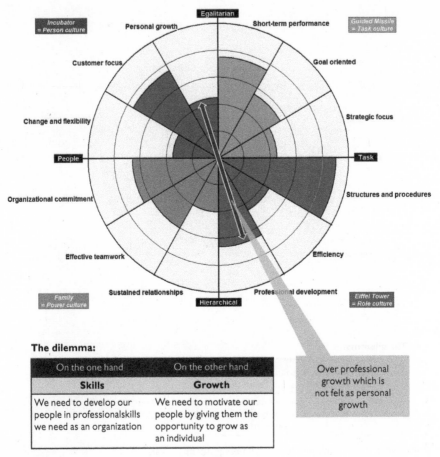

The dilemma:

On the one hand	On the other hand
Skills	**Growth**
We need to develop our people in professionalskills we need as an organization	We need to motivate our people by giving them the opportunity to grow as an individual

Over professional growth which is not felt as personal growth

FIGURE 18.9. OVP Definition: Skills Versus Growth

    6. Stability. Risk arises where there is an excess in professional growth that is not felt or aligned as personal growth (Figure 18.9).

Again we find a compromise between the need for personal growth and professional development. Innovation thrives when both are reconciled.

In Perspective

In our consulting we have captured, encoded, and trawled through some 44,000 dilemmas with which organizations wrestle. Linguistic analysis and data mining shows this raw database can be reduced and clustered to a manageable series of frequently recurring dilemmas that embrace the life cycle stages we have described.

It is those organizations that successfully reconcile the dilemmas by making connections between different orientations that survive in the ever-changing world. HR has a key role to facilitate this mindset change.

Ultimately, people are still the unique and scarce entity. But the challenge for HR is not to think itself as human-resource management but the management of resourceful humans.

And that really would be innovation!

The new concepts described here are explored in detail in the recently published *Riding the Whirlwind: Connecting People and Organizations in a Culture of Innovation* by Fons Trompenaars, published by Infinite Ideas Limited, October 2007, ISBN-13: 978-1905940363. See: www.ridingthewhirlwind.com.

Further scenarios and explanation is given in Appendix A (Creating a Culture of Innovation App).

Developing Digital Leaders
The Critical Role of Dilemma Reconciliation

Fons Trompenaars and Lucas de Jong de Abril

ALTHOUGH MUCH has been written and hypothesized about leadership competencies and styles, the advent of leadership in the digital age has further complicated the issue. In this chapter, we propose a model of reconciliation based on seven golden "dilemmas" that digital leaders face. The approaches to these dilemmas are culturally defined. The premise is that, by thinking and acting to reconcile these issues, leaders are better able to work digitally *and* cross-culturally.

Limitations of Established Frameworks

Attempts to map the personality traits, effective behavioral competencies, contingency, and transformational styles of outstanding leaders have fascinated a diverse number of practitioners and researchers. But in spite of the extensive proliferation of such models and frameworks, leadership has remained elusive. Too many of these existing models are inadequate for today's world as we find that desirable characteristics or effective behaviors of leadership and other frameworks identified in the USA or Anglo-Saxon cultures do not transfer to modern global business. But neither do culturally biased French or Chinese frameworks. They also fail at home for an increasingly diverse workforce. And if we subscribe to situational leadership, how do leaders assess these situations, and what is appropriate?

All of such published models of leadership tend to lack any coherent underlying rationale or base pre-proposition that predicts effective leadership behaviors. These models tend to seek the same end, but differ in approach as they try to encapsulate the existing body of knowledge about what makes an effective leader. Because of the methodology adopted there is no underlying rationale or unifying theme that defines the holistic characteristic of leadership. This creates considerable confusion for today's world of the transcultural leader. Which paradigm should he or she fit into? Which meanings should a leader espouse, his or her own or those of the foreign culture? Since most of our management theory comes from the USA and other English-speaking countries, there is a real danger of ethnocentrism. We do not know, for example, how the lists cited fare outside the USA, or how diverse conceptions of leadership may be. Do different cultures necessitate different styles? Can we reasonably expect other cultures to follow a lead from outside those cultures?

A Proposed New Metatheory of Leadership

Much attention has been given to the recognition of and respect for cultural differences. However, if we stop at only these first two stages we run the risk of supporting only stereotypical views on cultures. Our response was to progress from basic cross-cultural awareness training and consulting to developing the global minds of leaders and beyond.

A new metatheory of leadership is needed to tackle how leaders will deal with value dilemmas as a result of digital transformations. We can infer from our research findings that successful leaders in the current epoch of digitalizing situations and multicultural surroundings need to operate with a people-oriented style in order to accomplish their task. Leaders will have to be participative in order to be able to take autocratic decisions of a higher level. They will have to think logically, fed by a nonlogical intuition. Finally leaders must be very sensitive to the situation in order to make consistent decisions regardless of the situation.

We claim that our work is unique in that our focus has been to extend research on leadership to giving much more attention to the reconciliation of differences after the identification of these differences. We have accumulated a significant body of evidence that leaders lead by reconciling values across the whole management spectrum. The new question is therefore to ask what we can do to help leaders make business, and digitalization in particular, more effective once we cross cultural or diversity boundaries.

Our solution that we have been using since the late nineties was based on this reconciliation of cultural differences. It is a series of behaviors that enables effective interaction with those of contrasting value systems.

Why do leaders face such dilemmas, and why are they important? All organizations need stability and agility, long-term and short-term decisions, tradition and innovation, planning and laissez-faire, digital and analogue. The challenge for leaders is to fuse these opposites, not to select one extreme at the expense of the other. As a leader you have to inspire well as listen. As a professional, you need to master your materials, and at the same time you need to be passionately at one with the mission of the whole organization. You need to apply your brilliant analytic skills in order to place these contributions in a larger context. You are supposed to have priorities and put them in a meticulous sequence, while parallel processing is in vogue. You have to develop a brilliant strategy and at the same time have all the answers to questions in case your strategy misses its goals.

Dilemmas of Digital Leaders

These digitalization dilemmas seem to be universal for all leaders globally. The approach to these dilemmas seem to be culturally defined.

Readers of our more recent books and other publications will know that we make extensive use of the Internet for collecting primary data from participants from our client organizations. In addition to the main Trompenaars' cross-cultural database, we have also collected and indexed some 45,000 dilemmas faced by leaders in their respective organizations across the world gathered over the last 14 years. Coding and subsequent analysis of these dilemmas using clustering and data mining algorithms reveals a frequently reoccurring series of "golden dilemmas" that provide a basis for a structured approach to diagnosing challenges for leaders that owe their origin to cultural value differences.

TABLE 19.1. Generic Dilemmas Faced by Leaders

Standard and adaptation	Standardized products/services	Customized products/services
Individual and team	Keeping data to yourself	Sharing data publicly
Passion and control	Be cool	Show passion
Analysis and synthesis	High tech	High touch
Doing and being	Bottom-up	Top-down
Past, present, and future	Traditional mindset	Inventive mindset
Short and long term	Fast learning	Reliable products
Push and pull	Keep control	Go with the flow

Frequently Reoccurring Digitalization Dilemmas

At the generic level, the following represent the principal "golden dilemmas" faced by digital leaders:

Dilemma 1: Standard and Adaptation

It is remarkable how often leaders mentioned this dilemma. Do we have to globalize our approach, or do we just have to localize? Is it more beneficial for our organization to choose mass production than focus on specialized and customized products? Effective leaders found the solution in the "transnational organization" where best local practices are globalized on a continuous basis. "Mass customization" is the keyword for reconciling standardized production and specialized adaptations.

How does this manifest itself in the digital space? On the one hand, we strive for robust digital products and services to benefit from a common universal identity and branding (as well as cost savings through economies of scale). On the other hand, we try to develop and offer unique and customized digital products and services adapted to the needs and tastes of local markets

We talk a lot about the importance of being agile. But we have seen many organizations going over the top in agility, lacking all kind of stable points. The reconciliation of both desirable states can be best described by what we observed during the 2019 Rugby World Cup in Japan. What can we learn from the extreme strategies that teams have displayed? We

FIGURE 19.1. Agility Dilemma

have seen the robust play of Wales, but they lost against Japan. We have seen the very creative and agile play of England, but they lost the finals against the South Africans. What can we learn from the Japanese and South African game? Both teams had found the stable stepping-stones from which they could be agile. The Japanese had minimally 40 percent (and sometimes 80 percent) more passes than their opponents. They trained to make the passing game their stable process so they could take more advantage from their agility and won games by doing it (Figure 19.1). The Springboks showed their strength first against the English and became agile in the latter stages of the game. So we see that the dilemma is universal while it is culture that defines where to start the process of reconciliation.

Dilemma 2: Individual Privacy and Public Sharing of Data

A second general leadership dilemma is the integration of team spirit with individual creativity and a competitive mindset. The effective leader knows how to make an excellent team out of creative individuals. The team is stimulated to support brilliant individuals, while these individuals deploy themselves for the greater whole. This has been called co-opetition.

In the digital space the most frequently mentioned dilemma is the tension between keeping data to yourself and sharing data publicly (Figure

FIGURE 19.2. Privacy Dilemma

19.2). The reconciliation can be found in public clusters of privacy. This tension is very known in the social media advertising realm. Reconciliations are popping up quite recently where users are not only warned with a cookie announcement but also progressively involved in what they want to be informed by and thus want to share with others.

Dilemma 3: Passion and Control

Is a good leader an emotional and passionate person, or does the control of emotions make a better leader? Here there are two clear types. Passionate leaders without reason are neurotics, and neutral leaders without emotions are robots. Richard Branson regularly checks his passion with reason, and if we look at the more neutral Jack Welch, the former CEO of General Electric, we see a leader who gives his controlled reason meaning by showing passion once in a while.

For the digital world we find versions of this dilemma in the shape of the ethical use of AI in recruitment, for example. On the one hand, we want to rationally choose candidates on the basis of measurable and rational criteria. On the other hand, we want to positively discriminate in a passionate way to give minorities a chance and increase diversity. One of the possible reconciliations is to have a value-based recruitment process, where the cultural context is checked wherein with measurable competences can flourish (Figure 19.3).

FIGURE 19.3. Passion and Control Dilemma

Dilemma 4: Analysis and Synthesis

Is the leader of the twenty-first century a detached, analytical person who is able to divide the big picture into ready-to-eat pieces, always selecting for shareholder value? Or is it somebody who puts issues in the big picture and gives priority to the rather vaguely defined stakeholder value? At Shell, Van Lennep's "helicopter view" was introduced as a significant characteristic of a modern leader—the capability to ascend and keep the overview, while being able to zoom in on certain aspects of the matter. Jan Carlzon (SAS) called the integration of specific moments with profundity, as a part of client service, "moments of truth." This is another significant characteristic of the modern leader—namely, the ability to know when and where to go in deep. Pure analysis leads to paralysis, and the overuse of synthesis leads to an infinite holism and a lack of action.

Going for the Clicks That Stick

The challenge to financial service companies has come in part from the unbundling of services into specific pieces.

You can buy information, research, trading facilities, and advice from separate sources, and the combined fees may be less than those paid to six- and seven-figure professionals. While the Internet is overflowing with data, this is not the same as knowledge or information. We are informed by facts relevant to our questions and concerns. We "know" when we get answers to our propositions and hypotheses. The larger the Internet becomes, the more customers will need a guide to what is relevant to their concern.

The dilemma can be analyzed as follows. On the one axis we find low-cost specific data and transactions on the Internet. The risk here is that you create a high-tech solution where brokers are bypassed by technology. On the other, we find the rich, meaningful, diffuse personal relationships that brokers have developed with their clients. It maintains a high-touch environment where you are overpaying for your own dependence.

It is obvious that in specific cultures like the USA and northwest Europe, the Internet services can take a lot away from the traditional face-to-face business. This is true for financial services and for buying a dishwasher, a CD, a book, and even a car. However, in more diffuse cultures such as Arabs, Latinos, and most Asians, the relationships are seen as so crucial that one would never give this up for an anonymous service that you get through a click. I remember an American consultant of Merrill Lynch working in Saudi Arabia. The Saudis liked face-to-face contact rather than being served by data on the Internet. However, his American colleagues were telling him that he couldn't ignore the fact that the more Internet-driven competitors were gradually taking market share away.

Merrill Lynch found a situation where Charles Schwab high-level Internet services were eating away quite some market share. Merrill Lynch's answer was close to brilliant. They well understood that instead of relationships being eclipsed by the Internet, these get more and more important in interpreting the possible meanings of data flows, as what is available grows ever larger than what is relevant to each client.

Merrill Lynch's response to its dilemma was to refocus its efforts on reconciling new technology with customer service. Its strategy was announced by John Steffens at Forrester Conference in May 1999: "By combining technology with skilled advisors, clients are given the convenience of interacting when, how and where they want."

Then-CEO Dave Komansky clarified the policy:

> "Anyone, anywhere, at any time can log into the Internet to get free quotes, market data, and stock picks from a variety of chat rooms. Yet at Merrill Lynch we are confidently making unparalleled billion dollar investments in our Financial Consultants, research analysts and in our technology and products. We're doing this because we know success in the online world—as it was in the offline world—will be defined by meaningful content for the individual."[1]

FIGURE 19.4. High Tech Versus High Touch

We need high tech, but we also need high touch. The more those numbers rain down upon you, the more you need to talk to someone about these. Merrill Lynch is using the Internet to give better personal service (using high technology) to its high touch customers, but also uses the Internet to identify those high-tech customers for whom it makes good business sense to offer high touch.

Dilemma 5: Past and Future, Short Term and Long Term

Notably, effective leaders are able to plan in a rigorous, sequential way, but at the same time have the ability to stimulate parallel processes. This reconciliation, which we know as "synchronize processes to increase the sequential speed"—or "just in time" management—seems also to be very effective in integrating the long and short term.

MVP and Mindset

For the digital world the most challenging dilemmas are the traditional mindset of the existing organization versus the untested inventive mindset and the related focus on planning and optimization versus the rapid launch and fast learning.

In the digital world we regularly face the urge to "go digital." When we show our own digital products/services to our clients, they initially get excited, and it follows with a blank and staring face. How to do this with the

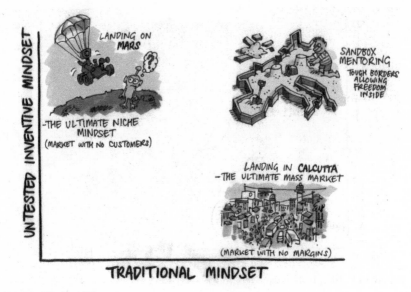

FIGURE 19.5. Mindset Dilemma

existing mindset? When everything changes and goes digital, one might end in the ultimate niche market, that piece of the market with no customers. Conversely, we find that following no paths will make you end in a market with no margins. Possible reconciliations are found in giving the organization clear traditional boundaries within which complete freedom can be given (Figure 19.5). Experienced mentors can give young nerds great perspectives in this process.

Similarly we find the necessity of the minimum viable product. A core component of the reconciliation between working products and comprehensive documentation is the Lean Startup methodology as it represents the build-measure-learn feedback loop.[2] The first step is figuring out the problem that needs to be solved and then developing a minimum viable product (MVP) to begin the process of learning as quickly as possible (Figure 19.6). Once the MVP is established, a start-up can work on tuning the engine. This will involve measurement and learning and must include actionable metrics that can demonstrate cause-and-effect questions.

The start-up will also utilize an investigative development method called the Five Whys, asking simple questions to study and solve problems along the way. When this process of measuring and learning is done correctly, it will be clear that a company is either moving the drivers of the business

FIGURE 19.6. Minimum Viable Product (MVP)

model or not. If not, it is a sign that it is time to pivot or make a structural course correction to test a new fundamental hypothesis about the product, strategy, and engine of growth.

Progress in manufacturing is measured by the production of high-quality goods. The unit of progress for lean start-ups is *validated learning*—a rigorous method for demonstrating progress when one is embedded in the soil of extreme uncertainty. Once entrepreneurs embrace validated learning, the development process can shrink substantially. When you focus on figuring the right thing to build, the thing customers want and will pay for, you need not spend months waiting for a product beta launch to change the company's direction. Instead, entrepreneurs can adapt their plans incrementally, inch by inch, minute by minute.

Dilemma 6: Push and Pull

This core competence for today's leaders is the ability to connect the voice of the market with the technology the company has developed and vice versa. This is not about technology push or market pull. The modern leader knows that the push of technology finally leads to the ultimate niche market, that part without any clients. If you only choose for the market, your clients will be unsatisfied. We believe that leaders are not simply "adding value," but synergizing through the integration (combining) of values. Thus a car that

FIGURE 19.7. Self-Driving Car

is both fast and safe, high-quality food that is also easy to prepare are the integration of values, not the result of "either-or" choices.

Self-Driving Car

With artificial intelligence we see many interesting developments unfolding, of which the self-driving car is one. But it is loaded with dilemmas. It was the CEO of Ford that at the end of 2018 predicted that the self-driving car would only be a success if the driver stays in control of what is controlling the driver. And it sounds reasonable knowing that one of the primary motivational forces of mankind, according to Daniel Pink, is self-mastery. A wonderful example of reconciliation is that we build cars where the driver controls what is controlling him or her (Figure 19.7).

Dilemma 7: Serving and Leading

"Getting things done" is an important characteristic of a manager. However, shouldn't we keep the rather vulgar "doing" in balance with "being," as in our private lives? As a leader you have to be yourself as well. From our research it appeared that successful leaders act the way they really are. They seem to be one with the business they are undertaking. One of the important causes of stress is that "doing" and "being" are not integrated. Excessive compulsion to perform, when not matching an individual's true personality, leads to ineffective behavior.

FIGURE 19.8. Servant Leadership

Servant Leadership

Our recent research reveals that the essential distinguishing characteristic of leaders in a diverse environment is their propensity to reconcile seemingly opposing values. In contrast, managers (rather than leaders) seem to have solvable problems. Managers are hired to solve one problem after the other: "Next problem, please." Leaders are hired to reconcile dilemmas.

Leaders are frequently suffering from insomnia because they were not able to resolve a dilemma they faced. It is difficult "not to have made it," but even more difficult not knowing "what to make." Then, even worse—the successful integration of conflicting values frequently leads to the creation of one or more new dilemmas. It is a continuous process.

In the preceding text we have seen what these dilemmas are that leaders in the digital age face. Of course you have to inspire as a leader, and you have also to listen. You need to follow the orders of HQ to fulfil the global strategy, and you have to have local success by adapting to regional circumstances. You have to decide when to act yourself but also when and where to delegate. As a professional you need to input your own day-to-day contribution and at the same time to be passionate about the mission of the whole. And you need to simultaneously use your brilliant analytical power while enabling the contribution of others (Figure 19.8). You need to develop an excellent strategy while simultaneously having answers to why the strategy misses its goal.

The view of leadership taken here is that leaders find themselves between conflicting demands and are subject to an endless series of paradoxes and dilemmas. There are nonstop culture clashes, and by culture we mean not simply the cultures of different nations, but those of different disciplines, functions, genders, classes, and so on. We will illustrate some well-known leadership dilemmas in this chapter, but their exact descriptions are less important than the capacity for transcultural competence or paradoxical problem-solving that underlies them all.

From Values to Performance

We have recently responded to these challenges by moving to a third phase in our approach in which we now focus on helping leaders by prioritizing and realizing the business benefits of reconciling cultural differences for competitive advantage.

The really exciting part of this third wave, based on our new dilemma database, is that we have been able more recently to converge on a number of key diagnostic measures that reveal how these meta-level dilemmas

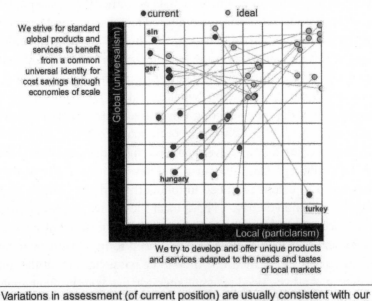

FIGURE 19.9. Measuring Current Versus Ideal Status of Golden Dilemmas

manifest for the leader and how these link to bottom-line business performance. We first help leaders make such "Golden Dilemmas" explicit and therefore tangible through our structured Dilemma Reconciliation Process. We then assess the current status of the dilemma against an ideal espoused state that would result when the business benefits had been realized (Figure 19.9). These vectors are then used to evaluate varying reconciliation strategies.

Leaders are now in a position to evaluate the business benefits against the costs and time scales to realize benefits and the degree to which the dilemma solution in located in one profit center or involves cooperation across a number of business units. The following example summarizes the top-level descriptions of the Golden Dilemmas faced by the top leadership of a major US organization and how they were subsequently placed on the dilemma relationship portfolio.

This type of analysis provides the leader with an objective evaluation of where the highest return on investment can be achieved and thus secures the best benefits to the business. In this particular case, the most important cultural dilemma that needed to be addressed was the need for technology push (what the company can make from its own intellectual capital) versus what the different markets want (what the organization could sell). When leaders are faced with major decisions involving high levels of funding and human capital, such analytical approaches help leaders to validate their tacit insights by making them explicit and open to debate.

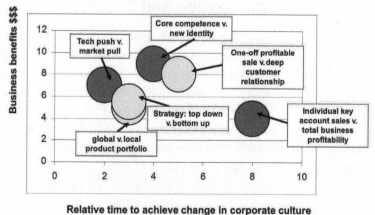

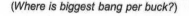

FIGURE 19.10. Digital Dilemma Portfolio Analysis

Transcultural Competence: The Propensity for Leaders to Reconcile Dilemmas

We have found that this competence in reconciling dilemmas is the most discriminating feature that differentiates successful from less successful digital leaders and thereby the performance of their organizations. But not unexpectedly, the perennial question reappeared! Is this competence innate or acquired? Can it be developed? Or more fundamentally, are leaders made or born? Furthermore, can the leader transform the organization such that it is continually eliciting and reconciling these dilemmas so it becomes the "reconciling organization"?

Many educational programs in our schools, universities, and within our organizations are based on presenting codified knowledge, which is dumped on the heads of the students. In order to break out from the imaginary square of the traditional principles of learning and to build a true learning organization, the leader needs to first distinguish a certain number of dilemmas that characterize an alternative learning process.

We have argued that the existing dominant theories of leadership, categorized in three main paradigms known as trait, behavioral, and situational theories, do not resolve main dilemmas leaders are facing. We believe our proposed metatheory resolves most black spots in existing leadership models.

Reconciling Dilemmas Between the Organization and Society

The tensions we have mentioned can all serve as challenges of a leader in creating learning organizations. But they can also definitely bring about real change if reconciled, which can result in companies' becoming, for example, more diversity-minded or more global. In all these dilemmas, one discovers an organizational principle that is based on the idea of integration. One will have to leave the Cartesian and deductive model behind, and to bring a synthesis of the dilemmas that form the basis of learning.

Nobody claims that combining values is easy; nevertheless, it is possible. The ever-expanding system of satisfaction of values will form the ultimate test for the leaders of this century. All organizations need stability and change, tradition and innovation, public and private interest, planning and laissez-faire, order and freedom, growth and decay. The consequence is that the systems and processes and challenges for leaders are changing to the world of dilemmas created by the evolving workplace and even more by digitalization.

To meet the challenges of today's ever globalizing world, leaders need to develop a new mindset of inquiry and support centered around the reconciliation of dilemmas—and thereby finally reveal their true worth. One approach to help leaders develop this capability that we are currently exploring is to develop a competency framework that specifies effective behavioral criteria based on our conceptual framework. Thus a conventional competency model that prescribes criteria for demonstrating "integrity" might include statements such as "to be direct, open, frank, and honest in the digital space." Such statements are often (unintentionally) culturally biased and do not embrace reconciliation. Thus, "to be direct, frank, and transparent" may work in the USA but be less effective in China (or dealing with Chinese members of your team located in the USA) for whom matters of "face" are different when facing criticism (even if the criticism is constructive). The equivalent behavior description that engenders a reconciliation approach would be "to develop your relationship with your team so that you can be open, direct, frank, and transparent." Similarly we have found that to start with high tech and then worry about high touch is more effective in the Western world. Amongst the Arabs, high touch is a better starting point from which one can introduce high-tech support. In all cultures the dilemma is similar, but the starting point is culturally defined. Extending this idea to the complete portfolio of competence descriptors can thereby induce a change of mindset through prescribing behaviors that are reconciling. Living and practicing these develops the aspiring leader to this new level.

Our own satisfaction derives from having reconciled our own intrinsic interest in researching the subject of culture with providing real operational support to our clients that we now know makes their organizations more sustainable.

20

Ethics Across Cultures

Did the Pedestrian Die?

Fons Trompenaars

THIS LAST chapter shows how different cultures might define integrity and ethical behavior differently. These definitions might work in a single culture, but what do we do when cultures meet in multicultural environments? People in all cultures, organizations, and institutions agree that the greatest leaders have integrity. In this chapter we suggest that integrity is creating wholeness through the integration of opposites. This is something that is not taught at educational institutions.

Many readers who have seen and heard me at one of my conference presentations will immediately understand the subtitle of this chapter: Did the Pedestrian Die?[1] We discussed this story, created by Americans Stouffer and Toby,[2] earlier, but we repeat it here in the context of exploring what is often cited as corruption in business.

You are riding in a car driven by a close friend. He hits a pedestrian. You know he was going at least 35 miles per hour in an area of the city where the maximum allowed speed is 20 miles per hour. There are no witnesses. His lawyer says that if you testify under oath that he was driving only 20 miles per hour, it may save him from serious consequences. What right has your friend to expect you to protect him?

A. My friend has a definite right as a friend to expect me to testify to the lower figure.

B. He has some right as a friend to expect me to testify to the lower figure.

C. He has no right as a friend to expect me to testify to the lower figure.

What do you think you would do in view of the obligations of a sworn witness and the obligation to your friend?

D. Testify that he was going 20 miles an hour.

E. Not testify that he was going 20 miles an hour.

Figure 20.1. shows the result of putting these questions to a variety of nationalities. The percentage represents those who answered that the friend had no right or some right and would then not testify (C or B + E). North Americans and most north Europeans emerge as almost totally universalist in their approach to the problem. The proportion falls to less than 55 percent for the French and 33 percent for the Japanese, while in India more than 80 of respondents would lie to the police to protect their friend. Time and again in our workshops, the universalists' response is that as the seriousness of the accident increases, the obligation to help their friend decreases. They seem to be saying to themselves, "The law was broken, and the serious condition of the pedestrian underlines the importance of upholding the law." This attitude suggests that universalism is rarely used to the exclusion of particularism, rather that it forms the first principle in the process of moral reasoning. Particular consequences remind us of the need for universal laws.

Particularist cultures, however, are rather more likely to support their friend as the pedestrian's injuries increase. They seem to reason, "My friend needs my help more than ever now that he is in serious trouble with the law." Universalists would regard such an attitude as corrupt and unethical. What if we all started to lie on behalf of those close to us? Society would fall

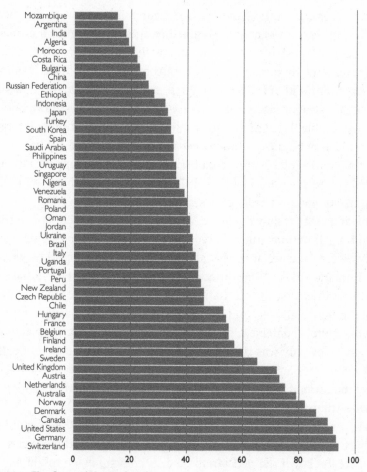

FIGURE 20.1. The Car and the Pedestrian

apart. There is merit to this argument, but particularism, which is based on a logic of the heart and human friendship, may also be the chief reason that citizens would not break laws in the first place. Do you love your children, or present them with a copy of the civil code? And what if the law becomes a weapon in the hands of a corrupt elite? You can choose what you call corruption. The more universalist cultures would say that the particularists are corrupt because you can't trust them since they would help their friends. The particularistic cultures, on the contrary, would call the universalists corrupt because you can't trust them since they would not even help their friends. The question becomes, by what you want to be corrupted: a friend or an abstract system?

Do you remember the discussion in Chapter 4? Let us help your memory.

In a workshop we were giving some time ago, we presented this dilemma. There was one British woman, Fiona, among the group of French participants. Fiona started the discussion of the dilemma by asking about the condition of the pedestrian. Without that information, she said, it would be impossible to answer the question. When the group asked her why this information was so indispensable, Dominique, an employee of a French airline, interjected: "Naturally, it is because if the pedestrian is very seriously injured or even dead, then my friend has the absolute right to expect my support. Otherwise, I would not be so sure." Fiona, slightly irritated but laughing, said, "That's amazing. For me it is absolutely the other way around."

This illustration shows that we "anchor" our response in one of the two principles. All nations might agree that universals and particulars should ideally be resolved—that is, that all exceptional cases should be judged by more humane rules. What differs is their starting points. We have since posed this dilemma in international workshops and conferences across many different cultures, and also to some 140,000 managers captured in our cross-cultural database, also made available in our free app Culture for Business.[3] Not only was the initial reaction different in different cultures, but the course of action the passenger would finally take, such as lying to protect their friend, was also dependent on the answer to the question, "Did the pedestrian die?"

While all could readily identify with the dilemma, this response was clearly culturally determined. A British person might feel more concerned to respect the law if the pedestrian died. A French person might feel more obligated to help their friend, arguing that friends are more important than unknown pedestrians.

Global Differences

Internationally operating organizations have known this dilemma in its manifestation of developing strict rules against corruption. Their integrity offensive often ended in universalist rules dictated from HQ by people who didn't think in dilemmas. It was black or it is white. In predominantly Protestant countries the value of integrity became very popular. It is by far the most quoted value—obviously because it is hardly practiced in most organizations. (If it was, why mention it?) Let's check if the value of integrity truly helps.

I was giving a workshop at one of the largest financial institutions in the USA. I started to ask their international top 80 people who in the audience would like to be in this situation. As I have experienced before, no one in the crowd raised their hand. So I asked why not? And the prevailing answer was that this is a dilemma.

Obviously this organization had *integrity* as their first value. So I followed by asking the following question: "If you lived the value of integrity seriously in your organization, what would you do in the car accident dilemma." A North American stood up and said he didn't understand the question: "How can you have integrity if you don't tell the truth in court? And a good friend would never ask me to lie." Fortunately we were interrupted by a South Korean who said, "I disagree, John, how can you have integrity if you don't help your friend?" It was fun to see that all 80 international participants, representing 40 countries, understood both. As a human being we share the dilemma. There is no one who wouldn't say, "We like to help friends in difficult situations, that is what friends are for." And at the same time, "We have to respect the laws that are made to protect our children from being hit by a car, and therefore we have to tell the truth." That is why it is a dilemma. And by the dialogue I realized that we as human beings share the same dilemmas. But I also realized that when we have to make a decision our cultural context numbs half of our logic.

What I liked about the discussion was that obviously amongst Americans you would have a preference not to lie, while in South Korea there is a tendency to help your friend in this case. But what about in a multicultural environment consisting of Swedish, Chinese, American, and South Korean participants? This is the challenge an ever internationalizing world is facing. And the reason I mention this particular organization out of many is that they had a second value: *We respect the culture of others* (Figure 20.2). So I

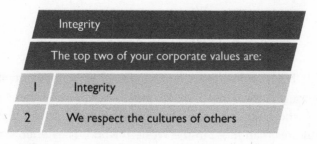

Integrity		
The top two of your corporate values are:		
1	Integrity	
2	We respect the cultures of others	

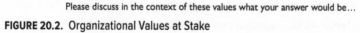

Please discuss in the context of these values what your answer would be...

FIGURE 20.2. Organizational Values at Stake

was ready for a nice afternoon because I asked the crowd to sit in groups of five and discuss what the two main values would do for you in deciding whether or not to help a friend in a multicultural group.

It is astonishing how few participants ever come up with an answer that pleases all cultures ranging from particularist to universalist. Is it a lack of intelligence or experience? No, obviously not. It is the unconscious bias we have in the way we have asked the question. There is an assumption that by choosing between a friend and the truth you'll find more or less integrity. You don't! So in view of the dichotomous question, the answer that works in all cultures is nonexistent. We need to go back to the etymological root of the word *integrity*. Most versions refer to *wholeness*. The one I prefer is that integrity is *creating wholeness through the integration of opposites*. Think about yin and yang. It is a whole that consists of two opposites. It is synthesis built out of thesis and antithesis. It is understanding that the cylinder includes the shadows representing the rectangle and the ellipse (Figure 20.3).

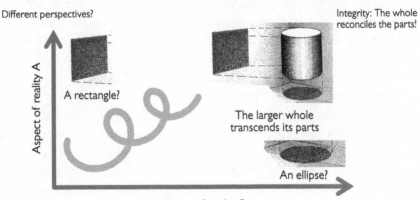

FIGURE 20.3. How Do We Perceive Reality?

A Japanese Approach

Nice words, but how does this work in practice? How can we create a whole out of opposing particularist and universalist viewpoints? Often I found that Japanese participants come more frequently with the answer that works in diverse cultures than those in the Western world. They often start by saying that their answer is not one of the possibilities. A good start. "What we would do in Japan is to convince our friend as a friend to tell the truth in court. And we will have to talk to the judge to lower the sentence for his courage." So you see that both the truth and the friendship is respected. Some Westerners come with the answer that "We should not lie but help our friend in many other ways like socially, financially, and legally". In both cases the friendship is deepened by the truth, and that is the real meaning of integrity.

Cultural Relativism

The arguments made above are very often seen as a culturally relativist position. Not at all! Not anything goes. Corruption is bad anywhere, and we should fight it everywhere. I once had a discussion with a Nigerian who called an American the most corrupt person in the world. Why? "After doing business he takes you out to dinner and pays for it. Very corrupt! I will never do that in the part of Nigeria where I live." And after asking him what the biggest problem is in Nigeria, he unequivocally answered, "Corruption!" So ethical behavior in a multicultural environment can only be achieved when we integrate value orientations on a higher level.

The Way Forward

This chapter presented just one particular dilemma that we identified and used to help both organizations and individual managers and leaders. Each element has been conceived, written, and then used all over the world; many were created after requests from clients, or developed from "moments of enlightenment" as we teased our research team or joked with fellow gurus. The individual dilemmas we face in our writings are on the one hand self-contained, but on the other hand form a whole that embraces the important issues facing the international leader and manager in today's ever-globalizing world.[4] Together they provide a comprehensive digest of best practice and learning for modern business management.

University education and too much training are still failing today's generation of potential leaders and managers. These are still based on Cartesian logic and scientific method where problems are defined as closed systems and where the variables selected are those that can be measured and controlled. Apparently, all we have to do is to evaluate alternate courses of action and select the one offering the lowest cost or highest margin. MBA students are still being taught to give sophisticated answers to the wrong type of question. Even in school laboratories pupils are told think in terms of keeping the temperature and pressure constant so they can study changes in volume. However, those who have to work in the real world know that a change in volume is not isothermal, but adiabatic: everything is connected to everything else. A problem is like surplus flab—tuck it in here, and it pops out somewhere else.

Billions of people in all cultures, organizations, and institutions agree on the greatness of Mandela, Gandhi, Muhammad Ali, and our religious icons. And what do these leaders have in common that their respect crosses cultures and institutions? Indeed they have integrity, the art of creating wholeness through bridging opposites. The crucial question for following up this chapter is whether ethical leadership is a reflection or a cause of this competence to integrate opposites. It is indeed true that most world-respected leaders have some quality that can be described as ethical. And it doesn't matter if the pedestrian died or not.

Self-Assessment Through the Integrity App

What is the app? The app is intended to make users better understand each other's approach to integrity and corruption.

The app is not primarily focused on "fighting corruption," but on awareness of situations that, from various perspectives, may remind the users of integrity and corruption.

How to use the app? For instance:
- Educational purposes
- When visiting other countries, the app prepares for sensitive situations
- When a company faces integrity issues, using the app prepares the employees for discussions about those issues
- Stakeholder discussions

What's next? Again, please see www.ridingthewavesofculture.com.

APPENDIX A

Supporting Diagnostic Tools and Apps

I N THIS appendix we describe our digital tools supporting the following areas:

1. Globalization
2. Culture Change
3. Mergers and acquisitions
4. Sustainability
5. Innovation
6. Diversity and inclusion
7. Leadership dilemmas
8. Financial performance

Globalization

Intercultural Awareness Profiler (IAP)

The Intercultural Awareness Profiler (IAP) questionnaire is designed to assess the personal orientation of choices that an individual makes when resolving intercultural business issues. Using a range of diagnostic questions, the questionnaire is able to elicit individual cross-cultural orientations against the Seven Dimensions of Culture model discussed in this book.

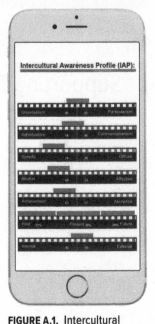

The Intercultural Awareness Profiler can be used in conjunction with workshops as well as in coaching situations. It allows users to perform a comprehensive personal analysis of their own cross-cultural orientation based on their individually generated profile and the personalized feedback provided.

FIGURE A.1. Intercultural Awareness Profiler (IAP)

Purpose

- Based on 30 years of research
- Regular testing for continued reliability and validation
- Active database
- Used worldwide
- Various methods of administering the questionnaire, depending on client needs
- Profiles available either in hard copy or online
- Questionnaire available in multiple languages
- Can be used in conjunction with the Culture for Business App, a self-paced e-learning tool

How to Download

Get more information and download here:

www.ridingthewavesofculture.com/iap.

Culture for Business App

This app provides clients with a better understanding of and detailed information on the differences across national cultures. It provides business travelers, international managers, or anyone who is interested in understanding other cultures with specific tips for meetings, management, and negotiations. Tips will be dependent on the difference between your score and the one of the country of interest—140 countries are available.

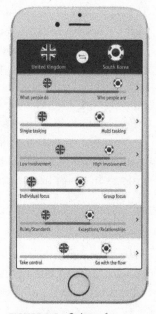

Purpose

To provide a better understanding of cultural differences, the reasons for cultural differences, and most important to increase users' cross-cultural management, communication, and cooperation capabilities.

FIGURE A.2. Culture for Business App

How to Download

Apps in the Google and Apple app stores: Culture for Business and web-based. Get more information and download here:

www.ridingthewavesofculture.com/cfb.

Intercultural Competence Profiler (ICP)

This app provides assessment and feedback rather than a mirror reflection of the respondent (and, therefore, we speak of "describing" instead of "scoring") on one's competence to Recognize, Respect, Reconcile, and Realize cultural differences: it is about how the respondent sees him/herself. This way we avoid cultural bias. Rather than giving advice, the app provides self-guiding reflection questions: we give guidance as to what respondents can reflect on to help improve these competencies.

This app uses a reconciled approach to development rather than a linear approach: we encourage the respondent to use the Dilemma Reconciliation Process in his or her personal development, instead of for instance SMART objectives.

Purpose

Self: Your personal profile is an indication of how you have described your knowledge and behaviors. It is not intended to be compared to those of others, because we all use different standards to describe ourselves.

360 Observers: When we use the observer version completed by people from your work environment, there is an "independent" measure against which you can compare your own assessment.

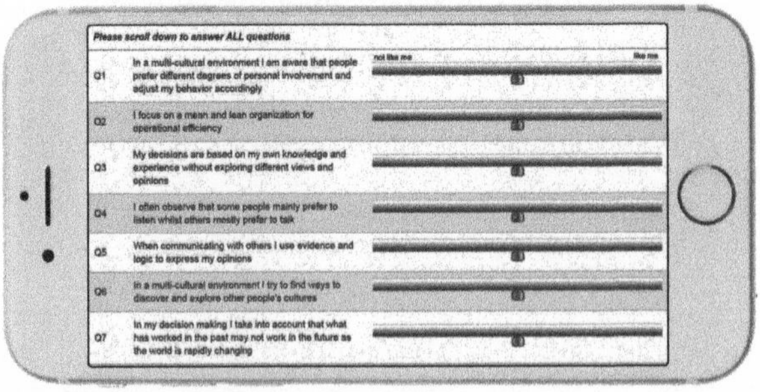

FIGURE A.3. Intercultural Competence Profiler (ICP)

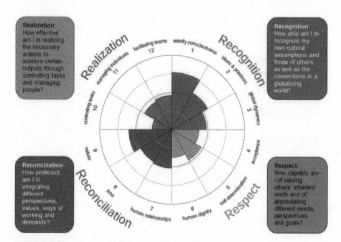

FIGURE A.4. Intercultural Competence Profiler (ICP)

How to Download

Get more information and download here:

www.ridingthewavesofculture.com/icp.

Globalization Index

This app enables respondents to consider and reflect on their organizations' readiness to be effective in international or global business. It uses the construct and model of Reconciliation to analyze responses from multiple-choice questions on the way in which their organization and various functional disciplines operate across the world.

Supplementary questions enable responses to be cross-referenced with the corporate culture and other aspects of global business performance and strategy. Respondents consider both the actual situation and ideal modes of operation for their organization.

Purpose

For the organization, this app is particularly suited to reviewing actual or intended strategic alliances, takeovers, and mergers with organizations of different national and corporate cultures. In addition, a range of options are presented to be considered by the organization in terms of possible changes in modes of working, systems, or structure to realize true globalization.

How Organizations operate in the world (by functional area)

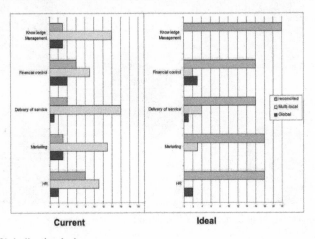

Current   Ideal

FIGURE A.5. Globalization Index

How your Organization operates in the world

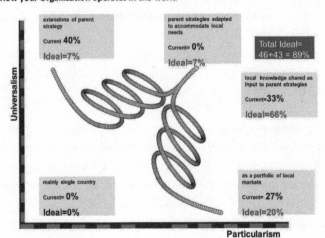

FIGURE A.6. Globalization Index

How to Download

Get more information and download here:

www.ridingthewavesofculture.com/glindex.

Culture Change

Corporate Culture Profiler (CCP)

The Corporate Culture Profiler (CCP) is a multifunctional instrument that enables participants to review and examine the interpretations employees give to relationships with each other and with the organization as a whole. Specifically, the CCP looks at the perceived current and idealized perceptions of issues such as Corporate Effectiveness (toward mission/goals), Efficiency, Loyalty, Learning, and Values, as well as possible other areas as per the request of the individual client.

This tool can be used within a group or organization internally, or with two groups involved in an integration process, allowing the leaders and/or teams to address key identified tensions and prioritize distribution of time and resources.

Like other corporate culture diagnostic tools, the CCP offers a simple diagnosis of the

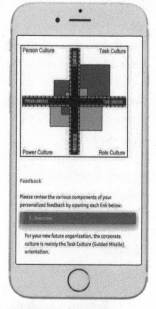

FIGURE A.7. Corporate Culture Profiler (CCP)

dominant culture in your organization using four typologies: Incubator, Family, Guided Missile, and Eiffel Tower. This could be helpful in either mergers/acquisitions, strategic change, diversity, globalization, or other related issues.

Purpose

- Provides a rigorous assessment of key issues rather than assumed needs
- Offers a road map for future action
- Benchmarking against THT's cultural, industry, or sector databases
- Secures engagement with organization/conference/workshop participants, as they feel their key issues are being addressed

How to Download

Get more information and download here:

www.ridingthewavesofculture.com/ccp.

Organization Values Profiler (OVP)

The Organization Values Profiler (OVP) is a multifunctional instrument that enables participants to review and examine the interpretations employees give to relationships with each other and with the organization as a whole. Specifically, the OVP looks at the perceived current and idealized perceptions of issues such as Corporate Effectiveness (toward mission/goals), Efficiency, Loyalty, Learning, and Values, as well as possible other areas as per the request of the individual client.

This tool can be used within a group or organization internally, or with two groups involved in an integration process, allowing the leaders and/or teams to address key identified tensions and prioritize distribution of time and resources.

Unlike other corporate culture diagnostic tools, the OVP goes beyond simple diagnosis and serves the basis for the reconciliation of the key tensions that owe their origin to mergers/acquisitions, strategic change, diversity, or globalization.

Purpose
- Maximizes participation of managers and leaders by connecting their viewpoints and problems to the wider organization
- Provides a rigorous assessment of key issues rather than assumed needs
- Offers a road map for future action
- Allows benchmarking against THT's cultural, industry, or sector databases
- Secures engagement with organization/conference/workshop participants, as they feel their key issues are being addressed

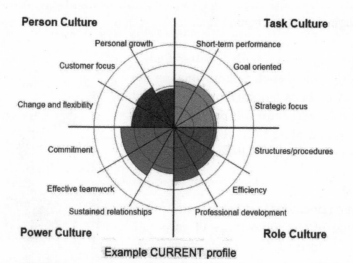

Example CURRENT profile

FIGURE A.8. Organization Values Profiler (OVP)

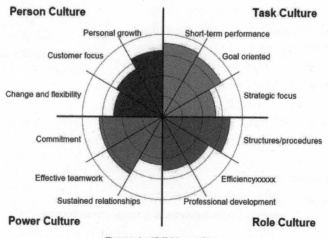

Example IDEAL profile

FIGURE A.9. Organization Values Profiler (OVP)

How to Download

Get more information and download here:

www.ridingthewavesofculture.com/ovp.

Managing Change App

App provides users with a better understanding of and detailed information on the
differences between current and desired
organizational cultures. It provides users a
new way of dealing with the tensions raised
by different corporate cultures.

Purpose

This app is intended to develop users' understanding of the importance of corporate
culture by providing example stereotypes
from different types of organization. In spite
of well-developed processes for due diligence, many mergers and acquisitions are
still failing to deliver the expected business
benefits due to clashes in corporate culture.

Use this app to explore our approach
based on extensive research and consulting
practice that integrates different cultures and
harnesses the best of both.

FIGURE A.10. Managing
Change App

This app enables you to quickly assess your organization's corporate culture and compare with your desired organizational culture.

How to Download

Get more information and download here:

www.ridingthewavesofculture.com/change.

Personal Values Profiler (PVP)

The PVP enables participants to review and examine their personal values
in the context of their professional work.

There are no right or wrong answers, and no orientation to any particular values is better or worse. People from different cultures or professions
will necessarily have different perspectives and will wish to pursue and
prioritize their interests that are not necessarily the same as others.

Exploring how you personally give priorities to different values and how these differ from other employees across an organization offers important insights into the relationships employees have with their organization.

This provides understanding of matters concerning resistance or support for change, the capacity for stability, sustainability, and innovation. These can exert a decisive influence on the overall ability of the organization to deal with the challenges and dilemmas it faces.

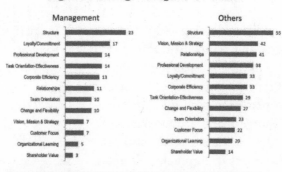

FIGURE A.11. Personal Values Profiler (PVP) App

Segment Ranking: Management v Others

Management		Others	
Structure	23	Structure	55
Loyalty/Commitment	17	Vision, Mission & Strategy	42
Professional Development	14	Relationships	41
Task Orientation-Effectiveness	14	Professional Development	38
Corporate Efficiency	13	Loyalty/Commitment	33
Relationships	11	Corporate Efficiency	33
Team Orientation	10	Task Orientation-Effectiveness	29
Change and Flexibility	10	Change and Flexibility	27
Vision, Mission & Strategy	7	Team Orientation	23
Customer Focus	7	Customer Focus	22
Organizational Learning	5	Organizational Learning	20
Shareholder Value	3	Shareholder Value	14

* Consistent pattern that Structure scores high for all groups, and with professional development and corporate efficiency whilst shareholder value lowest
* Remarkable differences are vision/mission and strategy

FIGURE A.12. Personal Values Profiler (PVP) App

Purpose

This PVP (Personal Values Profiler) is usually cross-linked to our OVP (Organization Values Profiler) to provide further important comparisons to corporate culture.

It has been developed by combining and extending our earlier frameworks based on our intellectual property. Each component has been subject to rigorous research and testing with extensive application in many client situations across the world and is also linked to our main corporate culture database of over 80,000 responses.

How to Download

Get more information and download here:

www.ridingthewavesofculture.com/pvp.

Mergers and Acquisitions

Dilemmas of Mergers and Acquisitions

This app provides users with a better understanding of and detailed information on the differences across organizational cultures. It provides users a new way of dealing with the tensions raised by different corporate cultures.

Purpose

This app is intended to develop users' understanding of the importance of corporate culture by providing example stereotypes from different types of organization. In spite of well-developed processes for due diligence, many mergers and acquisitions are still failing to deliver the expected business benefits due to clashes in corporate culture.

Use this app to explore our approach based on extensive research and consulting practice that integrates different cultures and harnesses the best of both.

FIGURE A.13. Dilemmas of Mergers and Acquisitions App

This app enables you to quickly assess your organization's corporate culture and compare with your new business partner organization.

How to Download

Get more information and download here:

www.ridingthewavesofculture.com/manda.

Sustainability

Ten Golden Dilemmas

We have identified "Ten Golden Dilemmas" that exist between five most important stakeholders. These dilemmas exist because *resources are scarce*. What is given to one segment of the cycle must be taken from another. Yet paradoxically, *values are abundant* or potentially so. The more innovative employees are and the faster they can learn, the better they will do on benchmarks. If these benchmarks are accurately aimed at what customers want, then customer satisfaction will rise, shortly after higher levels of quality are attained. The revenue generated by satisfied customers will increase shareholders' rewards, raising their readiness to invest. It all leads to sustainable results.

Purpose

The value conflicts between these segments, precipitated by scarcity at moments of time, have to be reconciled *over time*. It is difficult enough to resolve these dilemmas theoretically, but even this would not be enough to render the assessment methodology operationally. In order to do this, we need to demonstrate to assessors how the values we seek to reconcile should be measured.

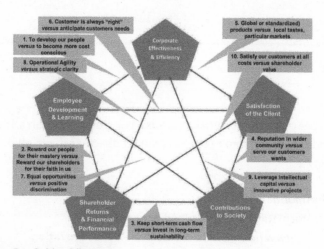

FIGURE A.14. Ten Golden Dilemmas

How to Download

Get more information and download here:

www.ridingthewavesofculture.com/sustainability.

Innovation

Dilemmas of Innovation

There are more aspects to innovation than simply assessment of creativity. Use this app to explore our integrated approach based on our extensive research and consulting practice. This quick assessment is based on only 12 questions collected from relevant employees.

The conceptual framework and methodology is based on the identification of key competing demands that will manifest as dilemmas and their measurements of current and ideal scenarios.

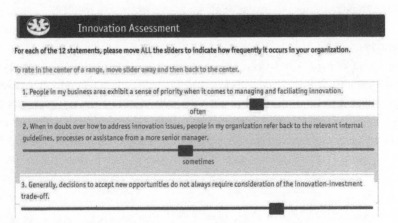

FIGURE A.15. Dilemmas of Innovation

Purpose

This app enables you to quickly assess your organization's Innovation Profile and gives you some personalized feedback and explanation of our methodology.

How to Download

Get more information and download here:

www.ridingthewavesofculture.com/innovation.

Individual Creativity App

This app measures your individual competence to innovate. It integrates the well-known Adaptor versus Innovator questionnaire of Kirton(KAI).

The model can also be used for measuring organizational fit, which is more important to adaptors than innovators. Adaptors are most likely to stay in organization where they fit and most likely to leave when they don't fit. Innovators are less strongly motivated by considerations of organizational fit to stay or leave since they are less likely to pay attention to whether or not they fit.

The main weakness of Kirton's assumptions perhaps lies in their succinctness and precision. Our interest is to see if we can extend Kirton's model so that it might be more appropriate when seeking to transfer these concepts to other cultures or multicultural situations.

Purpose

It was found that creative people move more effectively between intuition and thinking, that innovators extrovertly publish their introverted calculation and constantly learn by oscillating between judging and perceiving, and finally check their feelings through thinking. An additional finding is that culture often determines the side that respondents start from. So we are not saying that one culture is more creative than another—only that their starting point for looking at a problem is different.

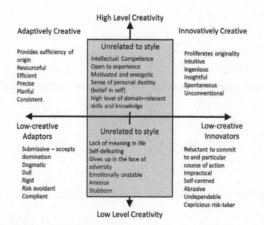

FIGURE A.16. Individual Creativity App

How to Download

Get more information here:

www.ridingthewavesofculture.com/kirton.

Creating a Culture of Innovation App

There are more aspects to innovation than simply assessment of creativity. Use this app to explore our integrated approach based on our extensive research and consulting practice.

Purpose

This app enables you to quickly assess your organization's Innovation Profile and gives you some personalized feedback and explanation of our methodology.

This quick assessment based on only 12 questions is obviously limited in terms of reliability, and we would normally recommend our comprehensive OIP (Organization Innovation Profiler) web tool based on some 46 diagnostics and responses collected from relevant employees.

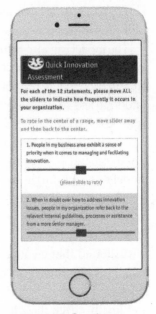

FIGURE A.17. Creating a Culture of Innovation App

The conceptual framework and methodology is the same—namely the identification of key competing demands that will manifest as dilemmas and their measurements of current and ideal scenarios.

How to Download

Get more information and download here:

www.ridingthewavesofculture.com/innovation/.

Diversity and Inclusion

Gender and Generational Diversity App

There are many differences between men and women and between generations. When we understand these differences, the way to reconciliation is much easier. The Gender and Generational Diversity App is an extension of our Culture for Business App.

The app can be used to provide a better understanding of gender differences, the reasons for those differences, and most important to increase users' cross-gender management skills, communication, and motivation capabilities.

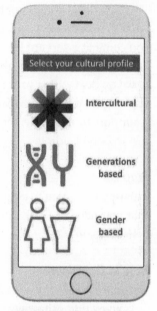

FIGURE A.18. Gender and Generational Diversity App

Purpose
- The app gives a variety of tips in dealing with different genders and generations in a variety of areas like motivation, career planning, rewarding, managing, and being managed.
- Tips are dependent on the delta between score individual/generation and gender of choice.

How to Download
Apps in the Google and Apple app stores: Culture for Business and web-based. Get more information and download here:

www.ridingthewavesofculture.com/cfb.

Leadership Dilemmas

Servant Leadership App

This app helps you to get better insights into what type of leader you are and how close you come to a servant leader: that leader that enables others to perform better. It looks at how you deal with a variety of dilemmas that you might face and how you react to them as a support to reconcile the meta dilemma of serving and leading.

Purpose

This app helps you to diagnose the dilemmas that you need to work on and is available in a 360 version.

How to Download

Get more information and download here:
www.ridingthewavesofculture.com /servantleader.

FIGURE A.19. Servant Leadership App

WebCue

The WebCue tool is an online interview questionnaire, which is used to draw out some of the basic issues or dilemmas that exist within an organization, before a particular event or in the context of a consulting intervention.

Through the WebCue, we anonymously collect and analyze the information from a specific group of respondents to uncover common thoughts, perceptions, or concerns. This information allows the user to better tailor interventions to the specific needs and circumstances of an organization and, thereby, to engage respondents more quickly into meaningful discussions. This could be in presentations, workshops, or consulting type projects. In addition, the WebCue may be used to validate findings from interviews, group sessions, or other organizational processes.

Purpose
- Information collected anonymously
- Highlights commonly shared dilemmas of the whole group rather than simple observations
- Questions tailored to clients' needs
- Customized client page introducing the tool
- Can incorporate additional client (survey) questions
- Asks respondents to think about relevant themes and issues before attending an event

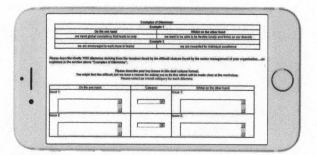

FIGURE A.20. WebCue

How to Download
Get more information here:

www.ridingthewavesofculture.com/webcue.

Intercultural Team App

The tool serves as an input to increase the awareness of the team's cultural orientation differences. In aggregate, it informs the position of groups and teams in comparison with other groups. Understanding one's own cultural profile is the first key step in enhancing job performance and bottom-line business results when working with other diverse cultures in your team.

Purpose

To provide a better understanding of cultural differences in a team, the reasons for cultural differences, and most important to increase the team leader's cross-cultural management and integration capabilities.

How to Download

Get more information and download here:
www.ridingthewavesofculture.com/itp.

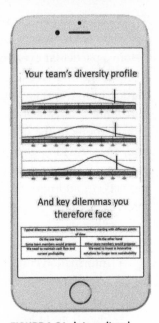

FIGURE A.21. Intercultural Team App

Financial Performance

Risk App

There are more aspects to risk than simply assessment of compliance. Use this app to explore our integrated approach based on our extensive research and consulting practice. This quick assessment based on only 12 questions is obviously limited in terms of reliability and we would normally recommend our comprehensive OIP (Organization Innovation Profiler) web tool based on some 46 diagnostics and responses collected from relevant employees.

The conceptual framework and methodology is the same—namely the identification of key competing demands that will manifest as dilemmas and their measurements of current and ideal scenarios.

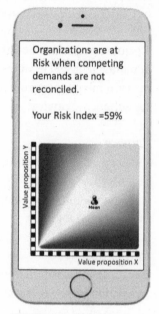

FIGURE A.22. Risk App

Purpose

This app enables you to quickly assess your organization's Risk Profile and gives you some personalized feedback and explanation of our methodology.

How to Download

Get more information and download here:

www.ridingthewavesofculture.com/risk.

Quality App

There are more aspects to quality than simply assessment of compliance. Use this app to explore our integrated approach based on our extensive research and consulting practice. This quick assessment based on only 12 questions identifies the key competing demands that will manifest as dilemmas and measurements of current and ideal scenarios for enhancing quality.

Purpose
This app enables you to quickly assess your organization's Quality Profile and gives you some personalized feedback and explanation of our methodology.

How to Download
Get more information and download here: **www.ridingthewavesofculture.com/quality.**

FIGURE A.23. Quality App

Supplier App

This app enables you to quickly assess your organization's corporate culture and compare with your new business partner or supplier organization. It provides users with a better understanding of and detailed information on the differences across organizational cultures. It provides users a new way of dealing with the tensions raised by different corporate cultures of buyer and supplier.

Purpose

This app is intended to develop users' understanding of the importance of corporate culture by providing example stereotypes from different types of organization. In spite of well-developed processes for selection, many procurement processes are still failing to deliver the expected business benefits due to clashes in corporate culture.

FIGURE A.24. Supplier App

How to Download

Get more information and download here: **www.ridingthewavesofculture.com/supplier.**

APPENDIX B

Technical Aspects of the Trompenaars' Databases

Peter Woolliams

THIS APPENDIX summarizes aspects of the development and analysis of the research database assembled by Trompenaars that underpins the main text. It is based on responses to various cross-cultural questionnaire instruments. The principal interest here is to review the data from the perspective of the level of national cultures, although extensive analysis of individual variations or variations through management function, industry sector, religion, and gender are also available. For a comprehensive review and detailed data and statistical analysis, research monographs are available.

We also mention the development of our additional complementary databases that support our more recent work, including the reconciliation database and text and keyword analysis.

The primary purpose of the Trompenaars database is to help managers structure their cross-cultural experiences in order to develop their competence for doing business and managing across cultures. In seeking to enhance the estimates of the average characteristics of managers in a given national culture, considerable efforts have been made to extend the size of the samples, reduce measurement errors, and maintain homogeneity. Issues our research team had identified in earlier and smaller versions of the database[1] were given priority.

The raw data set comprises some 155,000 cases from over 125 countries. This represents a sample size of nearly three times that of the original reviews. Analysis of the variety reveals functionally equivalent sets, since nearly all the selected managers were pursuing similar ends. However, it should be noted that the whole approach was not to seek an orthogonal dataset typified by classical market research. In the latter, a sample is targeted with the minimum number of cases to cover each attribute (country, gender, age, etc.). But this presumes we know what attributes to measure in advance and also has practical difficulties, for example, where does one find a young female Arab senior manager working in a Gulf country? Trompenaars therefore adopted the approach of collecting a larger dataset with extensive internal variety that enables a deductive analysis to be performed through data mining.

Work was also undertaken on improving the language of the questionnaire to make it more transparent across cultures and more acceptable where value systems and integrity are challenged. Cluster analysis was used to examine whether highly correlated items do in fact cluster around the concepts being tested. Validating interviews and cognitive mapping were also applied. Exhaustive quantitative analysis was applied to assess the validity of alternate questions and combinations of questions at both the "world level" and ecological (country) level.

Each of Trompenaars' dimensions is a scale based on a combination of finite alternatives to each of a series of finite alternatives, which therefore generates a combinatorial (binomial) rather than normal distribution. However, the central limit theorem suggests parametric methods may be applied to this nonparametric data in view of the large sample sizes. While this was accepted for convenience, analysis was also performed on a strict exact tests basis as a precaution. In fact, the latter shows the distributions to be leptokurtic (even more closely clustered than for a normal distribution).

Some authors have misinterpreted the origin of Trompenaars' rationale for these scales and derived incorrect conclusions therein. Thus in an early comment by Hofstede,[2] he had only used a subset of the data from individual questions or averages rather than the weighted combination of these questions that provide scale values for each of Trompenaars' dimensions. Saying that 65 percent of US managers chose the universalistic option when answering a question is not what Trompenaars means when he asserts that the typical US managers can be placed 65 percent along the universalistic–particularistic scale. Trompenaars combines responses from different questions to give a scale along each dimension, not a polarized bimodal measure at each end. These combinations are chosen and have constantly been redefined so as to maximize the discrimination between countries along each scale. The individual questions show not only high validity but also high reliability. Responses to component questions are by design not perfectly correlated within the scales. If they were, only one question would be required for each dimension! And as explained later, such results are validated by both earlier and more recent additional triangulation studies.

Cronbach's alpha test of reliability was applied to questions and combinations of questions. In some cases, and especially for corporate culture, questions were successively modified or removed where such change produced an increase in alpha. For each scale alpha was maximized, and the final design has the performance shown in Table B.1.

The scale for the time dimension, which is based on the circles test, required different treatment. With the wide diversity of diagrams, the aim was to identify common factors or underlying themes or cultural concepts that the respondents were trying to express. Thus the search was to find an algorithmic relationship with the coordinate system of their drawing and quantitative scales that could serve as the basis of cross-cultural discrimination.

TABLE B.1. Scale Variety Alpha

Universalism–particularism	0.71
Individualism–communitarianism	0.73
Specific–diffuse	0.63
Neutral–affective	0.75
Achievement–ascription	0.64
Internal–external	0.71
Time	0.74

As a result of extensive trials, it was concluded that three factors could be discerned that originated in the degree to which the circles overlapped, touched, or were separate and to the relative sizes of the circles. Earlier hand drawings were assessed visually. But since 2001 where the circles are drawn by the respondent directly on a computer screen, the scales were derived directly from the coordinates by integrating the area subtended at the base and the relative position of the center of gravity. Thus a scale from 100 (maximum overlap = synchronic culture) through to 0 (no overlap = sequential culture) was derived. A second scale assessed the relative component of past, present, and future orientation. A third scale could also be derived that measures a "time horizon" (short-term thinking and planning versus longer-term thinking and planning). In many ways, these scales suffered fewer problems than the other dimensions based on forced text questions.

The scales for corporate culture were examined, reviewed, and treated to the same degree of rigor to derive components with the reliabilities shown in Table B.2.

TABLE B.2. Cronbach's Alpha

Role culture	0.79
Task culture	0.75
Person culture	0.63
Power culture	0.74

In some situations, the set of scores on each dimension scales were subjected to a parabolic transform function to account for skew and kurtosis. This has the effect of maintaining the sequence and relationships between country scores, but makes the distribution more symmetrical for the purposes of presentation.

In addition to applying statistical tests of validity and reliability and reporting orientations along each cultural dimension, other types of analysis were performed to support the postulates and frameworks on which this book is based.

In particular, nonparametric data mining was used to investigate the variety within the data as well as investigating dimension reduction with factor analysis. This sought to ask two key questions:

1. What is the relative importance of each attribute (age, gender, religion, country, job function)?
2. How many dimensions of culture are required to explain the variety in the data?

Relative Importance of Attributes

For this discussion, the model can be considered in the following form (for each dimension):

$$\text{dimension score} =$$
$$c_1 \times \text{country} + c_2 \times \text{age} + c_3 \times \text{religion} + c_4 \times \text{gender} + c_5 \ldots \text{etc.}$$

It is tempting to "throw" established statistical techniques at the data to identify possible coefficients (c_1, c_2, c_3, etc.) using correlation and partial-correlation analysis or factor analysis. Some other authors have often done just that with their own more limited data sets or incomplete or extracted sets of the earlier data that have previously been published. This has been especially true of researchers with primarily a statistical mindset rather than open-minded inquirers or students with a genuine interest in trying to contribute to the debate and frameworks of cross-cultural analysis.

On examination of the data, it should be noted that these parametric methods are not strictly appropriate. Many of the data items are simply categories (nominal data) such as gender, religion, or management function. Classical statistical nonparametric methods are not readily available for this particular problem, and certainly none is included in industry standard statistical software. While analysis of variance and (categories) conjoint analysis can help with questionnaire design and testing, it cannot produce the analysis required here.

In order to explore the data set it is therefore appropriate to apply a different body of mathematics that is appropriate for this cause. Recent developments in relational database technology, database mining methods, and knowledge elicitation (expert systems) come to the rescue.

The basic principle is to find the relative importance of the various attributes in determining the goal attribute. The first step is to normalize (arrange) the data to the so-called third normal form in separate tables (as would be required for representation in a relational database).

For the full database, the amount of entropy for each attribute can be computed. This gives a measure of the uncertainty of classification of the goal by each attribute. As the entropy increases, the amount of uncertainty gained by adding each attribute increases. However, the quest is to find how much information there is when the value(s) of any particular attribute is (are) given. This can be found simply by weighting occurrences.

To explain the total variety, it would be necessary to use the same variety as there are cases. This is the same as saying that 30,000 respondents are all individuals and 30,000 attributes are required to describe them. Alternatively, one could use one attribute with 30,000 values (such as name!) to identify them uniquely. In the above parlance, "name" has the highest information content and lowest entropy. However, this is not the aim. Recall that Trompenaars is seeking to develop a model based on a number of dimensions (attributes) that help structure managers' experiences. The analysis attempted here is intended to support this aim by exploring the relative importance of different attributes rather than containing the total variety within the data set as an ideological statistician may prefer.

"Country" is confirmed to have the lowest entropy of classification and thus this corresponds to the least uncertainty. In other words, "country" has the highest information content and thus "country" is the major contributor in explaining the cultural orientation on the dimensions. Manager function, for example, has a smaller contribution. These computations support and justify the emphasis throughout this book on analysis at the ecological (country) level rather than that of individual respondent.

How Many Dimensions?

This is more difficult to answer because it partly depends on why the question is being posed.

A fundamental issue to consider is whether all the seven dimensions of the model are required and whether each is measuring a different aspect of culture. Culture is a construct that is derived from these individual dimensions, but are these dimensions themselves (orthogonal) individual? Perhaps there are alternative and simpler models of culture, such as

culture = c1 × (inherited characteristics)
  + c2 × (acquired characteristics)   (Equation i); or

culture = c1 × (relationships between people)
  + c2 × (relationship with nature)
  + c3 × (relationship or orientation to time)   (Equation ii)

In the former case one would only need two dimensions (and to determine the coefficients c1, c2), or three dimensions for the latter model. Thus possible interrelationships between the dimensions need to be explored.

Table B.3 shows the correlation between the dimensions. One can start the analysis with the use of parametric models by invoking the central limit theorem. If the correlations between the dimensions are zero, then they are individually and uniquely measuring a different aspect of culture. Using the average country scores from the database shows values that are not zero but are all less than .5. Bartlett's sphericity test can be used to consider the hypothesis that the correlation matrix is an identity matrix (i.e., the diagonals are 1 and the off-diagonal elements are 0). Thus the chi-square of the transformation of the determinant of the correlation matrix is computed.

This value is not low, and therefore the hypothesis that the correlation matrix is an identity matrix should not be rejected.

TABLE B.3. Correlations Between Dimensions

	UNPA	INDCOM	SPDI	NEAF	ACHASC	INTEXT
UNPA	1.0000	.1269	.4669	.1209	.4223	.4013
INDCOM	.1269	1.0000	.4236	.0697	.4397	.2753
SPDI	.4669	.4236	1.0000	−.0239	.4006	.4678
NEAF	.1209	.0697	−.0239	1.0000	.2177	−.0444
ACHASC	.4223	.4397	.4006	.2177	1.0000	.4976
INTEXT	.4013	.2753	.4678	−.0444	.4976	1.0000

Thus further probing is required to investigate whether there is any significance in the small off-diagonal correlation coefficients. However, Bartlett's test is strictly only valid for ratio data from a multivariate normal population, and the Trompenaars data is only intended to indicate ordinal/ranked measurements of cultural components, and country averages are being discussed, not individual responses. If individual cases are taken, much lower cross-correlations are found. This in itself may be sufficient to explain the small off-diagonal correlations here.

The partial correlation coefficients are a further indicator. If the dimensions share common factors, then again the off-diagonal correlation coefficients should be small when the linear effects of the other dimensions are controlled. Table B.4 shows that the off-diagonal partial correlation coefficients are again small, but not zero.

TABLE B.4. Partial Correlations

	UNPA	INDCOM	SPDI	NEAF	ACHASC	INTEXT
UNPA	−1.00000	−.33034	.28868	.04792	.45555	.05059
INDCOM	−0.33034	−1.00000	.55267	.08339	.22835	−.03604
SPDI	.28868	.55267	−1.00000	−.18283	.18540	.15654
NEAF	.04792	.08339	−.18283	−1.00000	.26277	−.16338
ACHASC	.45555	.22835	.18540	.26277	−1.00000	.34040
INTEXT	.05059	−.03604	.15654	−.16338	.34040	−1.00000

A better insight into the source of these small effects can be gained from computing the Kaiser–Meyer–Olkin (KMO) index.[3] This statistic compares the observed correlation coefficients to the partial correlation coefficients. If the sum of the squares of the partial coefficients between all dimensions is small compared to the sum of the squared total correlations, then the KMO will be close to 1. The small value of KMO indicates that correlation between the dimensions cannot be explained by the other variables. This is further evidence to support the need for all of the cultural dimensions.

The above statistics can be regenerated from the core of the original database. However slightly different correlations can be produced by taking different "cuts" of the data. As explained in the body of the book, there are changes over time that are easily subject to misinterpretation. If different datasets are "thrown" at a correlation matrix, then the inter-item correlations can vary considerably. By these changes are reduced if the data analysis is controlled for age, years worked abroad, etc., and thus basic reliability of the conceptual model is restored.

Using different cuts, we can demonstrate that the new generation of middle and senior managers who are well traveled and have more experience of working abroad tend to retain their ideographic country profile but show convergence to regional or global norms in terms of their nomothetic orientation for their industry or corporate sector. Far from diluting the reliability of the database, these smaller effects, which are now only discernable with our much longer and longitudinal datasets, simply mean that multivariate analysis is required to explain variety. This would also suggest that other research seeking single and simple score linear measures to provide a complete picture for country culture is insufficient.

The Score Values Shown Throughout This Book

Note that throughout this book, and where we have shown rank-order answers to our typical diagnostic questions (such as the Car Accident question 4.1 and similar bar charts), then these are based on cases with minimal experience of working abroad, and working for indigenous local employers. Thus a younger Italian who has limited overseas experience, working for an Italian local bank, in Italy, we have chosen to be more representative of more fundamental Italian culture than a well-traveled senior manager who has lived in New York for 10 years working for Goldman Sachs but who still likes to describe himself as Italian. And as discussed in the body of the book, their scores at the ideographic level tend to remain similar.

One can also use factor analysis to seek a smaller number of factors that can be used to represent the relationship between the dimensions of culture. The goal is to represent culture parsimoniously—that is, a desire to express culture with as few indicators (factors) as possible. If one can reduce the number, then not only is simplification achieved but new insights may arise. Ideally, the new factors should be interpretable because it would then be possible to derive the model of interest based on the constructs sought, rather than simply those that can be measured (the raw dimensions). Thus:

1. Can the not so directly measurable aspects of culture be extracted from the observable dimensions?
2. Can original data be explained by a model similar to Equation i or Equation ii above?
3. Are the observed correlations due to the sharing of common factors?

The KMO index above indicates that factor analysis is likely to be unsuccessful. Further, factor analysis is not simply multiple regression. The aim is not to try to express culture as a combination of dimensions but to combine dimensions into higher order factors that are not known in advance. However, the objective of factor analysis is to reduce the number of dimensions required to explain the data. Obtaining fewer factors by factor analysis does not mean that the seven-dimensional culture model is invalid or that the number of dimensions should be reduced. If the correlation coefficients had been higher, one might have expected to be able to extract valid factors because the interrelationships between the dimensions would have been due to the presence of these factors.

For the sake of completeness, principal components analysis can also be considered. Linear combinations of the observed dimensions are taken to estimate possible factors. The first component is the combination that accounts for the largest amount of the variance in the database. Successive components explain progressively smaller portions.

Table B.5 shows the eigenvalues for each factor. Having attempted to represent culture with two factors (similar to Equation i), this only explains some 50 percent of the variance and either seven replacement factors or all the original dimensions are required to account for the variance (cultural diversity). A scree plot of the data also reveals this. This result is not surprising, since both Bartlett's test[4] and the KMO index both indicated that there were unlikely to be underlying simpler factors.

TABLE A.5. Eigen Values

achasc	41.3% (cumulative)
indcom	52.5%
intext	76.6
time	85.7
neaf	92.7
spdi	97.3
unpa	100.0

Factor Matrix and Rotations

Again, little or no benefit is revealed, nor is any underlying model that justifies using these new factors rather than the original dimensions. If the rotation had achieved a simple structure, clusters of the dimensions would occur either near the ends of each axis or at their intersection. As expected, it is found that the original dimensions are widely scattered in the factor space.

Thus it cannot be concluded from the above discussion that fewer cultural dimensions can usefully explain the variance in the data. This could have been expected simply on the basis of the low correlations given above. However, further probing was undertaken with an open mind and to contribute to the debate. In addition, the question set is not ipsative (independent) because some questions are used for more than one scale and factor analysis does not correct for this in-built correlation.

One might also wish to reject the above discussion on the basis that the data collected is not genuine multivariate (ratio) normal data. If the data is ordinal or nonparametric, then one should really use nonmetric (MDS) multidimensional scaling rather than factor analysis to probe variety reduction. Here the original data has to be transformed into a matrix of cultural differences. Thus it is necessary to compute (for each country, for each dimension) the *difference* between each case and all other cases. Normally this is obtained by computing the Euclidean distance (square of the differences) to obtain a measure dissimilarity. In the MDS model, each country is represented in multidimensional space and arranged so that the distances between all pairs of cases (countries) is based on these differences—countries that score similarly on universalism–particularism will be closer together, etc. As with factor analysis, if the aim is to seek to reduce the number of dimensions, it may be possible to take combinations of cultural dimensions that cluster together, i.e., are measuring the same thing. It is necessary to assume that the data is always symmetric (the difference between the USA and Japan is the same as the cultural difference between Japan and the USA), and the analysis must be repeated for each dimension. Thus full (RMDS) replicated nonmetric multidimensional scaling algorithm (after McGee[5]) is required that applies the analysis of dissimilarity to each (cultural) dimension simultaneously. The plot of the RDMS stimulus coordinates produces a scatterplot with the dimensions spread between the axes. If the cultural dimensions were components of common factors, then the RDMS plots would show the dimensions more significantly clustered. Thus the same conclusion is reached by applying this nonparametric assessment, namely that the model of culture cannot simply be reduced to one or two new dimensions.

Finally, agglomerative hierarchical clustering should also be reviewed. Here the aim would be to try to form groups of countries with similar cultural orientations. However, it should be remembered that cluster analysis is a subjective rather than analytical technique. When group (cluster) membership is known, discriminant analysis can be applied. Here group (cluster) membership is not known, so again Euclidean distance is resorted to. Classically, the countries that are most similar would be clustered, then the next and so on. By transposition, attempts are made to cluster the cultural.

Only very weak clustering can be found. Again, this derives from the very weak correlation coefficients discussed above. The *sequence* of clustering shows a possible and interesting aspect, namely that there is more variety in ACHASC than the other dimensions. This has some face validity too. When two people first meet, the initial first greeting is either "Hi! I'm Mr. US, and I'm a lawyer," or "I'm Sheik Haasam, and I'm the brother of El Refaie." Does this confirm that on meeting someone we run our built-in survival program (shall we flee or fight?), and that who we are or what we do is the first thing we need to know about our assailant? As discussed elsewhere, in business applications other dimensions may have a higher priority in establishing the first point of cross-cultural communication.

In commenting on Trompenaars' earlier work, Hofstede's[6] exclusive use of parametric analysis is surprising. He should have used nonparametric methods such as correspondence analysis or homogeneity analysis for performing optimal scaling. However, all of these procedures are designed to set out to achieve dimension reduction rather than to identify the number of dimensions required to explain the variety in the original data. Saying that the data can be summarized as two or three statistical derived factors is not the same as claiming that Trompenaars' seven-dimensional model is not supported by his data or that fewer than seven dimensions are required. In particular there is the case of "outliers." Although, as Hofstede claims, responses to some of Trompenaars' questions may correlate for many countries, and therefore these dimensions might be combined, the separate dimensions are required for many specific cases (such as the Gulf countries, ignored by Hofstede) because for these countries they do not correlate. Thus for G7 countries compared to GCC (Gulf countries), different dimensions are required to explain these intercountry differences compared to the intra-G7 country differences.

Thus we may conclude in answer to the rhetorical question that, although fewer dimensions may be used to explain some of the data, in practice they are all required to explain the full diversity across the globe. In different practical situations (e.g., making comparisons between any two particular cultures), we can select those dimensions that best discriminate the two cultures. And let's remember that in the same way that gender correlates with height, just because two dimensions correlate is not the same as saying that they are measuring the same construct.

External Validation Studies

We have sought to triangulate our central database with other data sources as a means to strengthen our claims of reliability and validity.

For example, Fons often suggests in his conference presentations that universalistic cultures like the USA tend to have more lawyers to codify and/or to expose different interpretations of written laws. Thus we tried to correlate the number of lawyers per capita in a number of countries based on the number of practicing lawyers against our own scale of universalism. Such ideas are subject to all sorts of practical difficulties—notwithstanding the problem of accessing the external data. And what is the definition of a lawyer to include in the sample when in other countries we have a multiplicity of solicitors, procurators, notaries? In fact only in universalistic cultures might we have more precise (universal!) definitions of what a lawyer is in the first place!

We also started from the opposite perspective, namely what data did exist that we could access, and sought connections between such statistics and our own measures. Thus the CIA database has extensive data on the dwelling unit—that is, the number of people living together in a household unit. Do people live only in their nuclear family, or do they live with their grandparents and other elders? We did find that this parameter correlated highly with our individualism–communitarianism dimension for example, at least for major developed countries where other effects such as GDP might interfere with this measure. But generally, apart from face validity of such comparisons, there was insufficient to justify the supportive correlations we obtained.

But more successful was to take other surveys published by other but reliable sources where there were isolated areas of direct comparability—but most of these are surveys carried out at a particular time, so we compared their results with ours from the same period.

In the "Going Global Survey" for *TIME* by the market research company MORI, results were based on 1,225 face-to-face interviews conducted during February and March 2001. They surveyed 21- to 35-year-olds in Britain, France, Germany, and Italy about their hopes, habits, and hang-ups. The results depict a generation in transition, propelled by globalization into ever closer political and economic union but still firmly rooted in national and local identities. Though young Europeans share some of the same worries about biotechnology and the environment, what really binds them together is an avid embrace of change. Most young Europeans consider themselves to be primarily British, French, German, or Italian rather than European. Yet almost one-third now regard themselves more as Europeans than as nationals of their home country. The Italians see themselves as more European than the other nationalities surveyed, with two in five regarding themselves as more European than Italian. The Italians also have the greatest enthusiasm for integration.

The results of this survey correlate highly with our own idiographic-nomothetic analysis and support this divergence.

Around the same period, the *Wall Street Journal* published comparisons on issues faced by women compared to men in the workplace in the USA and five European countries. Their data correlates highly tensions deriving from our achievement–ascription dimension in our reconciliation database.

The Global Surveys (especially the Millennium survey) published by the well-respected and well-known Gallup polling organization shows similar high cross-validation in many areas.

Finally, the large socioeconomic database of the ongoing World Values Survey also included a number of key questions with very close working to our original cross-cultural questionnaire. Thus, question V46 in their survey shown below is very similar to our internal–external dimension question.

V46.   Some people feel they have completely free choice and control over their lives, while other people feel that what they do has no real effect on what happens to them. Please use this scale where 1 means "no choice at all" and 10 means " a great deal of choice" to indicate how much freedom of choice and control you feel you have over the way your life turns out (*code one number*):

NO CHOICE AT ALL   **A GREAT DEAL OF CHOICE**

1   2   3   4   5   6   7   8   9   10

And from our questionnaire:

Q. Of the following two statements, which do you believe to be more in line with your reality?	Your answer
When I make plans, I am almost certain that I can make them work.	
It is not always wise to plan too far ahead because many things turn out to be a matter of good or bad fortune anyhow.	

By taking comparable samples, again high degrees of correlation are found. The World Surveys Group do not derive inferences from their findings or offer comments, but seek to collect reliable data for other researchers to explore.

Dilemma Database

As discussed in the body of the book, we have collected some 12,000 of such dilemmas from our research and consulting, which includes around 1,000 related to mergers and acquisitions. We observe that these dilemmas can be categorized and clustered as ten frequently recurring dilemmas in the minds of leaders and senior managers. We describe these as the Ten

Golden Dilemmas. Every partner organization seems to have different priorities when focusing on these golden dilemmas that need to be reconciled in order to achieve future success and sustainability for the organization.

We have sought to categorize and then correlate these dilemmas against corporate and national culture characteristics. We have used KWIC analysis (keyword in context) and linguistic methods to semi-automate this mining. We have constructed "dictionaries" of frequently recurring keywords that correlate highly with the corresponding corporate culture stereotypes. Such analysis is indicative of the Sapir[en dash]Whorf hypothesis in that the semantic structure of a language shapes or limits the ways in which a speaker forms conceptions of the world, although we might argue the reverse is also true.

The principal finding is again to confirm that there are frequently recurring dilemmas faced by all cultures, but it is how these are interpreted and how these are approached that is culturally determined.

Further Research

The suite of Trompenaars' cross-cultural databases is one of the largest and richest sources of social constructs. Research is continuing to refine the instruments (particularly to avoid polarized dilemma options), to extend the number and variety of subcases, and to apply further methods of analysis such as neural networks. Access to the data is offered to bona fide researchers and to client companies with particular interests or needs. Again, the reader is referred to the research monographs for comprehensive treatment of the summary presented here.

The research team has recently applied AI methods to explore the databases, including both supervised and unsupervised learning, CHAID, and neural networks. These give further support and extend the findings from the advanced statistics as described in this appendix and will appear in the formal academic press in due course.

Notes

CHAPTER 1

1. Schein, E., *Organizational Culture and Leadership*, Jossey-Bass, San Francisco, 1985.
2. Collingwood, R. G., *Essay on Metaphysics*, Gateway, Chicago, 1974.
3. See for example: http://www.cerium.ca/L-Europe-et-la-culture?lang=fr.
4. Parsons, T., *The Social System*, Free Press, New York, 1951.

CHAPTER 2

1. Hofstede, G., *Culture's Consequences*, Sage, London, 1980.
2. Crozier, M., *The Bureaucratic Phenomenon*, University of Chicago Press, 1964.
3. Parsons, T., *The Social System*, Free Press, New York, 1951.
4. Schutz, A., *On Phenomenology and Social Relations*, University of Chicago Press, 1970.

CHAPTER 3

1. Geertz, C., *The Interpretation of Cultures*, Basic Books, New York, 1973.
2. Kluckhohn, F., and Strodtbeck, F. L., *Variations in Value Orientations*, Greenwood Press, Westport, CT, 1961.

CHAPTER 4

1. Stouffer, S.A., and Toby, J., "Role Conflict and Personality," *American Journal of Sociology*, LUI-5, 1951, pages 395–406.
2. Zurcher, L. A., Meadows, A., and Zurcher, S. L., "Value Orientations, Role Conflict and Alienation from Work: A Cross-Cultural Study," *American Sociological Review*, no. 30, 1965, pages 539–48.

CHAPTER 5

1. Parsons, T., and Shils, E. A., *Towards a General Theory of Action*, Harvard University Press, Cambridge, MA, 1951.
2. Hofstede, G., *Culture's Consequences*, Sage, London, 1980.
3. Tönnies, F., *Community and Society* (trans. C. P. Loomis), Harper & Row, New York, 1957.
4. Smith, A., *The Wealth of Nations*.

5. Weber, M., *The Theory of Social and Economic Organization*, Free Press, New York, 1947.
6. Simmel, G., *The Sociology of Simmel* (trans. K. H. Wolff), Glencoe, IL, 1950.
7. Bell, D., *The Cultural Contradictions of Capitalism*, Basic Books, 1976.
8. Bell, D., and Nelson, B., *The Idea of Usury*, Chicago University Press, 1969.
9. Lawrence, P. R., and Lorsch, J. W., *Organization and Environment: Managing Differentiation and Integration*, Irwin, Homewood, IL, 1967.
10. Hampden-Turner, C., *Charting the Corporate Mind*, Basil Blackwell, Oxford, 1991.

CHAPTER 7

1. Lewin, K., "Some Social-Psychological Differences Between the US and Germany," in Lewin, K., ed., *Principles of Topological Psychology*, 1936.
2. Feiffer, J., *Hold Me*, Knopf, New York, 1968.
3. Parsons, T., and Shils, E. A., *Towards a General Theory of Action*, Harvard University Press, Cambridge, MA, 1951, pages 128–33.
4. Dean, L. R., "The Pattern Variables: Some Empirical Operations," *American Sociological Review*, no. 26, 1961, pages 80–90.

CHAPTER 8

1. McClelland, D., *The Achieving Society*, Van Nostrand, New York, 1961.
2. Inzerilli, G., and Laurent, A., *The Concept of Organizational Structure*, Working Paper, University of Pennsylvania and INSEAD, 1979; "Managerial Views of Organizational Structure in France and the USA," *International Studies of Management and Organizations*, XIII, 1–2, 1983, pages 97–138.
3. Fons Trompenaars and Ed Voerman, *Servant Leadership Across Cultures*, McGraw-Hill, 2009.

CHAPTER 9

1. Kluckhohn, F., and Strodtbeck, F. L., *Variations in Value Orientations*, Greenwood Press, Westport, CT, 1960.
2. Durkheim, E., *De la division du travail social*, 7th ed., 1960.
3. Hall, E. T., *The Silent Language*, Anchor Press, Doubleday, NY, 1959.
4. Carroll, R., *Cultural Misunderstandings: the French-American Experience*, University of Chicago Press, 1987.

5. Cottle, T., "The Circles Test: An Investigation of Perception of Temporal Relatedness and Dominance," *Journal of Projective Technique and Personality Assessments*, no. 31, 1967, pages 58–71.
6. Cottle, T. J., and Howard, P., "Time Perception by Indian Adolescents," *Perceptual and Motor Skills*, no. 28, 1969, pages 599–612.
7. Buber, M. (Kauffman, W., ed.), *I and Thou*, Scribners' Books, New York, 1970.
8. Shell International, Group Planning Department, London (personal communication).

CHAPTER 10

1. Rotter, J. B., *Generalized Expectations for Internal Versus External Control of Reinforcement*, Psychological Monograph 609, 1966, pages 1–28. (Some items have been designed by CIBS.)
2. Trompenaars and Woolliams, *Marketing Across Cultures*, Capstone, 2004.
3. Ellul, J., *The Technological Society*, Vintage, New York, 1964.
4. Moscovici, S., *Essai sur l'histoire humaine de la nature*, Flammarion, Paris, 1977.
5. Mintzberg, H., *The Structure of Organizations*, Prentice-Hall, Englewood Cliffs, NJ, 1979.
6. Argyris, C., *Strategy Change and Defensive Routines*, Pitman, London, 1985.
7. Eric Ries, *The Lean Startup*, Random House, 2011.

CHAPTER 11

1. Connerley, M. L., and Pedersen, P. B., *Leadership in a Diverse and Multicultural Environment: Developing Awareness, Knowledge, and Skills*, 2005.
2. Iles, P. A., "Achieving Strategic Coherence in HRD Through Competence-Based Management and Organization Development," *Personnel Review*, 1993, emeraldinsight.com.
3. Boyatzis, R. E., *The Competent Manager: A Model for Effective Performance*, New York: John Wiley, 1982.
4. Boyatzis, R. E. Ibid.
5. Woodruffe, C., *Assessment Centres: Identifying and Developing Competence* (2nd ed.), London: Institute of Personnel and Development, 1993.
6. Woodruffe, C. Ibid.
7. Lawler, E. E., III, "From Job-Based to Competency-Based Organizations," *Journal of Organizational Behavior*, IS, 1994, 3–15.

8. Rhinesmith, Stephen H. "Global Mindsets for Global Managers," *Training & Development*, vol. 46, no. 10, Oct. 1992, p. 63+

9. Sheridan, E., *InterCultural Leadership Competencies for U.S. Business Leaders in the New Millennium*, 2005. Unpublished doctoral dissertation, University of Phoenix.

10. Hanvey, R. G., *An Attainable Global Perspective*, New York: The American Forum for Global Education, 2004. Retrieved from www.globaled.org/An.AttGlob_Persp_04_11_29.pdf.

11. Van der Zee, K. I., and Brinkmann, U., (2004). Construct Validity Evidence for the Intercultural Readiness Check Against the Multicultural Personality Questionnaire, *International Journal of Selection and Assessment*, I2, 285–290.

12. Lynn Rew, "Measuring Cultural Awareness in Nursing Students," July 2003, *Journal of Nursing Education* 42(6): 249-57

13. Hanvey, R. G., *An Attainable Global Perspective*, New York: The American Forum for Global Education, 2004. Retrieved from www.globaled.org/An.AttGlob_Persp_04_11_29.pdf.

14. Gove, P. B. *Webster's Third New International Dictionary*, G. & C. Merriam Co., Springfield, MA, 1981.

15. Kelly, B. O., *Perception of Professional Ethics Among Senior Baccalaureate Nursing Students*, 1987. Unpublished doctoral dissertation, the Ohio State University.

16. Trompenaars, F., and Hampden-Turner, C., *Building Cross-Cultural Competence*, New York: McGraw-Hill, 2003.

17. Adair, J., *How to Grow Leaders: The Seven Key Principles of Effective Leadership Development*, London: Kogan Page, 2006.

18. Adair, J., *Effective Leadership Development*, London: Chartered Institute of Personnel and Development, 2005.

19. Belbin, M. *Management Teams: Why They Succeed or Fail*, Butterworth-Heinemann, London, 2003.

CHAPTER 12

1. Hofstede, G., *Culture's Consequences*, Sage, London, 1980.

2. Inzerilli, G., and Laurent, A., "Managerial Views of Organization Structure in France and the USA," *International Studies of Management and Organizations*, XIII, 1–2, 1983.

3. Lawrence, P. R., and Lorsch, J. W., *Organization and Environment; Managing Differentiation and Integration*, Irwin, Homewood, IL, 1967.

4. Bartlett, C., and Ghoshal, S., *Managing Across Borders*, Hutchinson Business Books, London, 1990.

5. Ogilvy, J., Global Business Network, Emeryville, CA (personal communication).

6. Reich, R. B., *The Work of Nations: Preparing Ourselves for the 21st Century*, Knopf, 1991.

7. Goold, M., *Strategic Control*, The Economist Books/Business Books, London, 1990.

CHAPTER 13

1. Inzerilli, G., and Laurent, A., *The Concept of Organizational Structure*, Working Paper, University of Pennsylvania and INSEAD, 1979; "Managerial Views of Organizational Structure in France and the USA," *International Studies of Management and Organizations*, XIII, 1–2, 1983, pages 97–138.

2. Denison, Daniel R. *Corporate Culture and Organizational Effectiveness*. Wiley Series on Organizational Assessment and Change. Oxford, England: John Wiley & Sons, 1990, xvii.

3. Harrison, R., "Understanding Your Organization's Character," *Harvard Business Review*, May–June 1972.

CHAPTER 14

1. Hampden-Turner, C., *Charting the Corporate Mind*, Blackwell, London, 1992.

2. Senge, P., ed., *The Dance of Change: The Challengers to Sustaining Momentum in Learning Organizations*, Doubleday, New York, 2002.

3. Lewin, K., *Resolving Social Conflicts: Selected Papers on Group Dynamics*, Harper, New York, 1947.

4. Cameron, K., and Quinn, R., *Diagnosing and Changing Organizational Culture: Based on the Competing Values Framework*, Addison-Wesley Series on Organization Development, Addison-Wesley, Inc., Reading, MA, 1998.

5. Handy, C., *Understanding Organizations*, Penguin Business, Penguin Books, London, 1993.

6. Trompenaars, F., and Hampden-Turner, C., *21 Leaders for the 21st Century*, Capstone, London, 2002.

CHAPTER 16

1 Bennett, J. M., and Bennett, M. J., "Developing Intercultural Sensitivity: An Integrative Approach to Global and Domestic Diversity," in D. Landis, J. M. Bennett, and M. J. Bennett (Eds.), *Handbook of Intercultural Training*, 3rd ed., 147–65, Thousand Oaks, CA: Sage, 2004.
2 Bennett and Bennett, "Developing Intercultural Sensitivity."
3 Edward de Bono, *The Use of Lateral Thinking*, London: Jonathan Cape, 1967.

CHAPTER 17

1 *Economist*, January 9, 1999.
2. KPMG Consulting M&A Report 1999.
3. We owe very much to Allard Everts, who worked as a senior consultant at Trompenaars Hampden-Turner.
4. Collins, J., and Porras, J., *Built to Last*, New York: HarperBusiness, 1994.
5. Collins, J., and Porras, J., "Building Your Corporate Vision," *Harvard Business Review*, September–October 1996.
6. Ibid., 73.

CHAPTER 18

1 Kirton, M. J., "Adaptors and Innovators: A Description and Measure," *Journal of Applied Psychology* 61 (1976), 622–29.
2 Belbin, M. R., *Team Roles at Work*, London: Butterworth-Heinemann, 1981.

CHAPTER 19

1 Trompenaars, Fons, and Charles Hampden-Turner, 21 Leaders for the 21st Century, New York: McGraw Hill Higher Education, 2001.
2 Reis, Eric, The Lean Startup, London: Portfolio Penguin, 2011.

CHAPTER 20

1 Trompenaars, Fons, *Did the Pedestrian Die?*, Capstone, 2003.
2 Stouffer, S. A., and Toby, J., "Role Conflict and Personality," *American Journal of Sociology*, no. 56, 1951, pages 395–406.
3 Culture for Business (native) App. Refer to www.ridingthewavesof culture.com for access details from Apple App Store and Google Play.
4 Trompenaars, Fons, and Voerman, Ed, *Servant Leadership Across Cultures: Harnessing the Strength of the World's Most Powerful Leadership Philosophy*, London, Infinite Ideas, 2009.

APPENDIX B

1. Smith, P. B. Appendix to *Riding the Waves of Culture*, 1st ed., Nicholas Brealey Publishing, 1993; Smith et al., "National Cultures and Values of Organisational Employees", *Journal of Cross Cultural Psychology*, vol. 27, no. 2, March 1996.

2. Hofstede G., "Riding the Waves of Commerce," *International Journal of Intercultural Relations*, vol. 20, no. 2, pp.189–98, 1996; Hampden-Turner, C., and Trompenaars, F., "A Response to Hofstede," *International Journal of Intercultural Relations*, vol. 22, no. 4, pp.189–98, 1997.

3. Kaiser–Meyer–Olkin (KMO) index, see Kaiser, H., "Factor Analysis," *Psychometrika*, vol. 30, pp. 1–14, 1965.

4. Bartlett's test: ibid., pp. 1–14.

5. McGee, "Multi-dimensional Scaling, *Multi-variate Behavioural Research*, vol. 3, pp. 233–48, 1968.

6. Hofstede, "Riding the Waves of Commerce"; Hampden-Turner and Trompenaars, "A Response to Hofstede."

Index

Page numbers followed by *f* and *t* refer to figures and tables, respectively.

About the Authors

FONS TROMPENAARS is known all over the world for his work as consultant, trainer, motivational speaker, and author of many books on the subject of culture and business. He has spent more than 35 years helping Fortune 500 leaders and professionals manage and solve their business and cultural dilemmas to increase global effectiveness and performance, particularly in the areas of globalization, mergers and acquisition, HR, and leadership development.

Fons was voted one of the Top 20 HR Most Influential International Thinkers 2011 by *HR* magazine. He is also ranked in the Thinkers50 to be one of the most influential management thinkers alive in the last 10 years and shortlisted as making substantial strides in the contribution to the understanding of globalization and the new frontiers established by the emerging markets. In 2018 he was admitted to the Hall of Fame of the Thinkers50.

In 1989 he founded the Centre for International Business Studies, a consulting and training organization for international management, renamed Trompenaars Hampden-Turner in 1998. Fons has worked as a consultant for Shell, BP, ICI, Philips, Heineken, TRW, Mars, Motorola, General Motors, Nike, Cable and Wireless, SNC-Lavalin, CDPQ, and Merrill Lynch.

Fons Trompenaars studied Economics at the Free University of Amsterdam and later earned a PhD from Wharton School, University of Pennsylvania, with a dissertation on differences in conceptions of organizational structure in various cultures. He experienced cultural differences firsthand at home, where he grew up speaking both French and Dutch.

CHARLES HAMPDEN-TURNER is the Director of Research and Development for Trompenaars Hampden-Turner. He is also a Senior Research Associate at the Judge Institute of Management Studies at Cambridge University and a Fellow of the Cybernetics Society.

Charles's corporate work began in 1985, when he was appointed Royal Dutch Shell Senior Research Fellow at the London Business School, moving to the Cambridge University Judge Institute in 1992. He has consulted to, among others: Royal Dutch Shell, Rockwell Automation, Motorola, Advanced Micro Devices, Applied Materials, BZW, KPMG, AT Kearney, McKinsey, the British Council, Scottish Enterprise, CDPQ, and British Airways.

Charles Hampden-Turner graduated from Cambridge University and received his master's and doctorate degrees from Harvard University. He has taught at Harvard University, Brandeis University, and the University of Toronto.

A recipient of Guggenheim, Rockefeller, and Ford Foundation Fellowships, he is also a past winner of the Douglas McGregor Memorial Award and most recently has been appointed Goh Tjoei Kok Distinguished Visiting Professor at Nanyang Business School, Singapore. He has taught at the University of California and the Wright Institute.